CLIFF SHEATS'
L E A N
BODIES
COOKBOOK

CLIFF SHEATS'
LEAN BODIES
COOKBOOK

A Cooking Companion to Cliff Sheats' Lean Bodies

CLIFF SHEATS, M.S., C.N.N.

Certified Clinical Nutritionist

Fellow, American Council of Applied Nutrition

International and American Association for Clinical Nutritionists

AND

LINDA M. THORNBRUGH, M.S.

THE SUMMIT GROUP

FORT WORTH, TEXAS

THE SUMMIT GROUP

1227 West Magnolia, Suite 500, Fort Worth, Texas 76104

10   9   8   7   6

LIBRARY OF CONGRESS CATALOGING IN PUBLICATION DATA

Sheats, Cliff.

Cliff Sheats' lean bodies cookbook : a cooking companion to
    Cliff Sheats' lean bodies / Cliff Sheats, Linda Thornbrugh.
    p. cm.
    Includes index.
    ISBN 1-56530-008-4

1. Reducing diets – Recipes. 2. Reducing diets – Menus. 3. Nutrition.
I. Thornbrugh, Linda. II. Title. III. Title: Cliff Sheats' lean bodies.

RM222.2.S532 1992   641.563
                           QBI92-20076

Dedicated to Kathy,
Jonathan
and "Baby Sheats" number two.
My warmest appreciation to Linda Thornbrugh,
Kathy Coker, Chef Chris Lalonde,
Jeff and Maggie Robinson, the Lean Bodies staff,
The Summit Group and all of those
"Lean Bodies" who have "eaten their way"
into a healthier body.

CONTEN

T S

1

❦ *About Lean Bodies*

MANY OF YOU BECAME FAMILIAR with the Lean Bodies program by either attending my classes or reading my first book, *Cliff Sheats' Lean Bodies*. Whether or not you are familiar with the program, let me summarize it.

Lean Bodies really is revolutionary. Unlike other diets, most of which work by decreasing the body's caloric intake, the Lean Bodies program helps you lose bodyfat by actually increasing calories. That's right. Increasing your daily caloric intake to 1,800 or 2,500 or even 3,600 calories can help you shed the pounds. By eating the right combinations together with the right quantities of lean proteins, starchy carbohydrates, and lean, fibrous vegetables, you will dramatically speed up your metabolism and therefore burn bodyfat. It sounds unbelievable, but it's true.

I entered the field of nutrition because I was intrigued with how it had everything to do with restoring my health when I was much younger. While playing tennis in college, my teammates and I would eat chocolate candy bars for the quick energy they would provide so that we could play for longer periods of time. Call it a quick fix. As a result, over time, I got into the habit of eating candy – even to the point of substituting sugar for meals so as to keep my energy up. Eventually, I started feeling tired and weak all the time. My sugar "addiction" eventually led to full-blown hypoglycemia. Severe allergies followed and it became difficult to breathe, let alone do much of anything else.

For treatment of the allergies, I was put on various medications. In fact, there were so many of these medications that I had to carry them around with me all day. It got to where I would stuff them inside my tennis racket cover, which eventually was bulging with bottles and jars. Worse than that, however, all the medication accomplished was to aggravate my already failing health. This lasted for a few years and it wasn't until a friend at church told me about a Dr. Marshall Ringsdorf that I was able to start working toward a solution to my health problems.

Desperate, I went to see Dr. Ringsdorf. After one look at my blood tests, he told me all of my problems could be corrected with proper nutrition. I was floored! Dr. Ringsdorf took me off medication and put me on a high-protein, high-complex-carbohydrate, high-calorie diet, along with nutritional supplements. In two weeks, I felt so good that I decided to take a run. I went outdoors, ran a lap around the block and then stopped for a moment to see if I was all right. As I stood there feeling my heart pound away, I was overcome with emotion knowing that I had regained my strength. I was cured, so to speak.

It wasn't long before I started playing tennis again. And to think that a doctor had told me to quit the sport. Nine months later, I was playing professional tennis on a circuit where I was competing against world-class athletes.

A while later, I underwent a complete physical and I'll never forget what the doctor told me. He said, "There's no place to rate you on our scale. You're above 'excellent.' In fact, you are in the superior range."

As a result of these and other experiences, I decided to pursue a career in nutrition. With hindsight, I now realize that by enduring my early health problems, I was better able to understand what other people are going through and could recognize the vital role food plays when it comes to good health.

In the late 1980s, while in private practice and working with a cardiologist, I designed a revolutionary new fat-loss method.

This new approach to fat loss, called the Lean Bodies program, is based on the very latest research in nutrition and metabolism.

In my practice, I have worked with people suffering from a wide range of problems that include obesity, high blood pressure, high cholesterol, diabetes, hypoglycemia, and chronic fatigue. Although these problems varied from person to person, the afflicted have almost always had two things in common: 1) they were not eating enough food to fuel their bodies efficiently and 2) what little food they did eat was the wrong kind. Interestingly, the latest research shows that losing bodyfat means eating more calories, not less. Further research shows that the body's ability to build muscle depends less on exercise and more on eating habits than previously thought. In fact, 75 percent of the body's ability to gain lean mass is a matter of nutrition. Only 25 percent depends on exercise.

That is why the Lean Bodies program stresses food; plenty of food, healthy food, and good food. That's why the Lean Bodies cookbook was created – to give you many choices while you follow the Lean Bodies program. Lean Bodies is about eating, not fasting, and the delicious recipes in this new cookbook will help you really enjoy eating at the same time you are losing bodyfat and gaining energy.

For more information about the program or to receive a free brochure on Lean Bodies, please call 1-800-875-3346.

2

How To Use This Book

THE LEAN BODIES COOKBOOK is an integral part of the Lean Bodies nutritional program. Three basic criteria were used in developing the recipes for this cookbook. These recipes had to:

1) be lean and nutritious;

2) be easy to prepare; and

3) taste terrific.

Now that you are on the Lean Bodies program, you are learning to change your lifestyle. You are learning that eating healthy and nutritious food gives you energy, takes off extra pounds, and keeps you from feeling hungry. The recipes in this cookbook will help you achieve your Lean Bodies goal.

Recipes in *The Lean Bodies Cookbook* incorporate a variety of aromatic and flavorful herbs, spices, and seasonings. Get acquainted with these items and be sure to lay in a good shelf supply. The best way to learn about these flavor enhancers is through experimentation. Your best guide for which ones to use is your own personal palate.

If you like your foods well-seasoned, choose recipes that use basil, bay leaves, cayenne pepper, chili powder, cumin, dill weed, dry mustard, garlic, oregano, rosemary, sage, or thyme. If you like recipes that emphasize sweetness, choose those that contain cardamon, cinnamon, curry, ginger, marjoram, mint, or nutmeg.

Be creative as you experiment with these recipes. If you discover that you dislike one herb, find another herb that you do like, and make your own substitution. Tailor these recipes to satisfy your own taste buds.

Food Choices on the Lean Bodies Program

Lean Proteins

Egg whites

Fish

Bass

Catfish

Cod

Flounder

Grouper

Haddock

Hake

Halibut

Mackerel

Mahi mahi

Marlin

Ocean perch

Orange roughy

Red snapper

Salmon

Scrod

Shark

Sole

Swordfish

Trout

Tuna

Scallops

Shrimp

Chicken (white meat only)

Turkey (white meat only)

Starchy Carbohydrates

Barley

Black-eyed peas

Brown rice

Buckwheat

Bulgur

Butter beans

Chard

Corn

Garbanzo beans

Kasha

Kidney beans

Lentils

Lima beans

Millet

Navy beans

Old-fashioned oatmeal (not quick - cooking)

Peas

Pinto beans

Potatoes

Red beans

Rice cakes

Split peas

Sweet potatoes

Water chestnuts

White beans

Winter squash

Yams

Lean, Fibrous Vegetables

Alfalfa sprouts

Artichokes

Asparagus

Bamboo shoots

Bean sprouts

Beets

Bok choy

Broccoflower

Broccoli

Brussels sprouts

Cabbage

Carrots

Cauliflower

Celery

Collard greens

Cucumbers

Eggplant

Green, leafy vegetables

Green onions

Green peppers

Kale

Leeks

Mushrooms

Okra

Onions

Parsley

Parsnips

Radishes

Red cabbage

Rutabaga

Scallions

Snowpeas

Spinach

Summer squash

Tomatoes

Turnips

Turnip greens

Watercress

Zucchini

Herb And Spice List

Fresh Herbs

Chopped fresh chives

Chopped fresh cilantro

Chopped fresh mint

Chopped fresh parsley

Fresh mint sprigs

Fresh parsley sprigs

Grated fresh ginger root

Herbs and Spices

Allspice

Barbecue seasoning

Bay leaf or leaves

Black pepper

Caraway seeds

Cayenne pepper

Chili powder

Cinnamon

Crushed red pepper flakes

Curry powder

Dried basil

Dried celery flakes

Dried chervil

Dried cilantro

Dried dill weed

Dried lemon peel

Dried marjoram

Dried mint flakes

Dried orange peel

Dried oregano

Dried parsley flakes

Dried rosemary, crumbled

Dried summer savory

Dried tarragon

Dried thyme

Dried vegetable flakes

Dry mustard

Freeze-dried chives

Garlic powder

Ground cardamom

Ground cloves

Ground cumin

Ground ginger

Ground oregano

Ground sage

Horseradish

Instant minced onion flakes

Italian herb seasoning

Nutmeg

Onion powder

Paprika

Salt-free herb seasoning

Tumeric

White pepper

Whole cloves

Using Herbs and Spices

This list will give you some guidance, when you are altering recipes to suit your taste, to which herbs and spices are best used with which foods.

ITEM	PROTEINS	VEGETABLES	FOOD ITEMS
Basil	scrambled eggs	beans	chicken salads
	chicken	cauliflower	cucumber salads
	turkey	eggplant	green salads
	halibut	onions	seafood salads
	shrimp	peas	chowders
	tuna	squash	minestrone
		spinach	vegetable soups
		tomatoes	stuffings
		turnips	
Bay Leaves	halibut	beets	bean soups
	shrimp	carrots	bouillabaisse
		potatoes	broths
		tomatoes	corn chowders
			vegetable soups
Caraway		beets	deviled eggs
		broccoli	cole slaw
		cabbage	cabbage soup
		potatoes	chowder
		rice	
		turnips	
Cardamon		pea soups	

ITEM	PROTEINS	VEGETABLES	FOOD ITEMS
Cayenne Pepper			
	scrambled eggs		chowders
	fish		fish soups
			tomato soups
			seafood salads
			salad dressings
			Mexican foods
Celery Seeds	scrambled eggs	tomatoes	aspics
	turkey loaf		fish salads
	fish stew		potato salads
			all soups
			stuffings
Chervil	scrambled eggs	artichokes	deviled eggs
	chicken	beets	cole slaw
	turkey	broccoli	cucumber salads
	seafoods	eggplant	green salads
		potatoes	potato salads
		spinach	garnish
		tomatoes	stocks
			vegetable soups
			dips
			stuffings
Chili Powder	scrambled eggs	beans	chowders
	chicken		fish soups
	fish		spiced dishes
			salad dressings
			barbecue sauces

ITEM	PROTEINS	VEGETABLES	FOOD ITEMS
Chives	omelets	cabbage	green salads
		carrots	potato salads
		peas	bean soups
		potatoes	pea soups
			vichyssoise
Cilantro	seafood	beans	garnish
			stuffings
			dips
			Mexican dishes
			salad dressings
Cinnamon			barbecue sauce
			catsup
			fish marinades
Cloves	chicken	beets	barbecue sauce
	turkey loaf	sweet potatoes	catsup
	fish	tomatoes	marinades
Cumin	chicken	beans	deviled eggs
	turkey chili	cabbage	Mexican dishes
	turkey loaf	rice	chicken soups
	seafood		pea soups
			bean soups
Curry	scrambled eggs	artichokes	deviled eggs
	chicken	asparagus	marinades
	turkey	beans	chicken spreads
	seafoods	eggplant	tuna spreads

ITEM	PROTEINS	VEGETABLES	FOOD ITEMS
Curry, continued			
	tuna	onions	poultry salads
		rice	seafood salads
		tomatoes	vegetable salads
			potato salads
			chowders
			vegetable soups
			dips
Dill Seed	fish	cabbage	salad dressings
		carrots	vegetable soups
		cucumber	pickles
		turnips	
Dill Weed	scrambled eggs	beans	deviled eggs
	chicken	beets	cole slaw
	halibut	cabbage	vegetable salads
	shrimp	celery	seafood salads
	sole	cucumber	bean soups
		eggplant	chicken soups
		parsnips	chowders
		potatoes	pea soups
			dips
			seafood cocktails
Dry Mustard	scrambled eggs	beans	chicken spreads
	fish	cabbage	fish spreads
			potato soups
			dips
			cole slaw
			green salads
			salad dressings

ITEM	PROTEINS	VEGETABLES	FOOD ITEMS
Garlic	chicken		soups
	turkey		casseroles
			marinades
			salad dressings
			dips
Ginger	chicken	carrots	barbeque sauce
	fish	onions	catsup
	seafoods	squash	marinades
		sweet potatoes	stuffings
			chicken salads
			Chinese foods
Horseradish	fish	beets	
		potatoes	
Lemon Peel	fish	asparagus	stuffings
	omelets	carrots	marinades
		spinach	bouillabaise
			broth
			vegetable soups
Marjoram	scrambled eggs	asparagus	green salads
	chicken	beans	chicken salads
	turkey	broccoli	seafood salads
	halibut	cabbage	chowders
	tuna	carrots	onion soups
		mushrooms	tomato soups
		onions	vegetable soups
		peas	dips

ITEM	PROTEINS	VEGETABLES	FOOD ITEMS
Marjoram, continued		potatoes	
		spinach	
		zucchini	
Mint		carrots	garnish
		celery	cole slaw
		cabbage	green salad
		peas	bean soups
		potatoes	pea soups
		spinach	
		zucchini	
Nutmeg	chicken	carrots	stuffings
	turkey	cauliflower	poultry salads
	turkey loaf	onions	broths
	fish	potatoes	chowders
		squash	
		spinach	
Orange Peel	omelets	carrots	marinades
	chicken	squash	stuffings
	turkey	sweet potatoes	
Oregano	scrambled eggs	broccoli	bean salads
	chicken	cabbage	green salads
	shrimp	lentils	potato salads
		mushrooms	seafood salads
		onions	tomato soups
		tomatoes	minestrone
		zucchini	vegetable soups

ITEM	PROTEINS	VEGETABLES	FOOD ITEMS
Oregano, continued			stuffings
			marinades
Paprika	chicken	beans	deviled eggs
	fish	potatoes	stuffings
	seafoods	rice	tuna salad
			vegetable salads
			chowders
			garnish
			dips
Parsley	scrambled eggs	carrots	deviled eggs
	seafoods	potatoes	garnish
	fish	tomatoes	green salads
	chicken	vegetables	soups
			stock
			dips
			stuffings
Rosemary	scrambled eggs	beans	deviled eggs
	chicken	cauliflower	chicken soups
	halibut	cucumber	chowders
		mushrooms	pea soups
		peas	potato soups
		potatoes	spinach soups
		spinach	stuffings
		zucchini	
Sage	chicken	carrots	chicken soups
	turkey	eggplant	minestrone

ITEM	PROTEINS	VEGETABLES	FOOD ITEMS
Sage, continued			lima beans
			pea soups
		onions	potato soups
		peas	vegetable soups
		tomatoes	stuffings
Summer Savory			
	scrambled eggs	artichokes	deviled eggs
	chicken	asparagus	green salads
	turkey	beans	potato salads
	halibut	lentils	vegetable salads
	shrimp	rice	bean soups
	sole		chowders
			pea soups
			vegetable soups
			stuffings
Tarragon	scrambled eggs	cabbage	deviled eggs
	chicken	cauliflower	chicken salads
	turkey	celery	cole slaw
	halibut	mushrooms	eggs salads
	shrimp	peas	green salads
	sole	potatoes	seafood salads
		spinach	bean soups
		tomatoes	pea soups
			seafood cocktails
Thyme	scrambled eggs	asparagus	deviled eggs
	chicken	beans	aspics
	turkey	beets	chicken salads
	halibut	cabbage	cole slaw

ITEM	PROTEINS	VEGETABLES	FOOD ITEMS
Thyme, continued			
	scallops	carrots	tomato salads
	sole	onions	consumme
	cod	peas	gumbos
	tuna	sweet potatoes	pea soups
		zucchini	vegetable soups
			seafood cocktails
			stuffings
Tumeric	scrambled eggs	rice	marinades
	fish		seafood salads
			chowders
			curries
White Pepper	scrambled eggs		white sauces
	chicken		casseroles
	fish		

NOTE: Nutrient figures listed with each recipe in this book are based on *one* serving for *one* person, even where the recipe calls for serving two or more people. The only exceptions are the sauces, dressings and gravies listed in Chapter 14, where nutrients listed are for the entire serving provided for in the recipe.

Helpful Hints

Dry-Curd: Nonfat cottage cheese

Vegetable Flakes: Use whatever vegetable flakes you prefer.

3

CHAPTER THREE ❦ *Cooking In Bulk*

Doubling a recipe does not mean doubling the food preparation time. It does take some extra time to double or even triple a recipe. However, the time required to locate kitchen utensils and food supplies, mix the ingredients, cook the food items, clean up, and put away the food supplies is almost the same. You will have a larger quantity of ingredients to cut, chop, measure, and assemble. These activities are really a minor part of the whole operation. Here are suggestions for preparing large quantities of food items and freezing some for future use:

1. When making a casserole, increase the recipe and make enough for two, four, or six meals. Eat one today, refrigerate one for tomorrow, and freeze the remaining casseroles for next week or next month. Extra casseroles may be frozen unbaked for future baking or baked now for future defrosting and heating.

2. When making soups or chili, always increase the recipe. Soups and chili freeze wonderfully. For added reheating convenience, package the soups and chili in individual size servings. Freeze these foods in small, round, thin containers rather than in large, tall, rectangular containers. Food frozen in this manner defrosts much more efficiently.

3. To get maximum utilization from a small supply of appropriately designed freezing containers, remove the frozen article from its container and repackage the frozen article in freezer bags. Wash, store and reuse your containers as needed to freeze additional foods. Think big when purchasing chicken breasts. Instead

of buying 4 chicken breasts, purchase 8 or more. When you arrive home, cook and eat some of the chicken breasts and freeze the rest. Or skin, debone, and freeze all of the breasts for future use. You will find that, in total, it takes less time to handle larger quantities of chicken breasts once than to handle smaller quantities several times. Also, you save money by buying large quantities of chicken breasts when they are on sale.

Key Points for Freezing

Many food items that you will be using to prepare your Lean Bodies recipes can be purchased in quantity and stored in your freezer. Your freezer can also help you save money by allowing you to store large quantities of seasonal vegetables like tomatoes, corn on the cob, and asparagus that have been purchased at their flavor peak and their lowest price.

Purchase fresh herbs, freeze them, and keep plenty on hand for frequent use as ingredients and garnishes. Fresh herbs and spices accentuate the flavor and aroma of your recipes.

Prepare large quantities of soups, sauces, main dishes, and vegetables whenever time allows. These large quantities can then be broken down into family-sized and/or single servings and frozen for future use.

You can make the best use of your freezer by following these suggestions:

1. Select only quality foods for freezing.

2. Prepare fresh vegetables for freezing as soon as possible after gathering them from your garden or purchasing them from the market.

3. Cooked foods need to be cooled to room temperature or refrigerated before freezing.

4. Use storage bags and containers designed specifically for

freezing. Double bagging prolongs the freezer life of such delicate foods as asparagus, blueberries, tomatoes, herbs, and fish.

5. Label and date each frozen item.

6. Tray-freeze items like chicken breasts, stuffed peppers, ground turkey patties, and fish fillets. Place the items on a cookie sheet and leave space between each item. Do not wrap. Put the cookie sheet in the freezer. When all items are frozen, package them in a single storage bag or container. These items will now stay separated for easy removal of the exact quantity you need for defrosting and cooking.

7. Maintain correct storage temperature of zero degrees. Periodically check the freezer temperature with a freezer thermometer.

8. Foods have been frozen too long if their colors change or fade. Other indicators of excess freezing time are changes in consistency, broken-down starches , or limp vegetables. Food has suffered freezer burn if gray and white spots appear or food edges have dried out. This results from poor wrapping or storage in non-airtight containers.

9. To avoid spoilage, thaw food in the refrigerator or defrost in the microwave immediately prior to cooking or serving. Discard any defrosted food that appears spoiled or has an off odor.

10. Never refreeze food that has been completely thawed. Make sure that fish and poultry items are fresh if you are planning to freeze them. If food has been previously frozen, cook it before you refreeze it.

11. Undercook foods slightly when planning to freeze them. They will finish cooking during the reheating process.

12. In general, cooked food can be stored in the freezer for up to six months.

13. When freezing either cooked or ready-to-cook foods, consider the size and shape of the dish you will be using to defrost and

heat the food item for serving. Make your frozen foods match your food preparation dishes. This will speed defrosting and heating.

14. Line your heating container with aluminum foil. When the food is frozen, lift the foil out. Securely wrap the food with the foil and return to the freezer. When ready to use, remove from freezer and let stand for 3 minutes. Remove the foil and place the food in the original container for heating.

Pantry Shelf List

Baking powder

Baking soda

Bouillon:

> *No salt added, beef-flavored instant bouillon*

Butter / other sprinkles / products:

> *Bacon-flavored sprinkles*
>
> *Butter flavoring*
>
> *Butter-flavored mix*
>
> *Butter-flavored sprinkles*
>
> *Cheese-flavored sprinkles*

Canned goods:

> *Chicken broth*
>
> *Chopped green chilies*
>
> *Chopped jalapenos*
>
> *Chopped pimientos*
>
> *Mushrooms*
>
> *Tomato paste*
>
> *Tomato sauce*
>
> *Tomatoes*

Capers

Cornmeal

Cornstarch

Dijon mustard

Extracts and flavorings:

    Almond extract

    Banana extract

    Blackberry extract

    Coconut extract

    Lemon extract

    Maple flavoring

    Orange extract

    Pineapple extract

    Rum extract

    Strawberry extract

    Vanilla extract

Flour:

    Buckwheat

    Oat

    Rye

Freeze-dried mushrooms

Garlic cloves

Gelatins:

    Sugar-free flavored gelatins

    Gelatin, unflavored

Ketchup

Lemon juice

Liquid sauces:

    Hickory liquid smoke

    Kitchen Bouquet

    Low-salt soy sauce

    Tabasco sauce

    Worcestershire sauce

    Lime juice

Milk products:

  Dry-curd cottage cheese

  Evaporated skimmed milk

  Nonfat dry milk

  Nonfat yogurt

  Skim milk

Mustard

Non-stick cooking spray

Oat bran

Old-fashioned oatmeal

Picante sauce

Safflower oil

Sugar substitute

Vegetable juice

Vinegars:

  Balsamic

  Cider

  Red wine

  Rice wine

  Tarragon

  White wine

Wines:

  Dry cooking sherry

  Dry sherry

  Dry white wine

4

¶ *Eggs*

Helpful Hints

Use flavored sprinkles (butter, cheese, or bacon) to enhance the flavor of omelets, frittatas, or scrambled eggs.

In recipes substitute 2 egg whites for 1 whole egg.

Use skim milk only.

Use dry-curd cottage cheese only.

In recipes substitute evaporated skimmed milk for cream.

Use Mock Sour Cream (page 319) or nonfat yogurt in place of sour cream.

Use chopped egg whites as a filling for enchiladas.

Fill deviled eggs with mixtures other than yolks. Use refried beans,tuna, chicken, spinach dip, or black bean dip.

Check the freshness of eggs by floating in water. Fresh sink; stale float.

Fresh eggs should keep 30 to 40 days if refrigerated properly. One- or two-week-old eggs peel easily.

Spin egg to verify if it's cooked. Cooked eggs spin. Uncooked eggs wobble.

Eggs at room temperature beat more easily than cold ones.

To hard-boil eggs, place in a saucepan. Cover with cold water. Place over medium-high heat. Bring to a boil. Reduce heat. Cook 10 minutes. Drain. Cover with cold water. Cool. Refrigerate at once.

Basic Scrambled Eggs

6 egg whites
2 tbsp. skim milk
1 tbsp. prepared butter-flavored mix
¼ tsp. salt-free herb seasoning

In a small bowl, combine egg whites, milk, prepared butter mix, and seasonings. Beat with a fork or wire whisk until well blended. Spray a medium skillet with nonstick cooking spray. Heat skillet over medium heat. Pour in egg mixture. Cook until mixture begins to set on the bottom and around the edges. Gently stir until eggs are cooked but still soft and moist. Remove from heat and serve immediately. Serves 2.

(Serving = 1 lean protein)
NUTRIENTS: 107 calories; 16.4 grams of protein; 0.1 grams of fat; 8.8 grams of carbohydrates; 228 mg of sodium; 406 mg of potassium; and 210 mg of calcium.

Scrambled Eggs with Chilies and Onion

1 Basic Scrambled Eggs (page 31)

1 tsp. instant minced onion flakes

¼ tsp. chili powder

2 tbsp. chopped green chilies

Prepare Basic Scrambled Eggs, adding onion and chili powder to unbeaten egg mixture. Beat until well blended. Stir in green chilies. Continue according to recipe instructions for making scrambled eggs. Serves 2.

(Serving = 1 lean protein)
NUTRIENTS: 112 calories; 16.6 grams of protein; 0.1 grams of fat; 10.3 grams of carbohydrates; 238 mg of sodium; 437 mg of potassium; and 213 mg of calcium.

Scrambled Eggs with Herbs

1 Basic Scrambled Eggs (page 31)

1 tbsp. freeze-dried chives

1 tsp. dried celery flakes

Prepare Basic Scrambled Eggs, adding chives and celery flakes to unbeaten egg mixture. Beat until well blended. Continue according to recipe instructions for making scrambled eggs. Serves 2.

Variation 1: Substitute ¼ teaspoon garlic powder and 1 teaspoon dried parsley flakes for chives and celery flakes.

Variation 2: Substitute 1 teaspoon instant minced onion flakes for celery flakes.

Variation 3: Substitute 1 teaspoon dried parsley flakes and ¼ teaspoon dried thyme for chives and celery flakes.

(Serving = 1 lean protein)
NUTRIENTS: 108 calories; 16.5 grams of protein; 0.1 grams of fat; 9.3 grams of carbohydrates; 228 mg of sodium; 419 mg of potassium; and 213 mg of calcium.

Scrambled Eggs with Green Onions

1 Basic Scrambled Eggs (page 31)
¼ tsp. dried tarragon
2 tbsp. chopped green onion

Prepare Basic Scrambled Eggs, adding tarragon to unbeaten egg mixture. Beat until well blended. Stir in green onion. Continue according to recipe instructions for making scrambled eggs. Serves 2.

(Serving = 1 lean protein)
NUTRIENTS: 112 calories; 16.7 grams of protein; 0.1 grams of fat; 10.2 grams of carbohydrates; 229 mg of sodium; 435 mg of potassium; and 216 mg of calcium.

Scrambled Eggs with Peppers and Pimientos

1 Basic Scrambled Eggs (page 31)
¼ tsp. dried thyme
¼ tsp. dry mustard
2 tbsp. finely chopped green pepper
2 tbsp. chopped pimientos

Prepare Basic Scrambled Eggs, adding thyme and dry mustard to unbeaten egg mixture. Beat until well blended. Stir in green pepper and pimientos. Continue according to recipe instructions for making scrambled eggs. Serves 2.

(Serving = 1 lean protein)
NUTRIENTS: 108 calories; 16.5 grams of protein; 0.1 grams of fat; 9.3 grams of carbohydrates; 228 mg of sodium; 417 mg of potassium; and 210 mg of calcium.

Scrambled Eggs with Shrimp and Mushrooms

1 Basic Scrambled Eggs (page 31)
¼ cup chopped cooked shrimp
One 4-oz. can sliced mushrooms, drained
1 tbsp. chopped green onion

Prepare Basic Scrambled Eggs. Stir shrimp, mushrooms, and green onion into beaten egg mixture. Continue according to recipe instructions for making scrambled eggs. Serves 2.

(Serving = 1 lean protein)
NUTRIENTS: 149 calories; 22.9 grams of protein; 0.4 grams of fat; 13.2 grams of carbohydrates; 786 mg of sodium; 696 mg of potassium; and 236 mg of calcium.

Scrambled Eggs Florentine

1 Basic Scrambled Eggs (page 31)
⅛ tsp. cayenne pepper
1 tsp. lemon juice
½ cup frozen chopped spinach, thawed and drained

Prepare Basic Scrambled Eggs, adding pepper and lemon juice to unbeaten egg mixture. Beat until well blended. Stir in spinach. Continue according to recipe instructions for making scrambled eggs. Serves 2.

(Serving = 1 lean protein)
NUTRIENTS: 118 calories; 17.9 grams of protein; 0.3 grams of fat; 10.9 grams of carbohydrates; 254 mg of sodium; 573 mg of potassium; and 266 mg of calcium.

Scrambled Eggs with Sprouts and Onion

1 Basic Scrambled Eggs (page 31)
1 tsp. instant minced onion flakes
⅓ cup alfalfa sprouts

Prepare Basic Scrambled Eggs, adding onion flakes to unbeaten egg mixture. Beat until well blended. Stir in sprouts. Continue according to recipe instructions for making scrambled eggs. Serves 2.

(Serving = 1 lean protein)
NUTRIENTS: 122 calories; 17.5 grams of protein; 0.3 grams of fat; 11.0 grams of carbohydrates; 230 mg of sodium; 439 mg of potassium; and 218 mg of calcium.

Scrambled Eggs with Tomatoes

1 Basic Scrambled Eggs (page 31)
½ tsp. dried oregano
½ tsp. dried parsley flakes
¼ cup finely chopped tomatoes

Prepare Basic Scrambled Eggs, adding oregano and parsley to unbeaten egg mixture. Beat until well blended. Stir in tomatoes. Continue according to recipe instructions for making scrambled eggs. Serves 2.

Variation: Substitute ⅛ teaspoon curry powder for oregano and ⅛ teaspoon garlic powder for parsley.

(Serving = 1 lean protein)
NUTRIENTS: 113 calories; 16.8 grams of protein; 0.2 grams of fat; 14.4 grams of carbohydrates; 229 mg of sodium; 480 mg of potassium; and 214 mg of calcium.

Scrambled Eggs with Turkey

1 Basic Scrambled Eggs (page 31)
⅛ tsp. hickory liquid smoke
¼ tsp. paprika
2 tsp. chopped pimientos
⅓ cup chopped cooked turkey breast

Prepare Basic Scrambled Eggs, adding liquid smoke and paprika to unbeaten egg mixture. Beat until well blended. Stir in pimientos and turkey. Continue according to recipe instructions for making scrambled eggs. Serves 2.

(Serving = 1 lean protein)
NUTRIENTS: 151 calories; 25.8 grams of protein; 0.6 grams of fat; 9.0 grams of carbohydrates; 247 mg of sodium; 528 mg of potassium; and 210 mg of calcium.

Basic Omelet

4 egg whites
1 tbsp. water
¼ tsp. salt-free herb seasoning

In a small bowl, combine egg whites, water, and seasoning.
Beat vigorously with a fork or wire whisk until well blended.
Spray a 9-inch skillet or omelet pan with nonstick cooking
spray. Heat skillet over medium-high heat. Pour in beaten egg
mixture. As soon as bottom of omelet begins to set, slip a thin-
bladed spatula well under the edges and lift to allow uncooked
eggs to flow underneath. Cook until eggs no longer run freely
and top of omelet is creamy yet still soft. Remove skillet from
heat. Fold omelet almost in half. Remove omelet to serving
plate. Serves 1.

(Serving = 1 lean protein)
*NUTRIENTS: 67 calories; 14.4 grams of protein; 0.0 grams of fat; 1.1
grams of carbohydrates; 193 mg of sodium; 183 mg of potassium; and 21
mg of calcium.*

Apple Omelet

1 Granny Smith apple, shredded
2 tbsp. water
¼ tsp. orange extract
¼ tsp. coconut extract
¼ tsp. cinnamon
1 packet sugar substitute
2 Basic Omelets (page 37)

In a small microwaveable dish, combine apple and water. Microwave on high, 2 to 3 minutes, until apple is tender. Stir in orange extract, coconut extract, cinnamon, and sugar. Prepare one Basic Omelet. Fill omelet with 2 tablespoons filling. Fold omelet over filling. Repeat process for second omelet. Serve with extra filling spooned over omelets. Sprinkle with additional cinnamon. Serves 2.

(Serving = 1 lean protein)
NUTRIENTS: 129 calories; 19.2 grams of protein; 0.4 grams of fat; 11.5 grams of carbohydrates; 256 mg of sodium; 318 mg of potassium; and 21 mg of calcium.

Black Bean and Tomato Omelet

½ cup cooked black beans
½ cup chopped tomatoes
2 tbsp. lemon juice
¼ tsp. garlic powder
⅛ tsp. curry powder
1 tbsp. finely chopped fresh cilantro
2 Basic Omelets (page 37)

Combine black beans, tomatoes, lemon juice, garlic powder, curry, and cilantro. Prepare one Basic Omelet. Fill omelet with 2 tablespoons filling. Fold omelet over filling. Repeat process for second omelet. Serve with extra filling spooned over omelets. Serves 2.

(Serving = 1 lean protein)
NUTRIENTS: 156 calories; 23.3 grams of protein; 0.4 grams of fat; 14.1

grams of carbohydrates; 258 mg of sodium; 545 mg of potassium; and 41 mg of calcium.

Fresh Strawberry Omelet

1 cup sliced fresh strawberries
2 packets sugar substitute
½ cup dry-curd cottage cheese
2 tbsp. nonfat yogurt
½ tsp. vanilla extract
¼ tsp. cinnamon
2 Basic Omelets (page 37)

Mix sliced strawberries and sugar. Place cottage cheese, yogurt, vanilla, and cinnamon in a blender. Process until smooth. Prepare one Basic Omelet. Fill omelet with 2 tablespoons of strawberries. Fold omelet over strawberries. Repeat process for second omelet. Serve with remaining strawberries spooned over omelets. Top omelets and strawberries with blended cottage cheese. Serves 2.

(Serving = 1 lean protein)
NUTRIENTS: 155 calories; 26.0 grams of protein; 0.7 grams of fat; 8.8 grams of carbohydrates; 297 mg of sodium; 380 mg of potassium; and 100 mg of calcium.

Shrimp Omelet

½ cup finely chopped mushrooms
1 tbsp. finely chopped green onion
¾ cup chicken broth, defatted

1 cup chopped cooked shrimp

½ tsp. butter-flavored sprinkles

1 tbsp. chopped fresh parsley

1 tbsp. cornstarch

2 tbsp. dry sherry

2 Basic Omelets (page 37)

In a small saucepan, combine mushrooms, onion, and broth. Simmer until vegetables are tender. Stir in shrimp, butter sprinkles, and parsley. Dissolve cornstarch in sherry. Add to vegetables. Heat and stir until thickened. Prepare one Basic Omelet. Fill omelet with 2 tablespoons filling. Fold omelet over filling. Repeat process for second omelet. Serve with extra filling spooned over omelets. Serves 2.

(Serving = 1 lean protein)
NUTRIENTS: 328 calories; 34.9 grams of protein; 1.3 grams of fat; 18.1 grams of carbohydrates; 648 mg of sodium; 789 mg of potassium; and 70 mg of calcium.

Shrimp Egg Foo Yung

1 cup chicken broth, defatted

1 tbsp. low-salt soy sauce

1 tbsp. dry cooking sherry

1 tsp. dried parsley flakes

1 tbsp. cornstarch

1 tbsp. water

6 egg whites

¼ tsp. garlic powder

¼ tsp. white pepper

1 tsp. salt-free herb seasoning

1 cup chopped cooked shrimp

1½ cups bean sprouts, drained

1 cup sliced mushrooms

¼ cup chopped green onion

In a small saucepan, combine broth, soy sauce, sherry, and parsley. Bring to a boil over medium heat. Dissolve cornstarch in water and add to broth. Cook and stir until sauce is thickened. Remove sauce from heat and cover to keep warm. In a medium bowl, beat egg whites, garlic powder, pepper, and herb seasoning until well blended. Add remaining ingredients and mix. Spray a large skillet with nonstick cooking spray. Heat skillet over medium heat. Ladle one-fourth of egg mixture into skillet. Cook until egg mixture is set and lightly brown. Turn and cook other side. Remove to serving platter and keep warm while cooking the other 3 omelets. Spray skillet with non-stick cooking spray as needed. Serve with warm sauce. Serves 2.

Variation: Serve over cooked brown rice, cooked potatoes, or cooked bulgur.

(Serving = 1 lean protein; 1 lean, fibrous vegetable)
NUTRIENTS: 288 calories; 33.4 grams of protein; 2.5 grams of fat; 22.0 grams of carbohydrates; 551 mg of sodium; 1000 mg of potassium; and 110 mg of calcium.

Breakfast Turkey Succotash

6 egg whites

1 tsp. instant minced onion flakes

1 tsp. salt-free herb seasoning

1 tsp. dried celery flakes
½ tsp. paprika
1 cup chopped, cooked turkey breast
1 cup cooked lima beans
1 cup cooked corn
2 tbsp. chopped pimientos

In a large bowl, beat egg whites, onion flakes, herb seasoning, celery flakes, and paprika until well blended. Stir in remaining ingredients. Spray a large skillet with nonstick cooking spray. Heat skillet over medium heat. Pour in egg mixture. Cook until mixture begins to set on the bottom and around the edges. Stir until eggs are cooked. Remove from heat and serve immediately. Serves 2.

(Serving = 1 lean protein; 1 starchy carbohydrate)
NUTRIENTS: 363 calories; 55.2 grams of protein; 5.0 grams of fat; 21.3 grams of carbohydrates; 242 mg of sodium; 1099 mg of potassium; and 32 mg of calcium.

Italian Fritatta

½ cup chopped green pepper
¼ cup chopped onion
One 14½-oz. can tomatoes, chopped
1 cup broccoli florets
One 4-oz. can mushrooms, drained
1 tsp. dried oregano
½ tsp. dried basil
¼ tsp. garlic powder

2 cups cooked brown rice

6 egg whites

⅓ cup nonfat yogurt

1 tsp. cheese-flavored sprinkles

⅛ tsp. black pepper

Preheat oven to 375 degrees. In a medium skillet, combine green pepper, onion, tomatoes, and broccoli. Sauté until vegetables are tender. Stir in mushrooms, oregano, basil, garlic powder, and brown rice. Spray an ovenproof baking dish with nonstick cooking spray. Pour vegetable mixture into baking dish. In a medium bowl, combine egg whites, yogurt, cheese sprinkles, and pepper. Pour over vegetable mixture. Bake 15 to 20 minutes until eggs are set. Serves 2.

(Serving = 1 lean protein; 1 starchy carbohydrate; ½ lean, fibrous vegetable)
NUTRIENTS: 381 calories; 23.0 grams of protein; 2.5 grams of fat; 67.6 grams of carbohydrates; 1256 mg of sodium; 1221 mg of potassium; and 163 mg of calcium.

Tuna and Potato Fritatta

2 cups shredded cooked potatoes

One 7-oz. can water-packed albacore tuna, drained

⅓ cup dry-curd cottage cheese

2 tbsp. chopped pimientos

6 egg whites

⅓ cup nonfat yogurt

2 tsp. dried dill weed

1 tbsp. instant minced onion flakes

½ tsp. salt-free herb seasoning

Preheat oven to 375 degrees. Spray an ovenproof baking dish
with non-stick cooking spray. Combine potatoes, tuna, cottage
cheese and pimientos. Spoon mixture into baking dish. In a
medium bowl, combine egg whites, yogurt, dill weed, onion
flakes, and herb seasoning. Beat until well blended. Pour over
potato mixture. Bake 15 to 20 minutes until eggs are set.
Serves 2.

(Serving = 1 lean protein; 1 starchy carbohydrate)
*NUTRIENTS: 274 calories; 37.5 grams of protein; 1.4 grams of fat; 25.7
grams of carbohydrates; 220 mg of sodium; 819 mg of potassium; and 113
mg of calcium.*

Breakfast Bean Enchiladas

One 14½-oz. can tomatoes
½ cup coarsely chopped onion
1 clove garlic
½ tsp. ground cumin
½ tsp. ground oregano
1 tsp. salt-free herb seasoning
⅛ tsp. ground cloves
2 tbsp. tomato paste
6 corn tortillas
6 hard-boiled egg whites, chopped
2 cups cooked kidney beans
One 4-oz. can chopped green chilies
2 tsp. dried celery flakes
½ cup dry-curd cottage cheese
¼ cup chopped green onion

Preheat oven to 350 degrees. Combine tomatoes, onion, garlic, cumin, oregano, herb seasoning, cloves, and tomato paste in a blender. Blend until smooth. Pour mixture into medium saucepan. Bring to a near boil, reduce heat, cover, and simmer 20 minutes. Warm tortillas until soft and pliable. Combine egg whites, kidney beans, green chilies, and celery flakes. Divide mixture among tortillas. Top with cottage cheese. Roll up tortillas. Spray an 8" x 11" baking dish with nonstick cooking spray. Place enchiladas in the dish, seam side down. Cover enchiladas with sauce. Sprinkle with green onion. Cover. Bake for 30 minutes. Serves 2.

Note: This recipe may be prepared ahead of time. Cover unbaked enchiladas and refrigerate several hours or overnight. Bake when ready to eat.

(Serving = 1 lean protein; 1 starchy carbohydrate)
NUTRIENTS: 465 calories; 30.4 grams of protein; 4.4 grams of fat; 79.9 grams of carbohydrates; 607 mg of sodium; 1308 mg of potassium; and 236 mg of calcium.

Breakfast Rice Enchiladas

¼ cup chopped onion
One 8-oz. can tomatoes, chopped
2 tbsp. chopped green chilies
1 tsp. dried cilantro
1 tsp. chili powder
⅛ tsp. garlic powder
6 corn tortillas
6 egg whites, beaten

2 cups cooked brown rice
½ cup dry-curd cottage cheese

In a small saucepan, combine onion, tomatoes, green chilies, cilantro, chili powder, and garlic powder. Bring to a boil. Reduce heat. Cover and simmer sauce for 10 minutes. Warm tortillas until soft and pliable. Spray a medium skillet with non-stick cooking spray. Heat skillet over medium heat. Combine beaten egg whites and rice. Pour into skillet and cook until egg whites are scrambled. Stir in cottage cheese. Remove from heat. Divide egg mixture among tortillas. Roll up tortillas. Arrange enchiladas on two serving plates. Spoon sauce over enchiladas and serve.

Note: This recipe may be prepared ahead of time. Place filled enchiladas in 8" x 11" baking dish. Spoon sauce over enchiladas, cover, and refrigerate. When ready to serve, heat enchiladas in 350 degree oven for 20 minutes or microwave for 5 to 6 minutes. Serves 2.

Variation: Substitute cooked potatoes or cooked pinto beans for rice.

(Serving = 1 lean protein; 1 starchy carbohydrate)
NUTRIENTS: 522 calories; 25.5 grams of protein; 4.8 grams of fat; 95.0 grams of carbohydrates; 1005 mg of sodium; 722 mg of potassium; and 192 mg of calcium.

Poached Cowboy Eggs

½ cup chopped onion
½ cup chopped green pepper
1 tbsp. safflower oil

½ cup chopped tomatoes

One 8-oz. can tomato sauce

1 tsp. chili powder

½ tsp. salt-free herb seasoning

½ tsp. dried oregano

⅛ tsp. ground cumin

6 egg whites

2 cups cooked pinto beans

6 corn tortillas

1 tbsp. chopped fresh cilantro

In a medium skillet, sauté onion and green pepper in oil until tender. Add tomatoes, tomato sauce, chili powder, herb seasoning, oregano, and cumin. Reduce heat. Cover. Simmer for 20 minutes. Make impressions in sauce and pour egg whites into impressions. Cover and cook until eggs are poached. Heat previously cooked pinto beans. Wrap tortillas in a damp towel and warm in microwave. Divide beans among tortillas. Roll up tortillas. Arrange filled tortillas on two serving plates. Spoon poached eggs and sauce over tortillas. Garnish with cilantro. Serves 2.

(Serving = 1 lean protein; 1 starchy carbohydrate; ¼ lean, fibrous vegetable)
NUTRIENTS: 584 calories; 31.5 grams of protein; 11.5 grams of fat; 94.7 grams of carbohydrates; 371 mg of sodium; 2200 mg of potassium; and 297 mg of calcium.

Potato Deviled Eggs

6 hard-boiled eggs

1 cup mashed potatoes

1 tbsp. tarragon vinegar

1 tsp. mustard

1 tsp. freeze-dried chives

⅛ tsp. tumeric

Cut eggs in half, lengthwise. Remove and discard yolks.
Combine remaining ingredients and mix well. Fill egg halves
with potato mixture. Chill before serving. Serves 2.

(Serving = 1 lean protein; ½ starchy carbohydrate)
NUTRIENTS: 140 calories; 13.4 grams of protein; 2.7 grams of fat; 14.9
grams of carbohydrates; 485 mg of sodium; 501 mg of potassium; and 48
mg of calcium.

Tuna Deviled Eggs

6 hard-boiled eggs

½ 7-oz. can water-packed albacore tuna, drained

1 tbsp. nonfat yogurt

⅛ tsp. dry mustard

1 tsp. dried vegetable flakes

⅛ tsp. onion powder

Cut eggs in half, lengthwise. Remove and discard yolks. Mash
tuna. Combine with remaining ingredients. Fill egg halves with
tuna mixture. Chill before serving. Serves 2.

(Serving = 1 lean protein)
NUTRIENTS: 96 calories; 20.3 grams of protein; 0.4 grams of fat; 1.2
grams of carbohydrates; 163 mg of sodium; 240 mg of potassium; and 23
mg of calcium.

Chinese Egg Scramble

½ cup freeze-dried mushrooms
1 cup chicken broth, defatted
4 egg whites, beaten
¼ cup chopped green onion
1 tsp. grated fresh ginger root
¼ tsp. garlic powder
½ tsp. salt-free herb seasoning
1 tbsp. low-salt soy sauce
½ cup frozen peas, thawed
1 cup cooked brown rice
½ cup bean sprouts, drained
⅓ cup chopped cooked chicken breast

Combine mushrooms and broth; set aside. Spray a medium
skillet with nonstick cooking spray. Add beaten egg whites.
Cook and stir until soft curds form. Remove eggs and set aside.
Add green onion, ginger root, garlic powder, herb seasoning,
soy sauce, peas, and reconstituted mushrooms. Cook and stir
over medium heat for 3 minutes. Add brown rice, bean
sprouts, and chicken. Cook 3 to 5 minutes until thoroughly
heated. Fold in eggs. Heat and serve. Serves 2.

*(Serving = 1 lean protein; 1 starchy carbohydrate; ½ lean,
fibrous vegetable)*
*NUTRIENTS: 274 calories; 21.9 grams of protein; 3.5 grams of fat; 39.9
grams of carbohydrates; 1489 mg of sodium; 378 mg of potassium; and
129 mg of calcium.*

Shirred Eggs and Potatoes

1½ cups thinly sliced cooked potatoes
½ cup chopped green onion
1½ cups cooked peas
One 8-oz. can tomato sauce
¼ tsp. dried marjoram
½ tsp. dried chervil
6 egg whites
dash paprika

Preheat oven to 350 degrees. Spray a shallow 1½ quart baking dish with nonstick cooking spray. Arrange potato slices, onion, and peas in the dish. Combine tomato sauce, marjoram, and chervil. Pour mixture over peas. Make six impressions with a spoon in the tomato sauce. Place one egg white in each impression. Sprinkle with paprika. Bake 25 to 30 minutes until eggs are set. Serves 2.

Note: This casserole may be prepared ahead of time. Cover unbaked casserole. Refrigerate several hours or overnight. Bake when ready to eat.

(Serving = 1 lean protein; 2 starchy carbohydrates)
NUTRIENTS: 267 calories; 21.8 grams of protein; 15.1 grams of fat; 31.0 grams of carbohydrates; 1117 mg of sodium; 1145 mg of potassium; and 103 mg of calcium.

Skillet Potatoes and Eggs

1 tbsp. safflower oil
1½ cups cubed, cooked potatoes
¼ cup chopped onion

6 egg whites
¼ tsp. garlic powder
1 tsp. dried parsley flakes
½ cup alfalfa sprouts
½ cup chopped tomatoes
¼ cup picante sauce

Heat oil in a medium skillet over medium-high heat. Add potatoes and onion. Cook until golden. Mix egg whites, garlic, and parsley until blended. Pour over potatoes. Cover and cook over low heat until eggs are set. Top with alfalfa sprouts and tomatoes. Garnish with picante sauce. Serves 2.

(Serving = 1 lean protein; 1 starchy carbohydrate; ½ lean, fibrous vegetable)
NUTRIENTS: 232 calories; 15.9 grams of protein; 7.7 grams of fat; 26.2 grams of carbohydrates; 311 mg of sodium; 691 mg of potassium; and 43 mg of calcium.

Huevos Rancheros

3 tbsp. chopped onion
3 tbsp. chopped green chilies
2 tbsp. water
8 egg whites
½ tsp. salt-free herb seasoning
6 corn tortillas
½ cup picante sauce, warmed
2 tbsp. chopped green onion

Spray a medium skillet with nonstick cooking spray. Sauté onion and green chilies in water until tender. Add egg whites and herb seasoning. Cook and stir until egg whites are scrambled. Wrap tortillas in a damp towel and warm in microwave. Divide scrambled eggs among tortillas. Roll up tortillas. Top with warmed picante sauce and green onions. Serves 2.

(Serving = 1 lean protein; ½ starchy carbohydrate)
NUTRIENTS: 309 calories; 21.8 grams of protein; 3.8 grams of fat; 48.1 grams of carbohydrates; 674 mg of sodium; 495 mg of potassium; and 159 mg of calcium.

5

❢ *Breakfast Grains*

Helpful Hints

Cereal can be prepared the night before. This
method also makes "portable" cereal.

Fill a wide-mouth quart thermos with boiling water
to heat it. Empty water from the thermos. Add 1 cup
of cereal such as barley, millet, rye, or buckwheat
with 3 cups boiling water. Seal. Keep overnight. In
the morning stir cereal before using. Prepare oatmeal
using 1 cup oatmeal with 2¼ cups boiling water.

You can also fill a crockpot with cereals or grains. Add water,
cinnamon, and vanilla. Allow to cook overnight. Cereal will be
ready when you awaken.

Read all cereal labels, avoiding added fat, sugar, and salt.

Choose whole grain cereals.

Use skim milk on cereal. Try sugar-free drink mixes as a
delicious alternative.

Replace butter with prepared butter-flavored sprinkles or
butter flavoring.

Enhance the flavor of nonfat yogurt by adding 2½ tablespoons
of sugar-free syrups (several recipes are in this book), or a cup
of strawberries, raspberries, or blackberries. You may also add
½ teaspoon of flavored extracts and 1 packet sugar substitute.

Heat crepes or tortillas 1 to 2 minutes in a microwave after
wrapping in a moist cloth or napkin.

Use leftover grains such as rice, millet, barley, or bulgur as cereal. Serve hot or cold with skim milk.

Mix leftover rice with dry-curd cottage cheese, adding cinnamon and vanilla.

Try topping a rice cake with dry-curd cottage cheese and fruit.

A baked potato topped with nonfat yogurt, Mock Sour Cream (page 321), or butter sprinkles makes an excellent breakfast change of pace. Heat or reheat in a microwave.

Try a baked sweet potato topped with cinnamon and sugar substitute.

Strawberry Yogurt Muesli

2 cups old-fashioned oatmeal, uncooked
1½ cups nonfat yogurt
4 packets sugar substitute
¼ tsp. dried lemon peel
2 tsp. strawberry extract
2 cups sliced fresh strawberries

In a medium bowl, combine oatmeal, yogurt, sugar substitute, lemon peel, and strawberry extract. Mix until well blended. Cover and refrigerate overnight. Before serving, stir in sliced strawberries. Serves 2.

(Serving = 1 starchy carbohydrate)
NUTRIENTS: 488 calories; 18.1 grams of protein; 9.6 grams of fat; 85.2 grams of carbohydrates; 47 mg of sodium; 719 mg of potassium; and 186 mg of calcium.

Apple Orange Muesli

2 cups old-fashioned oatmeal, uncooked

2 cups sugar-free orange-flavored drink

1 Granny Smith apple, grated

2 tsp. banana extract

¼ tsp. almond extract

1 cup skim milk

In a mixing bowl, combine oatmeal and orange drink. Cover and refrigerate overnight. Before serving, stir in grated apple, banana extract, and almond extract. Serve with milk. Serves 2.

(Serving = 1 starchy carbohydrate)
NUTRIENTS: 475 calories; 18.5 grams of protein; 7.9 grams of fat; 84.8 grams of carbohydrates; 67 mg of sodium; 636 mg of potassium; and 209 mg of calcium.

Chocolate Coconut Muesli

2 cups old-fashioned oatmeal, uncooked

1 tbsp. unsweetened cocoa

4 packets sugar substitute

1 cup water

1½ cups skim milk

1 tsp. chocolate extract

1 tsp. coconut extract

In a mixing bowl, combine oatmeal, cocoa, and sugar substitute. Add remaining ingredients. Mix until well blended. Cover and refrigerate overnight. Serves 2.

(Serving = 1 starchy carbohydrate)
NUTRIENTS: 456 calories; 20.4 grams of protein; 7.7 grams of fat; 77.2 grams of carbohydrates; 98 mg of sodium; 658 mg of potassium; and 280 mg of calcium.

Apple Oatmeal

4½ cups water
2 cups old-fashioned oatmeal, uncooked
1 Granny Smith apple, grated
2 tsp. maple flavoring
½ tsp. cinnamon
4 packets sugar substitute
2 cups skim milk

Bring water to a boil. Stir in oatmeal and grated apple. Cook 5 minutes, stirring occasionally. Remove from heat. Stir in maple flavoring, cinnamon, and sugar substitute. Serve with milk. Serves 2.

(Serving = 1 starchy carbohydrate)
NUTRIENTS: 519 calories; 22.6 grams of protein; 8.1 grams of fat; 90.8 grams of carbohydrates; 131 mg of sodium; 840 mg of potassium; and 360 mg of calcium.

Blueberry Oatmeal

4 cups water
2 cups old-fashioned oatmeal, uncooked
1 cup frozen, unsweetened blueberries
1 tsp. blackberry extract

¼ tsp. dried lemon peel

½ tsp. cinnamon

4 packets sugar substitute

2 cups skim milk

Bring water to a boil. Stir in oatmeal. Cook 3 minutes, stirring occasionally. Stir in frozen blueberries, blackberry extract, lemon peel, and cinnamon. Bring to a boil and cook 2 minutes, stirring occasionally. Remove from heat. Stir in sugar substitute. Serve with milk. Serves 2.

(Serving = 1 starchy carbohydrate)
NUTRIENTS: 528 calories; 22.9 grams of protein; 8.0 grams of fat; 92.7 grams of carbohydrates; 132 mg of sodium; 829 mg of potassium; and 362 mg of calcium.

Eggnog Oatmeal

4 cups water

2 cups old-fashioned oatmeal, uncooked

6 egg whites

2 tsp. vanilla extract

½ tsp. rum extract

½ tsp. cinnamon

¼ tsp. nutmeg

4 packets sugar substitute

2 cups skim milk

Bring water to a boil. Stir in oatmeal. Cook 5 minutes, stirring occasionally. Beat egg whites until frothy. Add to oatmeal and cook 1 to 2 minutes. Remove from heat. Stir in vanilla, rum,

cinnamon, nutmeg, and sugar substitute. Serve with milk.
Serves 2.

(Serving = 1 lean protein; 1 starchy carbohydrate)
NUTRIENTS: 529 calories; 33.3 grams of protein; 7.8 grams of fat; 81.0
grams of carbohydrates; 276 mg of sodium; 899 mg of potassium; and 364
mg of calcium.

Basic Oatmeal Pancakes

2½ cups old-fashioned oatmeal, uncooked
6 egg whites
1 cup skim milk
1 tbsp. safflower oil
1 tsp. baking powder
1 tsp. vanilla extract
Maple Syrup (page 68)

Place all ingredients in a blender or food processor. Blend 15 to
20 seconds, until smooth. Lightly spray griddle or electric
skillet with non-stick cooking spray. Heat until hot. For each
pancake, pour ¼ cup batter onto griddle. Cook pancakes until
edges are dry and bubbles appear on top. Turn and brown other
side. Makes 12 pancakes. Serve with Maple Syrup. Serves 2.

(Serving = 1 lean protein; 1 starchy carbohydrate)
NUTRIENTS: 599 calories; 28.7 grams of protein; 16.1 grams of fat;
86.1 grams of carbohydrates; 149 mg of sodium; 579 mg of potassium;
and 75 mg of calcium. (Does not include Maple Syrup.)

Buttermilk Oatmeal Pancakes

1½ cups old-fashioned oatmeal, uncooked
½ cup rye flour
4 egg whites
1 cup nonfat buttermilk
1 tbsp. safflower oil
½ tsp. baking soda
2 tsp. vanilla extract
Strawberry Syrup (page 68)

Place all ingredients in a blender or food processor. Blend 15 to 20 seconds, until smooth. Lightly spray griddle or electric skillet with nonstick cooking spray. Heat until hot. For each pancake, pour ¼ cup batter onto griddle. Cook pancakes until edges are dry and bubbles appear on top. Turn and brown other side. Makes 12 pancakes. Serve with Strawberry Syrup. Serves 2.

(Serving = 1 lean protein; 1 starchy carbohydrate)
NUTRIENTS: 431 calories; 21.9 grams of protein; 12.4 grams of fat; 57.5 grams of carbohydrates; 226 mg of sodium; 541 mg of potassium; and 188 mg of calcium. (Does not include Strawberry Syrup.)

Sweet Potato Pancakes

1 cup oat flour, uncooked
1 cup mashed cooked sweet potatoes
4 egg whites
1 cup skim milk
1 tbsp. safflower oil
1 tsp. vanilla extract

1 tsp. maple extract
½ tsp. cinnamon
Maple Syrup (page 68)

Place all ingredients in a blender or food processor. Blend 15 to
20 seconds, until smooth. Lightly spray griddle or electric
skillet with nonstick cooking spray. Heat until hot. For each
pancake, pour ¼ cup batter onto griddle. Cook pancakes until
edges are dry and bubbles appear on top. Turn and brown other
side. Makes 12 pancakes. Serve with Maple Syrup. Serves 2.

(Serving = 1 lean protein; 1 starchy carbohydrate)
NUTRIENTS: 538 calories; 23.9 grams of protein; 12.8 grams of fat;
82.6 grams of carbohydrates; 210 mg of sodium; 760 mg of potassium;
and 222 mg of calcium. (Does not include Maple Syrup.)

Blueberry Pancakes

1½ cups oat flour
½ cup buckwheat flour
4 egg whites
⅞ cup nonfat buttermilk
1 tbsp. safflower oil
½ tsp. baking soda
1 tsp. vanilla extract
1 tsp. blackberry extract
½ tsp. cinnamon
½ cup frozen unsweetened blueberries, thawed
Blueberry Syrup (page 69)

Place all ingredients, except blueberries, in a blender or food processor. Blend 15 to 20 seconds, until smooth. Add blueberries and blend until just mixed. Lightly spray griddle or electric skillet with nonstick cooking spray. Heat until hot. For each pancake, pour ¼ cup batter onto griddle. Cook pancakes until edges are dry and bubbles appear on top. Turn and brown other side. Makes 12 pancakes. Serve with Blueberry Syrup. Serves 2.

(Serving = 1 lean protein; 1 starchy carbohydrate)
NUTRIENTS: 456 calories; 22.1 grams of protein; 12.4 grams of fat; 63.8 grams of carbohydrates; 227 mg of sodium; 575 mg of potassium; and 192 mg of calcium. (Does not include Blueberry Syrup.)

Apple Oat Bran Pancakes

1 cup oat flour
1 cup oat bran
1 tsp. baking powder
4 egg whites
1¼ cups skim milk
1 tbsp. safflower oil
1 tsp. vanilla extract
½ tsp. cinnamon
¼ tsp. ground nutmeg
½ tsp. dried lemon peel
1 Granny Smith apple, grated
Ginger Syrup (page 70)

Place all ingredients in a blender or food processor. Blend 15 to 20 seconds, until smooth. Lightly spray griddle or electric skillet with nonstick cooking spray. Heat until hot. For each pancake, pour ¼ cup batter onto griddle. Cook pancakes until edges are dry and bubbles appear on top. Turn and brown other side. Add additional milk or water if batter becomes too thick. Makes 12 pancakes. Serve with Ginger Syrup. Serves 2.

(Serving = 1 lean protein; 1 starchy carbohydrate)
NUTRIENTS: 519 calories; 27.1 grams of protein; 14.0 grams of fat; 79.7 grams of carbohydrates; 185 mg of sodium; 827 mg of potassium; and 226 mg of calcium. (Does not include Ginger Syrup.)

Gingerbread Pancakes

1½ cups old-fashioned oatmeal, uncooked
½ cup rye flour
4 egg whites
1¼ cups skim milk
1 tbsp. safflower oil
1 tsp. baking powder
1 tsp. cinnamon
½ tsp. ground ginger
¼ tsp. ground nutmeg
1½ tsp. vanilla extract
½ tsp. rum extract
Lemon Syrup (page 71)
Whipped Topping (page 354)

Place all ingredients in a blender or food processor. Blend 15 to 20 seconds, until smooth. Lightly spray griddle or electric skillet with nonstick cooking spray. Heat until hot. For each pancake, pour ¼ cup batter onto griddle. Cook pancakes until edges are dry and bubbles appear on top. Turn and brown other side. Makes 12 pancakes. Serve with Lemon Syrup and top with Whipped Topping. Serves 2.

(Serving = 1 lean protein; 1 starchy carbohydrate)
NUTRIENTS: 545 calories; 28.3 grams of protein; 13.4 grams of fat;
80.9 grams of carbohydrates; 177 mg of sodium; 886 mg of potassium;
and 252 mg of calcium. (Does not include Lemon Syrup and Whipped
Topping.)

Buckwheat Pancakes

1¼ cups old-fashioned oatmeal, uncooked
¾ cup buckwheat flour
4 egg whites
1 cup skim milk
1 tbsp. safflower oil
1 tsp. baking powder
Apple Syrup (page 69)
Turkey Sausage (page 163)

Place all ingredients in a blender or food processor. Blend 15 to 20 seconds, until smooth. Lightly spray griddle or electric skillet with nonstick cooking spray. Heat until hot. For each pancake, pour ¼ cup batter onto griddle. Cook pancakes until edges are dry and bubbles appear on top. Turn and brown other side. Makes 12 pancakes. Serve with Apple Syrup and Turkey Sausage. Serves 2.

(Serving = ½ lean protein; 1 starchy carbohydrate)
NUTRIENTS: 506 calories; 24.6 grams of protein; 12.6 grams of fat;
76.2 grams of carbohydrates; 162 mg of sodium; 762 mg of potassium;
and 203 mg of calcium. (Does not include Apple Syrup and Turkey
Sausage.)

Hashbrown Pancakes

1 cup old-fashioned oatmeal, uncooked
¾ cup skim milk
¼ cup grated onion
2 egg whites
2 cups shredded new potatoes
1 tsp. salt-free herb seasoning
½ tsp. dried parsley flakes

Place oatmeal, milk, onion, and egg in a blender or food processor. Blend 15 to 20 seconds, until smooth. Stir in potatoes, herb seasonings, and parsley. Lightly spray griddle or electric skillet with nonstick cooking spray. Heat until hot. For each pancake, spoon ¼ cup batter onto griddle. Flatten batter with spoon. Cook until pancakes are golden brown and thoroughly cooked. Turn and brown other side. Makes 8 pancakes. Serve with scrambled eggs and picante sauce. Serves 2.

(Serving = 1 ½ starchy carbohydrate)
NUTRIENTS: 353 calories; 17.1 grams of protein; 4.0 grams of fat; 63.1 grams of carbohydrates; 102 mg of sodium; 850 mg of potassium; and 157 mg of calcium.

Oatmeal Waffles

¾ cup oat bran
¾ cup oat flour
½ cup buckwheat flour
2 tsp. baking powder
¼ tsp. cinnamon
1⅓ cups skim milk

2 tbsp. safflower oil

2 tsp. vanilla extract

3 egg whites

Maple Syrup (page 68)

Spray waffle iron with nonstick cooking spray and preheat.
In a mixing bowl, combine oat bran, oat flour, buckwheat flour,
baking powder, and cinnamon. Add milk, oil, and vanilla. Mix
well. Beat egg whites until stiff but not dry. Fold into batter.
Pour about 1 cup batter on preheated waffle iron. Close lid and
bake until waffles are golden brown. Check to see if waffles are
done when steam subsides. Makes 3 9-inch waffles. Serve with
Maple Syrup. Serves 2.

(Serving = ½ lean protein; 1 starchy carbohydrate)
NUTRIENTS: 536 calories; 24.8 grams of protein; 19.5 grams of fat;
72.2 grams of carbohydrates; 165 mg of sodium; 806 mg of potassium;
and 233 mg of calcium. (Does not include Maple Syrup.)

Strawberry Crepes

1 cup sliced fresh strawberries

2 packets sugar substitute

½ cup old-fashioned oatmeal, uncooked

½ cup oat bran

¼ cup oat flour

4 egg whites

1 cup skim milk

1 tbsp. safflower oil

1 tsp. vanilla extract

Strawberry Syrup (page 68)

Whipped Topping (page 354)

Combine strawberries and suger. Set aside. Prepare Whipped
Topping according to instructions. Place remaining ingredients
in a blender. Blend 20 to 30 seconds, until smooth. Cover and
let stand for 15 minutes. Lightly spray 7-inch skillet or crepe
pan with nonstick cooking spray. Heat until hot. Pour ⅓ cup
batter onto pan, until batter covers bottom of pan. Cook about
1 minute until underside of crepe is browned. Turn and brown
other side. Continue to make crepes until batter is used up.
Spray pan as required with cooking spray. Place cooked crepes
on a plate and cover to keep warm. Fill crepes with sweetened
strawberries. Top with Strawberry Syrup and Whipped
Topping. Makes 6 crepes.

(Serving = ½ lean protein; ½ starchy carbohydrate)
NUTRIENTS: 126 calories; 7.0 grams of protein; 3.9 grams of fat; 17.3
grams of carbohydrates; 55 mg of sodium; 221 mg of potassium; and 64
mg of calcium. (Does not include Strawberry Syrup and Whipped Topping.)

Maple Syrup

1 tbsp. cornstarch
1¼ cups water (divided)
4 packets sugar substitute
½ tsp. maple flavoring
1 tsp. vanilla extract

Dissolve cornstarch in ¼ cup water. In a small saucepan,
combine dissolved cornstarch and 1 cup water. Cook over
medium heat and stir until thickened. Remove from heat. Stir
in sugar substitute, maple, and vanilla. Serve warm. Makes 1¼
cups.

NUTRIENTS: 18 calories; 9.6 grams of carbohydrates.

Strawberry Syrup

2 tbsp. cornstarch

2 cups water (divided)

1 pkg. sugar-free, strawberry-flavored gelatin

Dissolve cornstarch in ¼ cup water. In a small saucepan, bring
1¾ cups water to a boil. Stir in dissolved cornstarch. Cook over
medium heat and stir until thickened. Remove from heat. Stir
in gelatin. Continue stirring until gelatin is dissolved. Serve
immediately. Makes 2 cups.

Note: This syrup may be prepared ahead of time and stored in
refrigerator. Heat in microwave until syrup is liquid and warm.

Variation: Substitute any flavor of gelatin (orange, lemon,
raspberry, etc.) for strawberry gelatin.

*NUTRIENTS: 59 calories; 6.0 grams of protein; 19.2 grams of carbohy-
drates; 8 mg of sodium; 180 mg of potassium.*

Apple Syrup

1 tbsp. cornstarch

1¼ cups water (divided)

1 Granny Smith apple, cored and grated

½ tsp. cinnamon

¼ tsp. ground ginger

1 tsp. vanilla extract

4 packets sugar substitute

Dissolve cornstarch in ¼ cup water. In a small saucepan, combine dissolved cornstarch, 1 cup water, grated apple, cinnamon, and ginger. Cook over medium heat and stir until thickened. Reduce heat. Simmer 5 minutes until apple is tender. Remove from heat. Stir in vanilla and sugar substitute. Serve warm. Makes 1¼ cups.

NUTRIENTS: 99 calories; 0.3 grams of protein; 0.5 grams of fat; 30.7 grams of carbohydrates; 1 mg of sodium; 159 mg of potassium; and 10 mg of calcium.

Blueberry Syrup

1 tsp. cornstarch
½ cup water
1 cup frozen, unsweetened blueberries, thawed and crushed
¼ tsp. lemon juice
6 packets sugar substitute
½ tsp. blackberry extract

In a small saucepan, combine cornstarch, water, and blueberries. Cook over medium heat and stir until thickened. Remove from heat. Stir in lemon juice, sugar substitute, and blackberry extract. Serve warm. Makes 1 cup.

NUTRIENTS: 118 calories; 0.9 grams of protein; 0.3 grams of fat; 34.6 grams of carbohydrates; 3 mg of sodium; 137 mg of potassium; and 13 mg of calcium.

Ginger Syrup

2 tsp. cornstarch

1 cup water

2 tsp. grated fresh ginger root

½ tsp. cinnamon

1 tsp. butter flavoring

½ tsp. vanilla extract

6 packets sugar substitute

In a small saucepan, combine cornstarch, water, ginger root, cinnamon, and butter flavoring. Cook over medium heat and stir until thickened. Reduce heat. Simmer 5 minutes. Remove from heat. Stir in vanilla and sugar substitute. Serve warm. Makes 1 cup.

NUTRIENTS: 36 calories; 19.2 grams of carbohydrates.

Raspberry Syrup

1 tsp. cornstarch

½ cup water

1 cup frozen, unsweetened raspberries, thawed and crushed

½ tsp. lemon juice

½ tsp. strawberry extract

6 packets sugar substitute

In a small saucepan, combine cornstarch, water, and raspberries. Cook over medium heat and stir until thickened. Remove from heat. Stir in lemon juice, strawberry extract, and sugar substitute. Serve warm. Makes 1¼ cups.

NUTRIENTS: 158 calories; 3.0 grams of protein; 1.2 grams of fat; 43.0 grams of carbohydrates; 2 mg of sodium; 414 mg of potassium; and 54 mg of calcium.

Lemon Syrup

1 tbsp. cornstarch
¼ cup lemon juice
1 cup water
½ tsp. dried lemon peel
⅛ tsp. nutmeg
¼ tsp. lemon extract
8 packets sugar substitute

Dissolve cornstarch in lemon juice. In a small saucepan, combine dissolved cornstarch, water, lemon peel, and nutmeg. Cook over medium heat and stir until thickened. Remove from heat. Stir in lemon extract and sugar substitute. Serve warm. Makes 1¼ cups.

NUTRIENTS: 18 calories; 9.6 grams of carbohydrates.

Basic Cornbread

1½ cups cornmeal
½ cup rye flour
2 tsp. baking powder
1 cup skim milk
3 egg whites
2 tbsp. safflower oil

Preheat oven to 400 degrees. In a mixing bowl, combine cornmeal, rye flour, and baking powder. Add milk and egg whites. Stir until blended. Add oil. Blend gently. Spray 9" x 9" x 2" baking pan with nonstick cooking spray. Pour mixture into pan. Bake 18 to 20 minutes until top is golden brown and edges begin to separate from pan. Serves 4.

(Serving = ¼ lean protein; ½ starchy carbohydrate)
NUTRIENTS: 300 calories; 11.1 grams of protein; 8.7 grams of fat; 45.8 grams of carbohydrates; 679 mg of sodium; 378 mg of potassium; and 219 mg of calcium.

Garden Cornbread

2 cups cornmeal
1 cup oat flour
1 tsp. allspice
2 tsp. baking powder
½ cup hot water
3 egg whites
¾ cup skim milk
2 tbsp. safflower oil
1 tsp. butter flavoring
½ cup frozen corn, thawed
½ cup grated zucchini
¼ cup grated carrot

Preheat oven to 400 degrees. In a large mixing bowl, combine cornmeal, flour, allspice, and baking powder. Add remaining ingredients. Stir until blended. Spray 9" x 9" x 2" baking pan with nonstick cooking spray. Pour mixture into pan. Bake

25 to 30 minutes or until edges begin to separate from pan.
Serves 4.

(Serving = ¼ lean protein; 1 starchy carbohydrate)
NUTRIENTS: 421 calories; 13.9 grams of protein; 10.8 grams of fat;
68.9 grams of carbohydrates; 949 mg of sodium; 459 mg of potassium;
and 257 mg of calcium.

———————

Black Bean Cornbread

½ cup chopped onion
½ cup chopped green pepper
2 tbsp. safflower oil
¼ cup prepared butter-flavored mix
1½ cups cornmeal
1½ cups rye flour
2 tsp. baking powder
1 tsp. chili powder
½ tsp. salt-free herb seasoning
¼ tsp. garlic powder
1 cup cooked black beans
1 cup skim milk
3 egg whites
1 tsp. cheese flavored sprinkles

Preheat oven to 400 degrees. In a medium skillet, sauté onion
and green pepper in oil and prepared butter mix until tender. In
a large mixing bowl, combine cornmeal, rye flour, baking
powder, chili powder, herb seasoning, and garlic powder. Add
onion mixture, black beans, milk, and egg whites. Stir until
blended. Spray 9" x 9" x 2" baking pan with nonstick cooking

spray. Pour mixture into pan. Bake 25 to 30 minutes or until edges begin to separate from pan. Remove from oven. Garnish with cheese sprinkles. Serves 4.

(Serving = ¼ lean protein; ½ starchy carbohydrate; ¼ lean fibrous vegetable)
NUTRIENTS: 470 calories; 20.4 grams of protein; 9.8 grams of fat; 79.8 grams of carbohydrates; 684 mg of sodium; 865 mg of potassium; and 260 mg of calcium.

Cornbread Dressing

1 recipe Basic Cornbread (page 72)
1 cup chopped celery
½ cup chopped onion
¼ cup prepared butter-flavored mix
1 tsp. ground sage
1 tsp. dried parsley flakes
1 tsp. salt-free herb seasoning
¼ tsp. black pepper
¼ tsp. garlic powder
¼ tsp. dried rosemary, crumbled
One 14½-oz. can chicken broth, defatted
3 egg whites, beaten

Preheat oven to 350 degrees. In a large bowl, crumble cornbread into small pieces. In a medium skillet, sauté celery and onion in prepared butter mix until tender. Remove from heat. Stir in seasonings. Pour mixture over cornbread. Toss. Add broth and egg whites. Toss. Spray 2-quart dish with non-stick cooking spray. Spoon mixture into dish. Cover. Bake 45 minutes. Serves 4.

(Serving = ½ lean protein; ½ starchy carbohydrate; ¼ lean, fibrous vegetable)
NUTRIENTS:505 calories; 24.3 grams of protein; 10.4 grams of fat; 83.6 grams of carbohydrates; 1496 mg of sodium; 1030 mg of potassium; and 285 mg of calcium.

Corn Tortillas

1½ cups water
1 cup cornmeal
3 tbsp. prepared butter-flavored mix
1¼ cups oat flour
½ tsp. baking soda
1 tsp. salt-free herb seasoning

In a small saucepan, bring water to a boil. Stir in cornmeal and prepared butter mix. Reduce heat. Cover. Simmer 5 minutes. Set aside to cool. In a mixing bowl, combine flour, baking soda, and herb seasoning. Stir in cooled cornmeal. Knead for 3 minutes. Add water or flour if necessary to form soft dough. Divide dough into 12 pieces. Sprinkle a board and rolling pin with cornmeal. Roll each piece into a 6-inch circle. Spray griddle with nonstick cooking spray. Cook tortillas 1 to 2 minutes on each side until golden brown. Use immediately or prepare in advance and reheat. Serves 4.

(Serving = ½ starchy carbohydrate)
NUTRIENTS: 224 calories; 6.9 grams of protein; 3.3 grams of fat; 42.4 grams of carbohydrates; 408 mg of sodium; 179 mg of potassium; and 105 mg of calcium.

6

❦ *Fish and Seafood*

Helpful Hints

Consult the chart Using Herbs and Spices (page 12) to try new combinations of spices.

Fish odors can be removed from utensils and hands by washing in a solution of 1 quart water and 3 tablespoons baking soda.

A quick way to cook fillets is to oven broil or grill. Fillets ½ to 1½ inches thick grill best. Keep fillets moist by basting with lemon during cooking.

Marinating and basting keep fish moist during grilling or broiling, and they add flavor. More flavor is absorbed from a marinade than from basting.

Avoid overcooking fish. Flavor is lost when overcooked.

Low-fat salad dressings make excellent fish marinades.

Use leftover fish in salads for added protein.

Most fishes can be substituted for the fish specified in a recipe.

Sautéed vegetables make an excellent topping for fish.

Skewer the tail section and then the head section of shrimp to ensure that it will lie flat when grilling.

To barbecue fish less than ¾ inch thick, place in a greased, hinged wire basket. Spray the grill when barbecuing or grilling thicker fish.

Select frozen fish that is solid, tightly wrapped, not discolored, has no freezer burns, and shows no ice crystals.

Properly cooked fish flakes with a fork and turns translucent, opaque, or white. Shellfish turns opaque when done.

Double the cooking time if fish is frozen prior to cooking. Add 5 minutes for fish wrapped in foil or cooked in sauce.

Poached Bass with Mushrooms

4 dried Chinese black mushrooms
1 lb. bass fillets
1 tbsp. low-salt soy sauce
1 tbsp. dry sherry
1 tbsp. rice wine vinegar
2 tbsp. chopped green onion
2 cloves garlic, pressed
1 tsp. grated fresh ginger root
¼ tsp. salt-free herb seasoning
½ cup chicken broth, defatted
1 tbsp. cornstarch
2 tbsp. water

Rinse mushrooms and remove stems. Soak in hot water for 20 minutes. In a 10-inch skillet, arrange bass in a single layer. Combine soy sauce, sherry, vinegar, onion, garlic, ginger root, herb seasoning, and chicken broth. Drain mushrooms. Cut softened mushrooms into small pieces. Add to combined ingredients. Pour mixture over fish. Bring to a boil. Reduce heat. Cover and simmer 8 to 12 minutes until fish flakes easily with fork. Remove fish to a platter and keep warm. Mix cornstarch and water. Stir into pan juices. Heat and stir until sauce is thickened. Pour sauce over fish and serve. Serves 4.

(Serving = 1 lean protein)
NUTRIENTS: 127 calories; 21.9 grams of protein; 3.5 grams of fat; 1.5 grams of carbohydrates; 336 mg of sodium; 28 mg of potassium; and 7 mg of calcium.

Basil Baked Cod

1 lb. cod fillets
¼ cup chopped green onion
One 4-oz. can mushrooms, drained
2 tbsp. dry white wine
1 tbsp. low-salt soy sauce
½ tsp. dried basil
½ tsp. dried oregano
¼ tsp. garlic powder

Preheat oven to 375 degrees. Spray a 9" x 9" x 2" baking dish with nonstick cooking spray. Place fish in dish. Combine remaining ingredients and spoon over fish. Cover and bake for 15 minutes. Uncover and bake 10 to 15 minutes until fish flakes easily with fork. Serves 4.

(Serving = 1 lean protein)
NUTRIENTS: 101 calories; 21.0 grams of protein; 0.8 grams of fat; 1.8 grams of carbohydrates; 367 mg of sodium; 534 mg of potassium; and 20 mg of calcium.

Crispy Cornmeal Cod

1 lb. cod fillets

½ cup cornmeal

2 tbsp. oat bran

1 tsp. paprika

½ tsp. dry mustard

1 tsp. dried celery flakes

½ tsp. salt-free herb seasoning

¼ tsp. black pepper

½ teaspoon onion powder

1 egg white

2 tbsp. skim milk

Preheat oven to 375 degrees. Pat fish dry with paper towels. In a shallow dish, combine cornmeal, oat bran, paprika, dry mustard, celery flakes, herb seasoning, black pepper, and onion powder. In a second shallow dish, combine egg white and milk. Beat until well blended. Coat fish with egg mixture, then cornmeal mixture. Spray a baking sheet with nonstick cooking spray. Place fish on sheet. Bake 15 minutes. Turn fish. Bake 10 minutes until fish is browned. Serves 4.

(Serving = 1 lean protein)
NUTRIENTS: 155 calories; 22.9 grams of protein; 1.0 grams of fat; 12.7 grams of carbohydrates; 299 mg of sodium; 506 mg of potassium; and 66 mg of calcium.

Buttered Cod in Foil

1 lb. cod fillets

1 tbsp. prepared butter-flavored mix

1 tbsp. dry white wine

2 tbsp. lemon juice

1 tsp. dried vegetable flakes

½ tsp. dried oregano

½ tsp. salt-free herb seasoning

¼ tsp. onion powder

Preheat oven to 400 degrees. Spray nonstick cooking spray on four pieces of aluminum foil large enough to enclose fish. Place fish on foil. Combine remaining ingredients. Drizzle mixture over fish. Fold foil over fish. Crimp edges together securely. Place wrapped fish on a baking pan. Bake 15 to 20 minutes until fish flakes easily with a fork. Serve fish in its wrapping. Serves 4.

(Serving = 1 lean protein)
NUTRIENTS: 89 calories; 20.0 grams of protein; 0.3 grams of fat; 0.0 grams of carbohydrates; 79 mg of sodium; 434 mg of potassium; and 11 mg of calcium.

Curried Flounder

1 lb. flounder fillets

1 cup chopped tomatoes

¼ cup chopped green onion

1 tbsp. cornstarch

¼ cup chicken broth, defatted

¾ cup skim milk

1 tbsp. chopped fresh parsley

2 tsp. curry powder

½ tsp. dried basil

⅛ tsp. garlic powder

Preheat oven to 375 degrees. Spray a 9" x 9" x 2" baking dish with nonstick cooking spray. Arrange fish in dish. Spoon tomatoes and onions over fish. Dissolve cornstarch in chicken broth. Stir in remaining ingredients. Pour over fish. Cover. Bake 20 to 25 minutes until fish flakes easily with a fork. Serves 4.

(Serving = 1 lean protein)
NUTRIENTS: 116 calories; 19.3 grams of protein; 0.9 grams of fat; 8.2 grams of carbohydrates; 182 mg of sodium; 641 mg of potassium; and 133 mg of calcium.

Glazed Flounder

1 lb. flounder fillets

2 tbsp. nonfat yogurt

2 tsp. Worcestershire sauce

1 tsp. Dijon mustard

1 tsp. instant minced onion flakes

½ tsp. dried thyme

¼ tsp. dried lemon peel

2 tbsp. oat bran

Preheat oven to 350 degrees. Spray a 9" x 9" x 2" baking dish with nonstick cooking spray. Arrange flounder in dish. Combine yogurt, Worcestershire sauce, mustard, onion flakes, thyme, and lemon peel. Spread mixture evenly over flounder. Sprinkle with oat bran. Bake uncovered 25 to 30 minutes until fish flakes easily with a fork. Serves 4.

(Serving = 1 lean protein)
NUTRIENTS: 89 calories; 17.6 grams of protein; 0.9 grams of fat; 2.0 grams of carbohydrates; 68 mg of sodium; 439 mg of potassium; and 78 mg of calcium.

Flounder Florentine

1 lb. flounder fillets
1½ cups frozen chopped spinach, thawed
½ cup thinly sliced onion
¼ tsp. garlic powder
⅛ tsp. black pepper
¼ tsp. dry mustard
½ tsp. dried marjoram
½ cup chicken broth, defatted
1 tbsp. lemon juice
1 tbsp. cornstarch
¼ cup water

Arrange fish in a single layer in a 10-inch skillet. Spoon spinach over fillets. Arrange onion slices over fish and spinach. Combine garlic, pepper, dry mustard, marjoram, chicken broth, and lemon juice. Pour over fish. Bring to a boil. Reduce heat, cover, and simmer 8 to 10 minutes until fish flakes easily with a fork. Remove fish to a platter and keep warm. Mix cornstarch and water. Stir into pan juices. Heat and stir until sauce is thickened. Pour sauce over fish. Serve immediately. Serves 4.

(Serving = 1 lean protein; ½ lean, fibrous vegetable)
NUTRIENTS: 105 calories; 19.6 grams of protein; 0.9 grams of fat; 4.9 grams of carbohydrates; 309 mg of sodium; 701 mg of potassium; and 157 mg of calcium.

Oven-Fried Flounder with Dill

1 lb. flounder fillets
½ cup oat bran
2 tbsp. cornmeal
1 tsp. dried dill weed
1 tsp. dried parsley flakes
¼ tsp. black pepper
½ tsp. dried lemon peel
1 egg white
2 tbsp. skim milk

Preheat oven to 375 degrees. Pat fish dry with paper towels. In a shallow dish, combine oat bran, cornmeal, dill weed, parsley flakes, black pepper, and lemon peel. In a second shallow dish, combine egg white and milk. Beat until well blended. Coat fish with egg mixture, then bran mixture. Spray a baking sheet with nonstick cooking spray. Place fish on sheet. Bake for 15 minutes. Turn fish. Bake for 10 minutes until fish is browned. Serves 4.

(Serving = 1 lean protein)
NUTRIENTS: 130 calories; 20.3 grams of protein; 1.4 grams of fat; 9.8 grams of carbohydrates; 132 mg of sodium; 505 mg of potassium; and 90 mg of calcium.

Spanish-Style Grouper

1 lb. grouper fillets

½ tsp. paprika

½ tsp. salt-free herb seasoning

¼ tsp. black pepper

1 green pepper, cut into rings

1 tomato, sliced

1 tbsp. safflower oil

1 tbsp. lime juice

2 tsp. instant minced onion flakes

¼ tsp. garlic powder

1 tsp. dried parsley flakes

Preheat oven to 375 degrees. Spray a 9" x 9" x 2" baking dish with nonstick cooking spray. Place fish in dish. Sprinkle with paprika, herb seasoning, and pepper. Top with green pepper rings and tomato slices. Combine remaining ingredients and pour over fish. Cover and bake for 15 minutes. Uncover and bake 10 to 15 minutes until fish flakes easily with fork. Serves 4.

(Serving = 1 lean protein; ½ lean, fibrous vegetable)
NUTRIENTS: 142 calories; 22.5 grams of protein; 4.1 grams of fat; 3.3 grams of carbohydrates; 4 mg of sodium; 145 mg of potassium; and 7 mg of calcium.

Southwestern Haddock

½ cup chopped onion

½ cup chopped celery

2 tbsp. chopped fresh parsley

1 lb. haddock fillets

1 8-oz. can tomato sauce

2 tbsp. lemon juice

1 tbsp. chopped canned jalapenos

¼ tsp. garlic powder

½ tsp. salt-free herb seasoning

⅛ tsp. cinnamon

⅛ tsp. ground cloves

Preheat oven to 375 degrees. Spray a 9" x 9" x 2" baking dish with nonstick cooking spray. Combine chopped onions, celery, and parsley. Place in dish. Arrange fish over vegetables. Combine remaining ingredients and pour over fish. Cover. Bake 25 to 30 minutes until fish flakes easily with fork. Serves 4.

(Serving = 1 lean protein)
NUTRIENTS: 119 calories; 22.0 grams of protein; 0.3 grams of fat; 8.4 grams of carbohydrates; 419 mg of sodium; 654 mg of potassium; and 58 mg of calcium.

Poached Haddock with Garden Sauce

1 lb. haddock fillets

1 cup chopped tomatoes

½ cup sliced celery

½ cup shredded carrots

¼ cup sliced green onion

2 tsp. dried parsley flakes

½ tsp. salt-free herb seasoning

⅛ tsp. black pepper

¼ tsp dried rosemary, crumbled

1 tsp. red wine vinegar

½ cup chicken broth, defatted
1 tbsp. cornstarch
¼ cup water

Arrange fish in a single layer in a 10-inch skillet. Combine
tomatoes, celery, carrots, and green onion. Spoon over fish.
Combine parsley, herb seasoning, pepper, rosemary, red wine
vinegar, and chicken broth. Pour over fish. Bring to a boil.
Reduce heat. Cover and simmer 8 to 12 minutes until fish flakes
easily with a fork. Remove fish to a platter and keep warm. Mix
cornstarch and water. Stir into pan juices. Heat and stir until
sauce is thickened. Pour sauce over fish. Serve immediately.
Serves 4.

(Serving = 1 lean protein; ½ lean, fibrous vegetable)
*NUTRIENTS: 118 calories; 22.0 grams of protein; 0.4 grams of fat; 7.8
grams of carbohydrates; 278 mg of sodium; 570 mg of potassium; and 45
mg of calcium.*

Halibut Casserole Amandine

1 lb. halibut steaks
2 cups frozen French-style green beans
One 4-oz. can mushrooms, drained
1 cup skim milk
2 tbsp. oat flour
1 tbsp. cheese-flavored sprinkles
1 tbsp. instant minced onion flakes
1 tbsp. dry sherry
1 tsp. salt-free herb seasoning
⅛ tsp. white pepper
½ tsp. almond extract

Cut halibut steaks into 2-inch chunks. Place in a 9" x 9" x 2" microwaveable dish. Add frozen green beans and mushrooms. Combine remaining ingredients. Pour over fish and vegetables. Cover. Microwave on high 10 to 12 minutes until fish flakes easily with a fork. Stir 3 times during cooking. Serves 4.

(Serving = 1 lean protein; ½ lean, fibrous vegetable)
NUTRIENTS: 188 calories; 28.9 grams of protein; 2.1 grams of fat; 13.4 grams of carbohydrates; 233 mg of sodium; 827 mg of potassium; and 125 mg of calcium.

Lemon-Baked Halibut

1 lb. halibut steaks
1 tbsp. safflower oil
2 tbsp. lemon juice
2 tbsp. dry white wine
1 tsp. dried celery flakes
¼ tsp. garlic powder
⅛ tsp. black pepper
1 tsp. dried parsley flakes
½ tsp. dried dill weed

Preheat oven to 375 degrees. Spray a 9" x 9" x 2" baking dish with nonstick cooking spray. Place fish in dish. Combine remaining ingredients and pour over fish. Cover and bake for 15 minutes. Uncover and bake 10 to 15 minutes until fish flakes easily with fork. Serve with Tartar Sauce (below). Serves 4.

(Serving = 1 lean protein)
NUTRIENTS: 144 calories; 23.7 grams of protein; 4.8 grams of fat; 0.0

grams of carbohydrates; 61 mg of sodium; 510 mg of potassium; and 15
mg of calcium.

Tartar Sauce

½ cup nonfat yogurt

2 tbsp. shredded carrots

2 tbsp. shredded zucchini

1 tbsp. chopped onion

1 tbsp. chopped pimiento

½ tsp. dried parsley flakes

¼ tsp. dried dill weed

1 tsp. lemon juice

In a small bowl, combine all ingredients. Serve with baked
halibut. Makes ¾ cup.

NUTRIENTS: 78 calories; 4.5 grams of protein; 2.1 grams of fat; 10.8
grams of carbohydrates; 135 mg of sodium; 271 mg of potassium; and 149
mg of calcium.

Poached Halibut with Mushroom Sauce

1 cup freeze-dried mushrooms

1 tbsp. instant minced onion flakes

¾ cup chicken broth, defatted

1 lb. halibut steaks

2 tbsp. dry white wine

1 tbsp. lemon juice

¼ tsp. salt-free herb seasoning

⅛ tsp. black pepper

¼ tsp. dried tarragon

1 tbsp. cornstarch

2 tbsp. water

Combine freeze-dried mushrooms, onion flakes, and chicken broth. Set aside. Arrange fish in a single layer in a 10-inch skillet. Add wine, lemon juice, herb seasoning, pepper, and tarragon to broth mixture. Pour over fish. Bring to a boil. Reduce heat. Cover and simmer 8 to 12 minutes until fish flakes easily with a fork. Remove fish to a platter and keep warm. Mix cornstarch and water. Stir into pan juices. Heat and stir until sauce is thickened. Pour over fish. Serve immediately. Serves 4.

(Serving = 1 lean protein)
NUTRIENTS: 124 calories; 24.4 grams of protein; 1.6 grams of fat; 1.9 grams of carbohydrates; 340 mg of sodium; 514 mg of potassium; and 28 mg of calcium.

Buttery Broiled Halibut

1 lb. halibut steaks

3 tbsp. lemon juice

3 tbsp. prepared butter-flavored mix

½ tsp. onion powder

1 tsp. dried parsley flakes

½ tsp. salt-free herb seasoning

¼ tsp. paprika

lemon wedges

parsley sprigs

Cut fish into serving-size pieces. Arrange in shallow dish. Combine lemon juice, prepared butter mix, onion powder, parsley, herb seasoning, and paprika. Pour mixture over fish. Marinate for 1 hour. Turn occasionally. Broil fish 3 inches from heat, 5 minutes on each side, until fish flakes easily with a fork. Baste with marinade while broiling. Garnish with lemon wedges and parsley sprigs. Serves 4.

(Serving = 1 lean protein)
NUTRIENTS: 114 calories; 23.7 grams of protein; 1.4 grams of fat; 0.0 grams of carbohydrates; 61 mg of sodium; 510 mg of potassium; and 15 mg of calcium.

Barbecued Halibut

1 lb. halibut steaks
½ cup coarsely chopped tomatoes
¼ cup coarsely chopped onion
1 tbsp. lemon juice
1 tbsp. chopped fresh parsley
1 tsp. red wine vinegar
1 tsp. salt-free herb seasoning
¼ tsp. dry mustard
1 clove garlic
¼ tsp. dried oregano
½ tsp. dried rosemary

Cut halibut into serving-size pieces. Arrange in a shallow dish. In a blender, combine remaining ingredients. Blend until well mixed. Pour marinade over fish. Marinate 50 minutes. Turn occasionally. Broil halibut 3 inches from heat source, 5 minutes on each side, until fish flakes easily with a fork. Baste with marinade while broiling. Serves 4.

(Serving = 1 lean protein)
NUTRIENTS: 124 calories; 24.2 grams of protein; 1.4 grams of fat; 2.2 grams of carbohydrates; 63 mg of sodium; 591 mg of potassium; and 19 mg of calcium.

Poached Mahi Mahi with Cilantro

1 lb. mahi mahi fillets
¾ cup chicken broth, defatted
½ tsp. salt-free herb seasoning
¼ tsp. garlic powder
2 tbsp. chopped green onion
1 tbsp. chopped fresh cilantro

Arrange fish in a single layer in a 10-inch skillet. Combine remaining ingredients. Pour over fish. Bring to a boil. Reduce heat. Cover. Simmer 8 to 12 minutes until fish flakes easily with a fork. Remove fish to a platter and serve. Serves 4.

(Serving = 1 lean protein)
NUTRIENTS: 140 calories; 22.1 grams of protein; 4.8 grams of fat; 0.7 grams of carbohydrates; 279 mg of sodium; 13 mg of potassium; and 26 mg of calcium.

Orange Roughy with Gingered Vegetables

1 lb. orange roughy fillets
¾ cup chicken broth, defatted

2 cups thinly sliced carrots

1 cup thinly sliced onion

1 cup thinly sliced green pepper

1 cup chicken broth, defatted

¼ tsp. garlic powder

1 tsp. grated fresh ginger root

½ tsp. dried chervil

1 tbsp. cornstarch

⅓ cup rice wine vinegar

1 packet sugar substitute

Arrange fish in a single layer in a 10-inch skillet. Add ¾ cup broth and water. Bring to a boil. Reduce heat. Cover. Simmer 8 to 12 minutes until fish flakes easily with a fork. In a medium saucepan, combine carrots, onions, green pepper, 1 cup broth, garlic powder, ginger, and chervil. Bring to a boil. Reduce heat. Cover. Simmer 5 minutes. Dissolve cornstarch in vinegar. Add to vegetables. Heat and stir until thickened. Remove from heat. Stir in sugar substitute. To serve, remove fish to a platter. Pour vegetables over fish. Serves 4.

NUTRIENTS: 210 calories; 16.8 grams of protein; 9.2 grams of fat; 11.4 grams of carbohydrates; 690 mg of sodium; 286 mg of potassium; and 44 mg of calcium.

Lemon Broiled Orange Roughy

1 lb. orange roughy fillets

2 tbsp. lemon juice

2 tsp. Worcestershire sauce

1 tbsp. dry white wine

½ tsp. dried chervil

1 tsp. salt-free herb seasoning

½ tsp. onion powder

¼ tsp. paprika

Arrange fish in a shallow dish. Combine remaining ingredients.
Pour over fish. Marinate for 15 minutes. Turn occasionally.
Broil fillets 3 inches from heat source, 5 minutes on each side,
until fish flakes easily with a fork. Baste with marinade while
broiling. Serves 4.

(Serving = 1 lean protein)
*NUTRIENTS: 156 calories; 14.7 grams of protein; 8.5 grams of fat; 0.0
grams of carbohydrates; 9 mg of sodium; 0 mg of potassium; and 0 mg of
calcium.*

Orange Roughy Oriental

1 lb. orange roughy fillets

1 tsp. salt-free herb seasoning

¼ cup chopped green onion

1 tbsp. grated fresh ginger root

1 tbsp. safflower oil

1 tbsp. dry white wine

2 tbsp. low-salt soy sauce

Preheat oven to 375 degrees. Arrange fish in ungreased
9" x 9" x 2" baking dish. Sprinkle fish with herb seasoning.
Combine green onions, ginger, oil, wine, and soy sauce. Spoon
over fish. Cover and bake for 15 minutes. Uncover and bake 10
to 15 minutes until fish flakes easily with fork. Serves 4.

(Serving = 1 lean protein)
NUTRIENTS: 196 calories; 15.4 grams of protein; 12.8 grams of fat; 1.0 grams of carbohydrates; 310 mg of sodium; 50 mg of potassium; and 10 mg of calcium.

Grilled Perch with Dill

1 lb. perch fillets
1 tbsp. safflower oil
2 tbsp. lemon juice
1 tsp. dried dill weed
¼ tsp. dried thyme
½ tsp. salt-free herb seasoning
⅛ tsp. ground ginger

Arrange fish in a shallow dish. Combine remaining ingredients. Pour over fish. Marinate for 15 minutes. Turn occasionally. Spray grill with nonstick cooking spray. Grill fish 3 to 4 minutes on each side, until fish flakes easily with a fork. Baste with marinade while grilling. Serves 4.

(Serving = 1 lean protein)
NUTRIENTS: 130 calories; 20.4 grams of protein; 4.8 grams of fat; 0.0 grams of carbohydrates; 90 mg of sodium; 305 mg of potassium; and 23 mg of calcium.

Red Snapper Wrapped in Swiss Chard

2 cups thinly sliced carrots
1 cup sliced mushrooms
¼ cup chopped green onion

1 cup chicken broth, defatted

1 cup shredded Swiss chard

1 tsp. butter-flavored sprinkles

1 tbsp. dried celery flakes

½ tsp. dried thyme

½ tsp. dried marjoram

1 tsp. salt-free herb seasoning

1 lb. red snapper fillets

4 leaves Swiss chard

1 tbsp. cornstarch

2 tbsp. lemon juice

In a large skillet, simmer carrots, mushrooms, and onions in broth for 4 minutes. Add shredded Swiss chard, butter sprinkles, celery flakes, thyme, marjoram, and herb seasoning. Stir to combine. Divide fillets into four servings. Place on Swiss chard leaves. Form into rolls. Secure rolls with a toothpick. Place roll on top of sautéed vegetables. Bring to a boil. Reduce heat. Cover. Simmer 12 to 15 minutes until fish flakes easily with a fork. Remove fish to a serving platter and keep warm. Dissolve cornstarch in lemon juice. Add to vegetables. Heat and stir until sauce is thickened. Pour over fish rolls. Serve immediately. Serves 4.

(Serving = 1 lean protein; 1 lean, fibrous vegetable)
NUTRIENTS: 180 calories; 27.4 grams of protein; 1.9 grams of fat; 14.6 grams of carbohydrates; 679 mg of sodium; 1326 mg of potassium; and 183 mg of calcium.

Curried Snapper

1 lb. red snapper fillets

1 green pepper, cut into rings

1 tomato, sliced

1 small onion, thinly sliced

2 tbsp. dry white wine

2 tsp. dried vegetable flakes

¼ tsp. garlic powder

1 tsp. curry powder

2 tbsp. lemon juice

Preheat oven to 375 degrees. Spray a 9" x 9" x 2" baking dish with nonstick cooking spray. Place fish in dish. Arrange pepper rings, tomato slices, and onion slices on top of fish. Combine remaining ingredients. Spoon over fish. Cover and bake for 15 minutes. Uncover and bake 10 to 15 minutes until fish flakes easily with fork. Serves 4.

(Serving = 1 lean protein; ½ lean, fibrous vegetable)
NUTRIENTS: 129 calories; 23.5 grams of protein; 1.2 grams of fat; 5.5 grams of carbohydrates; 83 mg of sodium; 551 mg of potassium; and 32 mg of calcium.

Snapper With Jalapeno Salsa

1 lb. red snapper fillets

¼ cup vegetable juice

1 tbsp. finely chopped fresh cilantro

¼ tsp. garlic powder

2 tbsp. lemon juice

Preheat oven to 375 degrees. Spray a 9" x 9" x 2" baking dish with nonstick cooking spray. Place fish in dish. Combine remaining ingredients and pour over fish. Cover and bake for 15 minutes. Uncover and bake 10 to 15 minutes until fish fillets flake easily with a fork. Serve with Jalapeno Salsa (below). Serves 4.

(Serving = 1 lean protein; ¼ lean, fibrous vegetable)
NUTRIENTS: 109 calories; 22.6 grams of protein; 1.0 grams of fat; 0.7 grams of carbohydrates; 121 mg of sodium; 400 mg of potassium; and 20 mg of calcium. (Does not include Jalapeno Salsa.)

Jalapeno Salsa

1 cup chopped tomatoes
⅓ cup chopped onion
1 tbsp. chopped canned jalapenos
¼ tsp. salt-free herb seasoning
½ tsp. dried oregano
1 tbsp. chopped fresh cilantro
¼ tsp. garlic powder
1 tbsp. lime juice

In a small, microwaveable dish, combine all ingredients. Microwave on high 1 to 2 minutes until hot. Spoon over cooked snapper. Makes 1¼ cups.

NUTRIENTS: 19 calories; 0.8 grams of protein; 0.1 grams of fat; 4.0 grams of carbohydrates; 3 mg of sodium; 153 mg of potassium; and 8 mg of calcium.

Cajun Grilled Salmon

1 lb. salmon steaks
2 tbsp. prepared butter-flavored mix
1 tbsp. safflower oil
1 tbsp. lemon juice
1 tbsp. mustard
1 tbsp. chopped fresh parsley
½ tsp. salt-free herb seasoning
⅛ tsp. cayenne pepper

Cut salmon into serving-size pieces. Arrange in a shallow dish. Combine remaining ingredients. Pour mixture over salmon. Marinate 15 to 30 minutes. Turn occasionally. Spray grill with nonstick cooking spray. Grill salmon 4 to 5 minutes on each side until fish flakes easily with a fork. Brush with marinade while grilling. Serves 4.

(Serving = 1 lean protein)
NUTRIENTS: 276 calories; 25.5 grams of protein; 18.6 grams of fat; 0.0 grams of carbohydrates; 0 mg of sodium; 0 mg of potassium; and 90 mg of calcium.

Gingered Baked Salmon

1 lb. salmon steaks
2 tbsp. dry white wine
¼ tsp. Tobasco sauce
2 tbsp. lime juice
2 tbsp. chopped green onion
1 tbsp. grated fresh ginger root
1 tsp. dried vegetable flakes
¼ tsp. onion powder

Preheat oven to 375 degrees. Spray a 9" x 9" x 2" baking dish with nonstick cooking spray. Place fish in dish. Combine remaining ingredients. Spoon over fish. Cover and bake for 15 minutes. Uncover and bake 10 to 15 minutes until fish flakes easily with fork. Serves 4.

(Serving = 1 lean protein)
NUTRIENTS: 298 calories; 25.6 grams of protein; 15.2 grams of fat; 0.5 grams of carbohydrates; 1 mg of sodium; 8 mg of potassium; and 91 mg of calcium.

Asian Broiled Salmon

1 lb. salmon steaks
2 tbsp. low-salt soy sauce
2 tbsp. dry sherry.
1 tbsp. safflower oil
1 tsp. grated fresh ginger root
½ tsp. dry mustard
¼ tsp. garlic powder
½ tsp. salt-free herb seasoning

Cut salmon into serving-size pieces. Arrange in shallow dish. Combine remaining ingredients. Pour mixture over fish. Marinate 15 to 30 minutes. Turn occasionally. Broil fish 3 inches from heat source for 5 minutes on each side, until fish flakes easily with a fork. Baste with marinade while broiling. Serves 4.

(Serving = 1 lean protein)
NUTRIENTS: 282 calories; 26.0 grams of protein; 19.5 grams of fat; 0.1

grams of carbohydrates; 300 mg of sodium; 33 mg of potassium; and 97 mg of calcium.

_____

Skewered Shark

1 lb. shark steaks
½ lb. button mushrooms
1 green pepper
1 red onion
½ cup dry white wine
¼ cup lime juice
1 tbsp. Worcestershire sauce
½ tsp. garlic powder
1 tsp. dried oregano

Cut shark into 1-inch cubes. Arrange in a shallow dish. Clean mushrooms and remove stems. Seed green pepper and cut into 1-inch squares. Remove outer layers from onion and cut into 1-inch squares. Place prepared vegetables over fish cubes. Combine wine, lime juice, Worcestershire sauce, garlic powder, and oregano. Pour over shark and vegetables. Marinate for 50 minutes or cover, refrigerate, and marinate overnight. Thread fish, mushrooms, green pepper, and onions onto skewers. Grill 8 to 10 minutes. Turn frequently. Brush with marinade while grilling. Serves 4.

(Serving = 1 lean protein; ½ lean, fibrous vegetable)
NUTRIENTS: 164 calories; 23.9 grams of protein; 4.8 grams of fat; 5.8 grams of carbohydrates; 14 mg of sodium; 320 mg of potassium; and 12 mg of calcium.

Asparagus Stuffed Sole

1 lb. asparagus spears

1 lb. sole fillets

1 cup chopped tomatoes

1 4-oz. can mushrooms, drained

¼ cup chopped onion

2 tsp. dried celery flakes

1 tsp. dried mint flakes

¼ tsp. garlic powder

½ cup chicken broth, defatted

1 tbsp. cornstarch

2 tbsp. water

Rinse asparagus and break off tough root ends. Cook asparagus in a small amount of boiling water for 5 minutes until partially tender. Drain. Place asparagus across fish fillets. Roll fish around asparagus and fasten with wooden toothpicks. Place fish rolls in a medium skillet. Combine tomatoes, mushrooms, onion, celery flakes, mint flakes, garlic, and chicken broth. Pour over fish rolls. Bring to a boil. Reduce heat. Cover and simmer 8 to 12 minutes until fish flakes easily with a fork. Remove fish to a platter and keep warm. Dissolve cornstarch in water. Mix with pan juices. Heat and stir until sauce is thickened. Spoon sauce over fish rolls and serve. Serves 4.

(Serving = 1 lean protein; 1 lean, fibrous vegetable)
NUTRIENTS: 133 calories; 22.1 grams of protein; 1.3 grams of fat; 8.5 grams of carbohydrates; 414 mg of sodium; 782 mg of potassium; and 38 mg of calcium.

Steamed Sole Rouladen

1 lb. sole fillets

2 tbsp. low-salt soy sauce

2 tbsp. dry white wine

2 tsp. grated fresh ginger root

1 tsp. dried summer savory

½ tsp. onion powder

½ tsp. salt-free herb seasoning

1 cup julienned carrots

1 cup julienned zucchini

¼ cup chopped green onion

1 tsp. cornstarch

¼ cup chicken broth, defatted

Arrange fillets in a shallow dish. Combine soy sauce, wine, ginger root, summer savory, and onion powder. Pour over fish. Marinate while preparing vegetables. Remove fillets from marinade. Sprinkle fillets with herb seasoning. Roll up fillets. Secure rolls with a toothpick. Place carrots and zucchini in steamer basket. Arrange rolled fillets, seam side down, on vegetables. Sprinkle with green onions. Bring water in steamer pot to a boil. Add steamer basket. Cover. Steam for 12 to 15 minutes until fish flakes easily with a fork. While fish is steaming, dissolve cornstarch in chicken broth. In a small saucepan, combine dissolved cornstarch and soy marinade. Cook over medium heat until sauce is thickened. When fish and vegetables are done, remove to serving platter. Top with thickened sauce and serve. Serves 4.

(Serving = 1 lean protein; ½ lean, fibrous vegetable)
NUTRIENTS: 124 calories; 20.4 grams of protein; 1.9 grams of fat;

7.1 grams of carbohydrates; 635 mg of sodium; 625 mg of potassium; and 44 mg of calcium.

Sole Dijon

1 lb. sole fillets

¼ cup dry white wine

2 tsp. Dijon mustard

2 tbsp. lemon juice

1 tsp. capers, drained

½ tsp. caraway seeds

⅛ tsp. white pepper

Preheat oven to 375 degrees. Spray a 9" x 9" x 2" baking dish with nonstick cooking spray. Place fish in dish. Combine remaining ingredients and pour over fish. Cover and bake for 15 minutes. Uncover and bake 10 to 15 minutes until fish flakes easily with fork. Serves 4.

(Serving = 1 lean protein)
NUTRIENTS: 90 calories; 19.0 grams of protein; 0.9 grams of fat; 0.0 grams of carbohydrates; 89 mg of sodium; 388 mg of potassium; and 14 mg of calcium.

Baked Swordfish with Potatoes

½ cup chopped onion

2 cloves garlic, pressed

1 cup chicken broth, defatted

One 14½-oz. can tomatoes, chopped

One 8-oz. can tomato sauce

1 tbsp. dried parsley flakes

½ tsp. salt-free herb seasoning

¼ tsp. ground oregano

⅛ tsp. dried thyme

1 tbsp. lemon juice

1 lb. swordfish steaks

3 cups thinly sliced potatoes

Preheat oven to 375 degrees. In a medium skillet, simmer onion and garlic in broth until tender. Add tomatoes, tomato sauce, parsley, herb seasoning, oregano, thyme, and lemon juice. Bring to a boil. Reduce heat. Cover and simmer 15 minutes. Spoon half of sauce into an ungreased 9" x 13" x 2" baking dish. Place fish in dish. Arrange potatoes around fish. Spoon remaining sauce over fish and potatoes. Cover and bake 30 minutes. Uncover and bake 10 to 20 minutes until potatoes are fork tender. If sauce starts to dry out, add water. Serves 4.

(Serving = 1 lean protein; 1 starchy carbohydrate)
NUTRIENTS: 264 calories; 26.5 grams of protein; 5.3 grams of fat; 28.3 grams of carbohydrates; 844 mg of sodium; 843 mg of potassium; and 44 mg of calcium.

Lemon Broiled Swordfish

1 lb. swordfish steaks

2 tbsp. dry white wine

2 tbsp. lemon juice

1 tbsp. low-salt soy sauce

2 cloves garlic, pressed

1 tsp. dried parsley flakes

½ tsp. salt-free herb seasoning

⅛ tsp. black pepper

Cut swordfish into serving-size pieces. Arrange in shallow dish. Combine wine, lemon juice, soy sauce, garlic, and parsley. Pour mixture over fish. Marinate for 30 minutes. Turn occasionally. Season with herb seasoning and pepper. Broil fish 3 inches from heat source for 5 minutes on each side, until fish flakes easily with a fork. Baste with marinade while broiling. Serves 4.

(Serving = 1 lean protein)
NUTRIENTS: 137 calories; 22.0 grams of protein; 5.0 grams of fat; 0.1 grams of carbohydrates; 150 mg of sodium; 17 mg of potassium; and 4 mg of calcium.

Grilled Swordfish with Cilantro Butter

1 lb. swordfish steaks
3 tbsp. lime juice
2 tsp. grated fresh ginger root
1 tbsp. prepared butter-flavored mix
1 tbsp. chopped fresh cilantro
½ tsp. salt-free herb seasoning
⅛ tsp. white pepper

Cut swordfish into serving-size pieces. Arrange in shallow dish. Combine lime juice, ginger root, prepared butter mix, and cilantro. Pour mixture over swordfish. Marinate 40 to 50 minutes. Turn occasionally. Spray grill with nonstick cooking spray. Remove swordfish from marinade. Season with herb seasoning and pepper. Grill swordfish 4 to 5 minutes on each side, until fish flakes easily with a fork. Baste with marinade while broiling. Serves 4.

(Serving = 1 lean protein)
NUTRIENTS: 134 calories; 21.8 grams of protein; 4.5 grams of fat; 0.0 grams of carbohydrates; 0 mg of sodium; 0 mg of potassium; and 0 mg of calcium.

Smoky Baked Tuna Steak

1 lb. tuna steaks
¼ cup dry white wine
2 tbsp. lime juice
1 tsp. liquid smoke
2 tbsp. chopped green onion
½ tsp. paprika
¼ tsp. white pepper
1 tbsp. chopped fresh parsley

Preheat oven to 375 degrees. Cut tuna steaks into serving-size pieces. Spray a 9" x 9" x 2" baking dish with nonstick cooking spray. Place fish in dish. Combine remaining ingredients. Pour over fish. Cover and bake for 20 to 25 minutes until fish flakes easily with a fork. Serves 4.

(Serving = 1 lean protein)
NUTRIENTS: 153 calories; 28.1 grams of protein; 3.4 grams of fat; 0.5 grams of carbohydrates; 43 mg of sodium; 8 mg of potassium; and 1 mg of calcium.

Tuna Oriental

1 cup chopped celery
½ cup chopped onion

1 cup chicken broth, defatted

Two 7-oz. cans water-packed albacore tuna, drained

One 4-oz. can mushrooms, drained

One 16-oz. can bean sprouts, drained

1 tbsp. low-salt soy sauce

One 6-oz. pkg. frozen snowpeas

1 tbsp. cornstarch

2 tbsp. water

In a medium skillet, simmer celery and onion in broth until tender. Add tuna, mushrooms, bean sprouts, soy sauce, and snowpeas. Cover. Simmer 8 to 10 minutes until snowpeas are tender. Dissolve cornstarch in water. Add to tuna mixture. Heat and stir until thickened. Serves 4.

(Serving = 1 lean protein; 1 lean, fibrous vegetable)
NUTRIENTS: 203 calories; 34.3 grams of protein; 2.3 grams of fat; 14.2 grams of carbohydrates; 733 mg of sodium; 487 mg of potassium; and 65 mg of calcium.

Tuna with Peas and Carrots

1 cup chopped onion

1 cup chopped celery

1 clove garlic, pressed

2 cups chicken broth, defatted

Two 7-oz. cans water-packed albacore tuna, drained

2 cups frozen peas

1 cup sliced carrots

1 tsp. paprika

½ tsp. salt-free herb seasoning

½ tsp. dried basil

2 tbsp. cornstarch

2 tbsp. water

In a large skillet, simmer onion, celery, and garlic in broth until tender. Add tuna, peas, carrots, paprika, herb seasoning, and basil. Cover. Simmer 15 to 20 minutes until peas and carrots are tender. Dissolve cornstarch in water. Add to tuna mixture. Heat and stir until thickened. Serves 4.

(Serving = 1 lean protein; ½ starchy carbohydrate; ½ lean, fibrous vegetable)
NUTRIENTS: 233 calories; 33.9 grams of protein; 1.8 grams of fat; 20.4 grams of carbohydrates; 904 mg of sodium; 638 mg of potassium; and 123 mg of calcium.

Tuna Florentine

1 lb. fresh spinach

¼ cup chopped green onion

One 8-oz. can water chestnuts, thinly sliced

Two 7-oz. cans water-packed albacore tuna, drained

2 tbsp. low-salt soy sauce

1 tsp. grated fresh ginger root

1 tbsp. lemon juice

⅛ tsp. garlic powder

⅛ tsp. black pepper

½ cup chicken broth, defatted

Wash spinach thoroughly and drain. Combine all ingredients in a large skillet. Cover. Simmer 15 minutes until spinach is wilted. Stir occasionally. Serves 4.

(Serving = 1 lean protein; ½ lean, fibrous vegetable)
NUTRIENTS: 189 calories; 32.8 grams of protein; 2.2 grams of fat; 10.8 grams of carbohydrates; 733 mg of sodium; 866 mg of potassium; and 150 mg of calcium.

Oven-Fried Tuna Patties

Two 7-oz. cans water-packed albacore tuna, drained
½ cup finely chopped onion
½ cup finely chopped celery
½ cup old-fashioned oatmeal
½ cup oat bran
¼ cup skim milk
2 egg whites, beaten
2 tbsp. lemon juice
2 tbsp. chopped fresh parsley
1 tsp. dried dill weed
1 tsp. salt-free herb seasoning
¼ cup oat flour

Preheat oven to 375 degrees. In a large bowl, combine all ingredients except oat flour. Mix well. Shape into 8 patties. Dust lightly with oat flour. Spray a cookie sheet with nonstick cooking spray. Place tuna patties on cookie sheet. Bake for 15 minutes. Turn patties. Bake for 10 minutes until browned. Serves 4.

(Serving = 1 lean protein; ¼ starchy carbohydrate; ¼ lean, fibrous vegetable)
NUTRIENTS: 258 calories; 35.3 grams of protein; 3.0 grams of fat; 24.2 grams of carbohydrates; 93 mg of sodium; 515 mg of potassium; and 57 mg of calcium.

Tuna-Stuffed Peppers

4 large green peppers

½ cup chopped onion

½ cup chopped celery

¼ cup chicken broth, defatted

Two 7-oz. cans water-packed albacore tuna, drained

3 cups cooked brown rice

1 tsp. Italian herb seasoning

1 tsp. dried parsley flakes

One 8-oz. can tomato sauce

2 tbsp. lemon juice

¼ cup old-fashioned oatmeal

Preheat oven to 350 degrees. Cut the top off of each green
pepper and remove seeds. Place peppers in a pot of boiling
water. Boil for 5 minutes. Remove peppers from water and
drain. In a medium skillet, simmer onion and celery in broth
until tender. Add remaining ingredients. Stir until combined.
Remove from heat. Cut peppers in half, lengthwise. Fill
peppers with tuna mixture. Spray an 8" x 11" x 2" baking dish
with nonstick cooking spray. Arrange filled peppers in dish.
Sprinkle peppers with oatmeal. Bake peppers for 30 minutes.
Serves 4.

*(Serving = 1 lean protein; 1 starchy carbohydrate; 1¼ lean, fibrous
vegetable)*
*NUTRIENTS: 371 calories; 34.9 grams of protein; 2.6 grams of fat; 53.4
grams of carbohydrates; 893 mg of sodium; 923 mg of potassium; and 78
mg of calcium.*

Sautéed Scallops with Vegetables

1 lb. bay scallops or quartered sea scallops
½ cup dry white wine
2 cloves garlic, pressed
1 cup sliced onion
1 cup sliced celery
1 cup frozen cut green beans, thawed
2 tsp. grated fresh ginger root
1 cup chicken broth, defatted
2 tbsp. low-salt soy sauce
One 4-oz. can mushrooms, drained
One 16-oz. can baby corn, drained
1 tbsp. cornstarch
1 tbsp. water

Rinse and drain scallops. Place scallops in a bowl. Add wine
and garlic. Marinate for 30 minutes. In a medium skillet,
simmer onions, celery, green beans, and ginger root in broth
for 5 minutes. Add soy sauce and mushrooms. Simmer for 15
minutes until beans are almost tender. Drain scallops. Add
scallops and baby corn to skillet. Cook 5 minutes. Dissolve
cornstarch in water. Add to skillet. Heat and stir until scallops
turn opaque and sauce is thickened. Serve immediately.
Serves 4.

*(Serving = 1 lean protein; ½ starchy carbohydrate; 1 lean, fibrous
vegetable)*
*NUTRIENTS: 239 calories; 22.4 grams of protein; 2.1 grams of fat; 32.2
grams of carbohydrates; 1330 mg of sodium; 875 mg of potassium; and 86
mg of calcium.*

Louisiana Spicy Scallops

1 lb. bay scallops or quartered sea scallops

½ cup dry white wine

2 cloves garlic, pressed

¼ tsp. cayenne pepper

1 tsp. black pepper

½ tsp. salt-free herb seasoning

1 tsp. dried parsley flakes

1 tbsp. Worcestershire sauce

2 tbsp. safflower oil

Rinse and drain scallops. Place scallops in a bowl. Add white wine and garlic. Marinate for 30 minutes. Combine all seasonings and set aside. Drain scallops. In a large skillet, heat Worcestershire sauce and oil over high heat. Add spices and scallops. Cook 4 to 5 minutes until scallops turn opaque. Serve immediately. Serves 4.

(Serving = 1 lean protein)
NUTRIENTS: 177 calories; 17.4 grams of protein; 7.0 grams of fat; 5.0 grams of carbohydrates; 291 mg of sodium; 477 mg of potassium; and 32 mg of calcium.

Buttery Broiled Scallops

1 lb. bay scallops or quartered sea scallops

3 tbsp. prepared butter-flavored mix

3 tbsp. lemon juice

3 cloves garlic, pressed

½ tsp. paprika

¼ tsp. white pepper

1 tsp. dried parsley flakes

Rinse and drain scallops. Place scallops in a bowl. Spray an
8" x 8" x 2" baking dish with nonstick cooking spray. Arrange
scallops in dish. Combine remaining ingredients. Pour over
scallops. Broil 4 inches from heat source 4 to 6 minutes until
scallops turn opaque. Serves 4.

(Serving = 1 lean protein)
*NUTRIENTS: 92 calories; 17.4 grams of protein; 0.2 grams of fat; 3.8
grams of carbohydrates; 289 mg of sodium; 449 mg of potassium; and 29
mg of calcium.*

Scallops in Cilantro Sauce

1 lb. bay scallops or quartered sea scallops
¾ cup chicken broth, defatted
2 tbsp. chopped green onion
¼ tsp. tumeric
1 tbsp. cornstarch
¼ cup dry white wine
¼ cup nonfat yogurt
1 tbsp. chopped fresh cilantro
2 tbsp. prepared butter-flavored mix
fresh cilantro leaves

Rinse and drain scallops. Thread scallops onto skewers and set
aside. In a small saucepan, combine broth, green onion, and
tumeric. Bring to a boil. Reduce heat. Simmer for 3 minutes.
Dissolve cornstarch in dry white wine. Add to broth. Heat and
stir until thickened. Add yogurt and cilantro. Remove from
heat. Cover and keep warm until scallops are cooked. Brush
scallops with prepared butter mix. Broil 4 inches from heat

source for 2 to 3 minutes on each side until scallops turn opaque. Place scallops on individual serving plates. Pour sauce over scallops. Garnish with fresh cilantro leaves. Serves 4.

(Serving = 1 lean protein)
NUTRIENTS: 122 calories; 18.2 grams of protein; 0.7 grams of fat; 8.2 grams of carbohydrates; 576 mg of sodium; 496 mg of potassium; and 52 mg of calcium.

Oven-Fried Scallops

1 lb. bay scallops or quartered sea scallops
½ cup dry white wine
¾ cup oat bran
½ tsp. salt-free herb seasoning
½ tsp. dried tarragon
½ tsp. onion powder
¼ tsp. white pepper
½ tsp. dried lemon peel

Preheat oven to 375 degrees. Rinse and drain scallops. Place scallops in a bowl. Add wine and marinate for 30 minutes. Spray a cookie sheet with nonstick cooking spray. Drain scallops. Place all dry ingredients in a plastic bag. Shake to mix. Add scallops, a few at a time, and shake to coat. Place scallops on cookie sheet. Bake 10 minutes. Turn and bake an additional 10 minutes, until browned. Serves 4.

(Serving = 1 lean protein)
NUTRIENTS: 168 calories; 20.2 grams of protein; 1.4 grams of fat; 15.1 grams of carbohydrates; 294 mg of sodium; 562 mg of potassium; and 32 mg of calcium.

Baked Scallops

1 lb. bay scallops or quartered sea scallops

2 cups sliced mushrooms

2 tbsp. chopped onion

½ cup dry white wine

½ tsp. dried marjoram

½ tsp. dried lemon peel

½ tsp. salt-free herb seasoning

¼ tsp. paprika

¾ cup skim milk

2 tbsp. oat flour

2 tbsp. water

¼ cup old-fashioned oatmeal

Preheat oven to 375 degrees. Rinse and drain scallops. In a medium skillet, combine scallops, mushrooms, onion, and wine. Heat and simmer 5 minutes. Add marjoram, lemon peel, herb seasoning, paprika, and skim milk. Blend oat flour with water. Add to skillet. Heat and stir until thickened. Spray a casserole dish with nonstick cooking spray. Pour mixture into dish. Sprinkle with oatmeal. Bake 10 to 15 minutes until bubbly. Serves 4.

(Serving = 1 lean protein)
NUTRIENTS: 195 calories; 22.1 grams of protein; 1.4 grams of fat; 17.9 grams of carbohydrates; 315 mg of sodium; 610 mg of potassium; and 104 mg of calcium.

Scallops in Garlic Sauce

1 lb. bay scallops or quartered sea scallops
1 cup sliced mushrooms
3 cloves garlic, pressed
½ cup chicken broth, defatted
½ cup chopped tomatoes
¼ cup chopped green onion
2 tsp. dried celery flakes
1 tsp. Italian herb seasoning
1 tbsp. cornstarch
2 tbsp. balsamic vinegar
1 tbsp. chopped fresh parsley

Rinse and drain scallops. In a medium skillet, simmer mushrooms and garlic in broth for 3 minutes. Add scallops, tomatoes, green onion, celery flakes, and Italian seasoning. Cook 5 minutes. Dissolve cornstarch in vinegar. Add to scallops. Heat and stir until scallops turn opaque and sauce is thickened. Garnish with parsley. Serves 4.

(Serving = 1 lean protein; ¼ lean, fibrous vegetable)
NUTRIENTS: 114 calories; 18.4 grams of protein; 0.5 grams of fat; 9.3 grams of carbohydrates; 476 mg of sodium; 534 mg of potassium; and 46 mg of calcium.

Southwestern Skillet Shrimp

1 cup chopped onion
1 clove garlic, pressed
¼ cup chicken broth, defatted
One 14½-oz. can tomatoes, chopped

1 tsp. dried cilantro

¼ tsp. salt-free herb seasoning

⅛ tsp. cayenne pepper

1 tsp. grated fresh ginger root

2 cups frozen cut green beans

1 tbsp. red wine vinegar

1 lb. shrimp, peeled and deveined

2 tbsp. cornstarch

2 tbsp. water

In a medium skillet, simmer onion and garlic in broth until tender. Add tomatoes, cilantro, herb seasoning, cayenne pepper, ginger root, green beans, and vinegar. Cover. Simmer 25 to 30 minutes until beans are almost tender. Add shrimp. Cook 5 minutes. Dissolve cornstarch in water. Add to skillet. Heat and stir until shrimp turns opaque and sauce is thickened. Serves 4.

(Serving = 1 lean protein; 1 lean, fibrous vegetable)
NUTRIENTS: 167 calories; 23.5 grams of protein; 1.3 grams of fat; 16.7 grams of carbohydrates; 396 mg of sodium; 667 mg of potassium; and 122 mg of calcium.

Minted Shrimp with Peas

1 cup chopped onion

2 cups chicken broth, defatted

½ cup uncooked brown rice

One 14 ½-oz. can tomatoes, chopped

2 tsp. dried mint flakes

1 tsp. dried parsley flakes

¼ tsp. garlic powder

¼ tsp. black pepper

1½ cups frozen peas

1 lb. shrimp, peeled and deveined

In a medium skillet, combine onions, broth, brown rice, tomatoes, mint flakes, parsley flakes, garlic powder, and pepper. Bring mixture to a boil. Reduce heat. Cover and simmer 40 minutes. Stir occasionally. Add peas. Simmer 10 minutes. Add shrimp. Simmer 5 to 7 minutes until shrimp turns opaque. Serves 4.

(Serving = 1 lean protein; 1 starchy carbohydrate)
NUTRIENTS: 225 calories; 26.5 grams of protein; 2.1 grams of fat; 24.7 grams of carbohydrates; 1163 mg of sodium; 657 mg of potassium; and 149 mg of calcium.

Shrimp with Snowpeas

1 cup freeze-dried mushrooms

1 cup chicken broth, defatted

¼ cup chopped green onion

1 tsp. grated fresh ginger root

1 cup shredded carrots

One 6-oz. pkg. frozen snowpeas

One 16-oz. can bean sprouts, drained

2 tbsp. low-salt soy sauce

1 lb. shrimp, peeled and deveined

1 tbsp. cornstarch

2 tbsp. water

In a small bowl, combine mushrooms and broth. Let stand for 5 minutes. In a medium skillet, simmer green onion, ginger root, and carrots in broth mixture for 3 minutes. Add snowpeas, bean sprouts, soy sauce, and shrimp. Cover and simmer 5 minutes. Dissolve cornstarch in water. Add to skillet. Heat and stir until shrimp turns opaque and sauce is thickened. Serves 4.

(Serving = 1 lean protein; 1 lean, fibrous vegetable)
NUTRIENTS: 182 calories; 26.4 grams of protein; 2.8 grams of fat; 16.3 grams of carbohydrates; 843 mg of sodium; 389 mg of potassium; and 129 mg of calcium.

Hot Barbecued Shrimp

1 lb. large shrimp, peeled and deveined
1 tbsp. low-salt soy sauce
2 tbsp. tomato paste
1 tbsp. red wine vinegar
1 tbsp. lemon juice
½ tsp. onion powder
¼ tsp. garlic powder
1 tsp. barbecue seasoning
¼ tsp. cayenne pepper
¼ tsp. black pepper
1 tsp. dried oregano

Spray an 8" x 8" x 2" baking dish with nonstick cooking spray. Place shrimp in dish. Combine remaining ingredients. Pour over shrimp. Cover and refrigerate several hours. Stir occasionally. When ready to bake, preheat oven to 350 degrees. Bake 15 to 20 minutes until shrimp turn opaque. Serves 4.

(Serving = 1 lean protein)
NUTRIENTS: 106 calories; 20.8 grams of protein; 1.3 grams of fat; 1.8 grams of carbohydrates; 309 mg of sodium; 266 mg of potassium; and 75 mg of calcium.

Shrimp Scampi

1 lb. shrimp, peeled and deveined
3 cloves garlic, pressed
¼ cup prepared butter-flavored mix
2 tbsp. lemon juice
2 tbsp. dry white wine
1 tbsp. tarragon vinegar
1 tbsp. low-salt soy sauce
1 tsp. dried parsley flakes
¼ tsp. black pepper
½ tsp. salt-free herb seasoning
½ tsp. paprika
⅛ tsp. Tabasco sauce

Place shrimp in a medium dish. Combine garlic, prepared butter mix, lemon juice, wine, and vinegar. Pour over shrimp. Marinate in refrigerator for 30 minutes. Place shrimp and marinade in a medium skillet. Combine remaining ingredients and add to skillet. Heat and stir 5 to 7 minutes until shrimp turn opaque. Serves 4.

(Serving = 1 lean protein)
NUTRIENTS: 106 calories; 20.8 grams of protein; 1.3 grams of fat; 1.8 grams of carbohydrates; 309 mg of sodium; 266 mg of potassium; and 75 mg of calcium.

Shrimp Creole

½ cup chopped onion
½ cup chopped celery
½ cup chopped green pepper
2 cloves garlic, pressed
1 cup vegetable juice
1 14 ½-oz. can tomatoes, chopped
1 tbsp. lemon juice
1 bay leaf
2 tsp. dried parsley flakes
1 tsp. paprika
½ tsp. salt-free herb seasoning
¼ tsp. cayenne pepper
1 lb. shrimp, peeled and deveined
3 cups cooked brown rice

In a medium skillet, cook onion, celery, green pepper, and garlic in vegetable juice for 5 minutes. Add tomatoes, lemon juice, bay leaf, parsley flakes, paprika, herb seasoning, and cayenne pepper. Cover and simmer 15 minutes. Add shrimp. Cover and simmer 5 to 7 minutes until shrimp turn opaque. Serve over hot rice. Serves 4.

(Serving = 1 lean protein; 1 starchy carbohydrate; ½ lean, fibrous vegetable)
NUTRIENTS: 318 calories; 26.0 grams of protein; 2.0 grams of fat; 49.1 grams of carbohydrates; 890 mg of sodium; 795 mg of potassium; and 115 mg of calcium.

Grilled Shrimp Teriyaki

1 lb. shrimp, peeled and deveined

2 tbsp. dry sherry

1 tbsp. low-salt soy sauce

1 tbsp. safflower oil

1 tsp. grated fresh ginger root

¼ tsp. garlic powder

1 packet sugar substitute

Place shrimp in a shallow dish. Combine remaining ingredients. Pour over shrimp. Cover. Marinate in refrigerator for several hours. Turn shrimp occasionally. Remove shrimp from marinade. Thread onto skewers. Spray grill with nonstick cooking spray. Grill shrimp 3 to 4 minutes on each side until shrimp turn opaque. Brush with marinade while grilling. Serves 4.

(Serving = 1 lean protein)
NUTRIENTS: 136 calories; 20.8 grams of protein; 4.7 grams of fat; 1.8 grams of carbohydrates; 309 mg of sodium; 266 mg of potassium; and 75 mg of calcium.

Shrimp in Garlic Sauce

6 dried Chinese black mushrooms

1 tbsp. cornstarch

2 tbsp. water

½ cup chicken broth, defatted

1 tbsp. low-salt soy sauce

1 tbsp. safflower oil

½ cup thinly sliced onion

4 cloves garlic, pressed

1 tsp. grated fresh ginger root
1 lb. shrimp, peeled and deveined
One 8-oz. can water chestnuts, drained and thinly sliced
1 cup frozen peas, thawed

Rinse mushrooms and remove stems. Cover with hot water. Soak for 20 minutes. In a small bowl, dissolve cornstarch in water. Add broth and soy sauce. Stir to blend. Set aside. Drain mushrooms. Cut into small pieces. Heat oil in wok or large skillet over high heat. Add onion, garlic, and ginger root. Stir-fry 1 minute. Add shrimp and water chestnuts. Stir-fry 2 minutes. Add mushrooms and peas. Stir-fry 3 minutes. Pour broth mixture into wok. Heat and stir until thickened. Serves 4.

(Serving = 1 lean protein; ¼ starchy carbohydrate)
NUTRIENTS: 202 calories; 23.6 grams of protein; 5.1 grams of fat; 16.3 grams of carbohydrates; 658 mg of sodium; 359 mg of potassium; and 132 mg of calcium.

Stir-Fried Shrimp with Broccoli

1 tbsp. cornstarch
1 tbsp. water
¾ cup chicken broth, defatted
1 tbsp. low-salt soy sauce
1 tbsp. safflower oil
1 lb. shrimp, peeled and deveined
2 cups chopped broccoli florets
2 tbsp. chopped green onion
1 tsp. grated fresh ginger root
1 8-oz. can bamboo shoots, thinly sliced
2 4-oz. cans mushrooms, drained

In a small bowl, dissolve cornstarch and water. Add broth and soy sauce. Stir to blend. Set aside. Heat oil in wok or large skillet over high heat. Add shrimp. Stir-fry for 3 minutes. Add broccoli, onion, and ginger root. Stir-fry for 2 minutes. Add bamboo shoots and mushrooms. Stir-fry for 1 minute. Pour broth mixture into wok. Heat and stir until thickened. Serves 4.

(Serving = 1 lean protein; 1 lean, fibrous vegetable)
NUTRIENTS: 184 calories; 25.1 grams of protein; 5.2 grams of fat; 11.1 grams of carbohydrates; 879 mg of sodium; 622 mg of potassium; and 115 mg of calcium.

Shrimp de Jonghe

1 lb. shrimp, peeled and deveined
¼ cup prepared butter-flavored mix
¼ cup dry sherry
2 tbsp. chopped fresh parsley
1 tbsp. finely chopped onion
⅛ tsp. Tabasco sauce
¼ tsp. garlic powder
½ tsp. salt-free herb seasoning
¼ tsp. dried tarragon
¼ tsp. dried chervil
¼ tsp. paprika
1 cup Oatmeal Pancake crumbs (page 59)

Preheat oven to 400 degrees. Spray an 8" x 8" x 2" baking dish with nonstick cooking spray. Arrange shrimp in dish. In a small bowl, combine prepared butter mix, sherry, parsley, onion, Tabasco sauce, and seasonings. Stir until blended. Add Oatmeal

Pancake crumbs. Toss to coat. Spoon over shrimp. Bake for 15
minutes until shrimp is opaque and crumbs are browned.
Serves 4.

(Serving = 1 lean protein)
*NUTRIENTS: 223 calories; 24.2 grams of protein; 2.8 grams of fat; 20.2
grams of carbohydrates; 160 mg of sodium; 353 mg of potassium; and 87
mg of calcium.*

Baked Shrimp with Mushrooms

1 lb. shrimp, peeled and deveined
2 cups sliced mushrooms
¼ cup chopped green onion
¼ cup chopped tomatoes
3 tbsp. chopped fresh parsley
¼ cup prepared butter-flavored mix
2 tsp. Worchestershire sauce
1 tbsp. lemon juice
¼ tsp. garlic powder
¼ tsp. chili powder
⅛ tsp. cayenne pepper
1 tsp. salt-free herb seasoning

Preheat oven to 425 degrees. Spray an 8" x 8" x 2" baking dish
with nonstick cooking spray. Arrange shrimp in dish. In a
medium skillet, sauté mushrooms, green onion, tomatoes, and
parsley in prepared butter mix until tender. Add Worcestershire sauce, lemon juice, and seasonings. Mix well and remove
from heat. Spoon over shrimp. Cover with foil. Bake 10 to 12
minutes until shrimp turns opaque. Serves 4.

(Serving = 1 lean protein)
NUTRIENTS: *120 calories; 21.8 grams of protein; 1.0 grams of fat; 4.8 grams of carbohydrates; 160 mg of sodium; 299 mg of potassium; and 86 mg of calcium.*

Spicy Grilled Shrimp

1 lb. shrimp, peeled and deveined
3 tbsp. lemon juice
1 tbsp. safflower oil
1 tsp. dried cilantro
½ tsp. instant minced onion flakes
1 tsp. grated fresh ginger root
1 clove garlic, pressed
¼ tsp. crushed red pepper flakes
¼ tsp. ground cumin
⅛ tsp. allspice

Place shrimp in a shallow dish. Combine remaining ingredients in a blender. Process until well blended. Pour over shrimp. Cover and marinate in refrigerator for several hours or overnight. Turn shrimp occasionally. Remove shrimp from marinade. Thread onto skewers. Spray grill with nonstick cooking spray. Grill shrimp 3 to 4 minutes on each side until shrimp turn opaque. Brush with marinade while grilling. Serves 4.

(Serving = 1 lean protein)
NUTRIENTS: *133 calories; 20.5 grams of protein; 4.3 grams of fat; 1.7 grams of carbohydrates; 159 mg of sodium; 250 mg of potassium; and 72 mg of calcium.*

Lemon Shrimp with Snowpeas

½ cup chopped green onion

2 cloves garlic, pressed

1 cup chicken broth, defatted

2 cups sliced mushrooms

1 lb. shrimp, peeled and deveined

2 cups snowpeas

1 tsp. salt-free herb seasoning

½ tsp. dried marjoram

¼ tsp. white pepper

1 tbsp. cornstarch

2 tbsp. lemon juice

2 tbsp. chopped fresh parsley

3 cups cooked wild rice

In a medium skillet, simmer onions and garlic in broth for 3 minutes. Add mushrooms, shrimp, snowpeas, herb seasoning, marjoram, and pepper. Cover and simmer 3 minutes. Dissolve cornstarch in lemon juice. Add dissolved cornstarch and parsley to shrimp. Cook and stir until shrimp turn opaque and sauce is thickened. Serve over hot rice. Serves 4.

(Serving = 1 lean protein; 1 starchy carbohydrate; ¾ lean, fibrous vegetable)
NUTRIENTS: 600 calories; 42.0 grams of protein; 2.3 grams of fat; 108.8 grams of carbohydrates; 540 mg of sodium; 553 mg of potassium; and 114 mg of calcium.

East Indian Shrimp Brochettes

1 lb. shrimp, peeled and deveined

2 tbsp. lemon juice

2 tbsp. chopped fresh mint

1 tsp. dried basil

½ tsp. ground cardamon

¼ tsp. ground cumin

½ tsp. chili powder

½ tsp. tumeric

¼ tsp. garlic powder

⅓ cup nonfat yogurt

Place shrimp in a medium dish. Combine remaining ingredients and pour over shrimp. Stir until shrimp are well coated with yogurt mixture. Cover. Chill and marinate for 50 minutes. Thread shrimp onto skewers. Broil 3 inches from heat source, 3 to 4 minutes on each side, until shrimp turn opaque. Brush with marinade while broiling. Serves 4.

(Serving = 1 lean protein)
NUTRIENTS: 113 calories; 21.2 grams of protein; 1.2 grams of fat; 2.7 grams of carbohydrates; 168 mg of sodium; 276 mg of potassium; and 94 mg of calcium.

7

Poultry

Helpful Hints

Refer to the chart Using Herbs and Spices (page 12) to try new combinations of spices.

Remove all skin from chicken or turkey before cooking.

Instead of frying poultry, broil, barbecue, steam, poach, or stir fry.

Chicken can be coated with oat bran before baking.

Wrap turkey in foil when baking to preserve moistness.

Use turkey in place of veal.

Raw chicken generally has a weight ratio of 5-to-4 to cooked chicken.

Turkey and chicken make excellent kabobs. They cook quickly and have excellent flavor. Marinate for succulent flavor.

Substitute rolled oats for bread crumbs when making turkey loaf.

Grill racks can be purchased at most hardware stores. These are useful when grilling fish or kabobs.

Stir-fry strips are best from boned, skinned chicken breasts.

Ground poultry cooks like beef. Substitute poultry when ground beef is called for. Be sure to drain any fat prior to serving.

Southwestern Chicken

2 whole chicken breasts, split and skinned

One 8-oz. can tomato sauce

1 cup water

One 4-oz. can chopped green chilies

1 tsp. chili powder

½ tsp. salt-free herb seasoning

¼ tsp. ground cumin

¼ tsp. garlic powder

Preheat oven to 350 degrees. Arrange chicken in 8" x 11" x 2" baking dish. Combine remaining ingredients. Pour over chicken. Bake 45 to 55 minutes until tender. Serves 4.

Variation: To make Easy Italian Chicken, substitute 1 4-oz. can mushrooms for green chilies; 1 teaspoon dried oregano for chili powder; and ¼ teaspoon dried marjoram for cumin.

(Serving = 1 lean protein)
NUTRIENTS: 167 calories; 27.8 grams of protein; 3.3 grams of fat; 6.1 grams of carbohydrates; 395 mg of sodium; 463 mg of potassium; and 37 mg of calcium.

Cheesy Chicken Rollups

One 6-oz. can tomato paste

1 cup water

1 tsp. Italian herb seasoning

¼ tsp. garlic powder

¼ tsp. black pepper

2 whole chicken breasts, split, skinned, and boned

1 egg white

½ cup dry-curd cottage cheese

2 tbsp. finely chopped green pepper

2 tbsp. finely chopped celery

1 tbsp. finely chopped fresh parsley

2 tbsp. oat bran

Preheat oven to 350 degrees. In a small saucepan, combine tomato paste, water, Italian herb seasoning, garlic powder, and pepper. Bring to a boil. Reduce heat. Simmer 10 minutes. Rinse chicken and pat dry. Pound between sheets of clear plastic wrap to ¼-inch thickness. In a small bowl, beat egg white until frothy. Add remaining ingredients. Mix well. Spoon mixture onto centers of chicken breasts. Roll up, eggroll fashion. Spoon half of tomato sauce into a 9" x 5" x 3" baking dish. Arrange chicken rolls in dish. Spoon remaining sauce over chicken rolls. Bake 45 to 55 minutes until tender. Serves 4.

(Serving = 1 lean protein)
NUTRIENTS: 215 calories; 31.4 grams of protein; 3.6 grams of fat; 15 grams of carbohydrates; 113 mg of sodium; 826 mg of potassium; and 72 mg of calcium.

Springtime Chicken

2 whole chicken breasts, split, skinned, and boned

⅓ cup oat flour

1 tbsp. safflower oil

One 14½-oz. can tomatoes, chopped

1 cup chicken broth, defatted

1 clove garlic, pressed

1 tsp. salt-free herb seasoning

1 tsp. dried basil
¼ tsp. paprika
⅛ tsp. black pepper
2 cups cauliflower florets
1 cup thinly sliced carrots
2 cups frozen green peas

Coat chicken with flour. In a deep skillet, brown chicken in oil.
Add tomatoes, broth, garlic, and seasonings. Bring to a boil.
Reduce heat. Cover. Simmer 25 minutes. Add cauliflower and
peas. Cover. Simmer 15 to 20 minutes until chicken is done and
vegetables are tender. Serves 4.

*(Serving = 1 lean protein; 1 starchy carbohydrate; 1 lean, fibrous
vegetable)*
*NUTRIENTS: 318 calories; 35.1 grams of protein; 8.2 grams of fat; 26.6
grams of carbohydrates; 664 mg of sodium; 827 mg of potassium; and 119
mg of calcium.*

Crispy Baked Chicken

¾ cup oat bran
½ tsp. dried basil
½ tsp. dried tarragon
½ tsp. dried celery leaves
½ tsp. paprika
¼ tsp. black pepper
2 whole chicken breasts, split and skinned

Preheat oven to 350 degrees. Combine all dry ingredients in a
plastic bag. Shake to mix. Pat chicken dry with paper towels.
Place one piece of chicken at a time in the bag. Shake to coat.

Arrange chicken in a shallow baking pan. Bake 25 minutes. Turn. Bake 20 to 25 minutes until done. Serves 4.

(Serving = 1 lean protein)
NUTRIENTS: 193 calories; 29.6 grams of protein; 4.2 grams of fat; 101.1 grams of carbohydrates; 66 mg of sodium; 305 mg of potassium; and 13 mg of calcium.

Cilantro Chicken

2 whole chicken breasts, split, skinned, and boned
2 tbsp. lime juice
2 tbsp. dry white wine
1 tbsp. low-salt soy sauce
1 clove garlic, pressed
1 tbsp. chopped fresh cilantro
½ tsp. chili powder
½ tsp. onion powder

Rinse chicken and pat dry. Arrange in a shallow dish. Combine remaining ingredients. Pour over chicken. Cover. Refrigerate 2 to 3 hours. Turn occasionally. Spray grill with nonstick cooking spray. Grill 7 to 9 minutes on each side. Baste with marinade while grilling. Serves 4.

Note: You can also use this recipe to prepare Chicken Fajitas. Serve with grilled onion, green pepper, corn tortillas, and Pico de Gallo.

(Serving = 1 lean protein)
NUTRIENTS: 151 calories; 27.0 grams of protein; 3.5 grams of fat; 0.4 grams of carbohydrates; 213 mg of sodium; 243 mg of potassium; and 17 mg of calcium.

Herbed Chicken Brochettes

1 lb. boneless chicken breasts
1 green pepper, cut into chunks
1 red pepper, cut into chunks
2 zucchini, cut into 1-inch chunks
2 yellow squash, cut into 1-inch chunks
½ cup dry white wine
¼ cup lemon juice
1 clove garlic, pressed
1 tbsp. chopped fresh parsley
1 tsp. dried oregano
½ tsp. dried basil
¼ tsp. black pepper

Cut chicken into1-inch cubes. Place chicken and vegetables in a
shallow dish. Combine remaining ingredients. Pour over
chicken and vegetables. Marinate 1 hour in the refrigerator.
Turn occasionally. Thread chicken and vegetables onto skewers.
Spray brochettes with nonstick cooking spray. Grill 8 to 10
minutes. Turn frequently. Brush with marinade while grilling.
Serves 4.

(Serving = 1 starchy carbohydrate)
*NUTRIENTS: 253 calories; 23.4 grams of protein; 2.6 grams of fat; 33.2
grams of carbohydrates; 386 mg of sodium; 1195 mg of potassium; and 87
mg of calcium.*

Asian Skewered Chicken

1 lb. boneless chicken breasts
½ lb. button mushrooms

2 cups broccoli florets

1 cup cherry tomatoes

½ cup dry white wine

2 tbsp. rice wine vinegar

2 tbsp. low-salt soy sauce

1 tbsp. safflower oil

1 tbsp. grated fresh ginger root

1 clove garlic, pressed

1 tsp. freeze-dried chives

⅛ tsp. crushed red pepper flakes

Cut chicken into1-inch cubes. Clean vegetables. Drain
thoroughly. Place chicken and vegetables in a shallow dish.
Combine remaining ingredients. Pour over chicken and vegetables. Marinate 1 hour in the refrigerator. Turn occasionally.
Thread chicken and vegetables onto skewers. Grill 8 to 10
minutes. Turn frequently. Brush with marinade while grilling.
Serves 4.

(Serving = 1 lean protein; 1 lean, fibrous vegetable)
*NUTRIENTS: 210 calories; 23.4 grams of protein; 6.8 grams of fat; 10.6
grams of carbohydrates; 326 mg of sodium; 607 mg of potassium; and 46
mg of calcium.*

Fragrant Baked Chicken Breasts

2 whole chicken breasts, split and skinned

2 cups water

1 onion, quartered

2 stalks celery with leaves, coarsely chopped

1 bay leaf

1 tsp. dried vegetable flakes
1 tsp. dried parsley flakes
½ tsp. salt-free herb seasoning

Preheat oven to 350 degrees. Place chicken breasts in a baking pan. Combine remaining ingredients. Pour over chicken. Cover. Bake 40 to 50 minutes until chicken is fork tender. Strain broth and refrigerate. Skim fat from broth and reserve for later use. Serves 4.

Note: This recipe freezes well. Use this recipe to prepare large quantities of cooked chicken breasts. Baking time will need to be increased when multiplying this recipe. When breasts are tender, remove from broth and cool. Remove bones. Cut chicken into strips. Package into single or multiple servings. Freeze for later use.

(Serving = 1 lean protein)
NUTRIENTS: 156 calories; 27.4 grams of protein; 3.2 grams of fat; 3.2 grams of carbohydrates; 97 mg of sodium; 345 mg of potassium; and 30 mg of calcium.

Enchilada Chicken Breasts

1 cup sliced onion
1 clove garlic, pressed
1 cup chicken broth, defatted
2 tbsp. cornstarch
¼ cup water
One 4-oz. can chopped green chilies
1½ cups frozen chopped spinach
2 tbsp. chopped fresh cilantro

½ tsp. chili powder

½ tsp. salt-free herb seasoning

1 tbsp. lime juice

2 whole chicken breasts, split and skinned

In a large, microwaveable casserole, combine onion, garlic, and broth. Microwave on high, uncovered, 3 minutes. Dissolve cornstarch in water. Add to casserole along with green chilies, spinach, cilantro, chili powder, herb seasoning, and lime juice. Stir to combine. Add chicken. Spoon sauce over chicken. Cover with wax paper. Microwave on high 8 minutes. Stir. Rotate dish ½ turn. Cover. Microwave 8 to 10 minutes until chicken is fork tender and no longer pink next to the bone. Remove wax paper. Let stand 5 minutes before serving. Serves 4.

(Serving = 1 lean protein; ½ lean, fibrous vegetable)
NUTRIENTS: 196 calories; 30.1 grams of protein; 3.6 grams of fat; 13.3 grams of carbohydrates; 496 mg of sodium; 541 mg of potassium; and 111 mg of calcium.

Chicken Breasts Mediterranean

2 whole chicken breasts, split and skinned

1 tbsp. cornstarch

2 tbsp. water

1 cup sliced onion

1 clove garlic, pressed

One 14½-oz. can stewed tomatoes

2 tsp. dried parsley flakes

½ tsp. salt-free herb seasoning

½ tsp. dried basil

¼ tsp. dried marjoram
¼ cup chicken broth, defatted
One 4-oz. can mushrooms, drained

In a large, microwaveable casserole, arrange chicken breasts.
Dissolve cornstarch in water. Combine with remaining ingredients. Pour sauce over chicken. Cover with wax paper. Microwave on high 8 minutes. Stir. Rotate dish ½ turn. Cover.
Microwave 8 to 10 minutes until chicken is fork tender and no
longer pink next to the bone. Remove wax paper. Let stand 5
minutes before serving. Serves 4.

(Serving = 1 lean protein; ½ lean, fibrous vegetable)
NUTRIENTS: 192 calories; 29.1 grams of protein; 3.4 grams of fat; 11.6
grams of carbohydrates; 434 mg of sodium; 584 mg of potassium; and 33
mg of calcium.

Cajun Chicken Breasts

4 whole chicken breasts, split and skinned
1 tsp. paprika
½ tsp. onion powder
¼ tsp. black pepper
⅛ tsp. red pepper
⅛ tsp. white pepper
⅛ tsp. garlic powder
1 tsp. dried summer savory
½ tsp. salt-free herb seasoning
2 tbsp. safflower oil

Preheat oven to 375 degrees. Arrange chicken on an ungreased baking sheet. Combine seasonings. Brush chicken with oil. Sprinkle chicken with seasonings. Bake 30 minutes. Turn. Bake 15 to 20 minutes until golden. Serves 8.

(Serving = 1 lean protein)
NUTRIENTS: 172 calories; 26.8 grams of protein; 6.5 grams of fat; 63 mg of sodium; 220 mg of potassium; and 13 mg of calcium.

Chicken with Sweet Peppers

½ cup chicken broth, defatted
1 cup sliced onion
1 clove garlic, pressed
2 medium green peppers, cut into strips
2 whole chicken breasts, split and skinned
1 tbsp. cornstarch
2 tbsp. water
1 tsp. dried celery flakes
½ tsp. salt-free herb seasoning
½ tsp. paprika
½ tsp. dried oregano
⅛ tsp. black pepper
1 cup chopped tomatoes

In a large, microwaveable casserole, combine broth, onion, garlic, and green peppers. Microwave on high, uncovered, 2 minutes. Add chicken. Dissolve cornstarch in water. Combine with remaining ingredients. Pour over chicken. Stir. Cover with wax paper. Microwave on high 8 minutes. Stir. Rotate dish ½ turn. Cover. Microwave 8 to 10 minutes until chicken is fork tender and no longer pink next to the bone. Remove wax paper. Let stand 5 minutes before serving. Serves 4.

(Serving = 1 lean protein, ½ lean, fibrous vegetable)
NUTRIENTS: 189 calories; 28.6 grams of protein; 3.5 grams of fat; 11.3 grams of carbohydrates; 260 mg of sodium; 526 mg of potassium; and 34 mg of calcium.

Chicken Florentine

2 whole chicken breasts, split and skinned
2 cups frozen chopped spinach, thawed
¼ cup chopped green onion
2 tbsp. chopped pimientos
One 4-oz. can mushrooms, drained
½ tsp. Italian herb seasoning
½ tsp. salt-free herb seasoning
1 tsp. dried parsley flakes
½ cup chicken broth, defatted

Preheat oven to 350 degrees. Arrange chicken breasts in a baking dish. Combine remaining ingredients. Pour over chicken. Cover. Bake 40 to 50 minutes until chicken is fork tender and no longer pink next to the bone. Serves 4.

(Serving = 1 lean protein; ½ lean, fibrous vegetable)
NUTRIENTS: 181 calories; 30.8 grams of protein; 3.6 grams of fat; 6.4 grams of carbohydrates; 464 mg of sodium; 639 mg of potassium; and 128 mg of calcium.

Tarragon Chicken

2 whole chicken breasts, split and skinned
1 tbsp. cornstarch

1 tbsp. water

1 4-oz. can mushrooms, drained

¼ cup sliced green onion

½ tsp. salt-free herb seasoning

2 tsp. dried parsley flakes

1 tsp. dried tarragon

⅛ tsp. black pepper

1 tsp. lemon juice

1 cup chicken broth, defatted

Arrange chicken breasts in a large, microwaveable casserole. Dissolve cornstarch in water. Combine with remaining ingredients. Pour over chicken. Cover with wax paper. Microwave on high 8 minutes. Stir. Rotate dish ½ turn. Cover. Microwave 8 to 10 minutes until chicken is fork tender and no longer pink next to the bone. Remove wax paper. Let stand 5 minutes before serving. Serves 4.

(Serving = 1 lean protein)
NUTRIENTS: 162 calories; 27.9 grams of protein; 3.4 grams of fat; 4.5 grams of carbohydrates; 572 mg of sodium; 310 mg of potassium; and 22 mg of calcium.

Lone Star Barbecued Chicken

2 whole chicken breasts, split, skinned, and boned

3 tbsp. lemon juice

2 tbsp. tomato paste

1 tsp. horseradish

1 tsp. instant minced onion flakes

¼ tsp. garlic powder

¼ tsp. paprika
⅛ tsp. crushed red pepper flakes
dash hickory liquid smoke
1 packet sugar substitute

Rinse chicken and pat dry. Arrange in a shallow dish. Combine remaining ingredients. Pour over chicken. Cover. Refrigerate several hours or overnight. Turn occasionally. Spray grill with nonstick cooking spray. Grill 7 to 9 minutes on each side. Baste with marinade while grilling. Serves 4.

(Serving = 1 lean protein; ½ lean, fibrous vegetable)
NUTRIENTS: 149 calories; 27.0 grams of protein; 3.1 grams of fat; 1.5 grams of carbohydrates; 66 mg of sodium; 290 mg of potassium; and 19 mg of calcium.

Tandoori Chicken

2 whole chicken breasts, split, skinned, and boned
3 tbsp. lemon juice
1 clove garlic, pressed
1 tbsp. grated fresh ginger root
2 tsp. paprika
½ tsp. ground cumin
¼ tsp. ground cardamom
¼ tsp. crushed red pepper flakes
¼ tsp. tumeric
¼ cup nonfat yogurt

Rinse chicken and pat dry. Pierce chicken with fork. Make diagonal slashes in chicken ½-inch deep. Arrange in a shallow bowl. Combine remaining ingredients. Pour over chicken. Cover. Refrigerate overnight. Turn occasionally. Spray grill with nonstick cooking spray. Grill 7 to 9 minutes on each side. Brush with marinade while grilling. Serves 4.

(Serving = 1 lean protein)
NUTRIENTS: 149 calories; 27.2 grams of protein; 3.3 grams of fat; 0.7 grams of carbohydrates; 70 mg of sodium; 240 mg of potassium; and 30 mg of calcium.

Broiled Lemon Chicken

2 whole chicken breasts, split, skinned, and boned
2 tbsp. lemon juice
1 tbsp. safflower oil
1 tbsp. white wine vinegar
2 cloves garlic, pressed
1 tsp. dried basil
½ tsp. dried lemon peel
¼ tsp. black pepper

Rinse chicken and pat dry. Arrange in a shallow dish. Combine remaining ingredients. Pour over chicken. Marinate 50 minutes or cover and refrigerate overnight. Broil 4 inches from heat source 6 to 8 minutes on each side. Brush with marinade while broiling. Serves 4.

(Serving = 1 lean protein)
NUTRIENTS: 172 calories; 26.8 grams of protein; 6.5 grams of fat; 63 mg of sodium; 220 mg of potassium; and 13 mg of calcium.

Easy Roast Turkey

One 5 to 5½ lb. turkey breast, skin removed
1 stalk celery, cut into chunks
1 small onion, quartered
1 tsp. butter-flavored sprinkles
1 tbsp. lemon juice
1 tsp. salt-free herb seasoning
¼ tsp. black pepper

Preheat oven to 325 degrees. Spray the center of a large piece of heavy-duty aluminum foil with nonstick cooking spray. Arrange turkey, celery, and onion on foil. Combine remaining ingredients. Drizzle over turkey. Fold ends of foil over turkey. Crimp edges together. Place in a shallow baking pan. Roast 2½ to 3 hours. Open foil last 20 minutes to brown turkey. Baste with pan juices. Serves 12.

(Serving = 1 lean protein)
NUTRIENTS: 247 calories; 51.4 grams of protein; 2.5 grams of fat; 1.9 grams of carbohydrates; 113 mg of sodium; 699 mg of potassium; and 5 mg of calcium.

Savory Turkey with Cabbage

1 lb. ground turkey breast, skin removed
1 cup chopped onion
1 tbsp. safflower oil
3 cups wedged cabbage
One 4-oz. can chopped green chilies
One16-oz. can tomato sauce
One 14½-oz. can tomatoes, chopped

1 tsp. garlic powder

½ tsp. Italian herb seasoning

½ tsp. dried basil

½ tsp. dried oregano

½ tsp. black pepper

4 cups cooked brown rice

In a large skillet, brown turkey and onion in oil. Arrange cabbage wedges over browned turkey. Combine remaining ingredients, except rice. Pour over cabbage. Bring to a boil. Reduce heat. Cover. Simmer 20 to 25 minutes until cabbage is tender. Serve over hot cooked rice. Serves 4.

(Serving = 1 lean protein; 1 starchy carbohydrate; 1 lean, fibrous vegetable)
NUTRIENTS: 486 calories; 37.1 grams of protein; 6.6 grams of fat; 70.8 grams of carbohydrates; 1406 mg of sodium; 1450 mg of potassium; and 122 mg of calcium.

Turkey Acapulco

1 lb. ground turkey breast, skin removed

½ cup chopped onion

1 tbsp. safflower oil

One 14½-oz. can tomatoes, chopped

¾ cup vegetable juice

½ tsp. garlic powder

¼ tsp. black pepper

½ tsp. ground cumin

2 tsp. chili powder

1 tsp. red wine vinegar

3 cups frozen corn

1 cup frozen lima beans

In a large skillet, brown turkey and onion in oil. Add remaining ingredients. Bring to a boil. Reduce heat. Cover. Simmer 20 minutes. Serves 4.

(Serving = 1 lean protein; 1 starchy carbohydrate)
NUTRIENTS: 389 calories; 37.7 grams of protein; 6.3 grams of fat; 52.3 grams of carbohydrates; 400 mg of sodium; 1253 mg of potassium; and 42 mg of calcium.

Southwestern Turkey and Beans

1 lb. ground turkey breast, skin removed

½ cup chopped onion

½ cup chopped green pepper

1 cup chopped celery

1 tbsp. safflower oil

3 cups cooked kidney beans

One 14½-oz. can tomatoes, chopped

One 8-oz. can tomato sauce

1 cup chicken broth, defatted

1 tsp. red wine vinegar

½ tsp. garlic powder

¼ tsp. cayenne pepper

1 tbsp. chopped fresh cilantro

1 tsp. dried parsley flakes

In a large skillet, brown turkey, onion, green pepper, and celery in oil. Add remaining ingredients. Bring to a boil. Reduce heat. Cover. Simmer 20 minutes. Serves 4.

(Serving = 1 lean protein; 1 starchy carbohydrate; ½ lean, fibrous vegetable)
NUTRIENTS: 223 calories; 30.8 grams of protein; 5.5 grams of fat; 15.7 grams of carbohydrates; 933 mg of sodium; 961 mg of potassium; and 48 mg of calcium.

Two Alarm Turkey Chili

1¼ lbs. ground turkey breast, skin removed
1 tbsp. safflower oil
One 8-oz. can tomato sauce
2 cups water
1 14½-oz. can tomatoes
2 tsp. instant minced onion flakes
½ tsp. garlic powder
1½ tsp. paprika
1 tbsp. ground cumin
1 tsp. ground oregano
1 tsp. salt-free herb seasoning
2 tsp. cayenne pepper
4 to 6 tbsp. chili powder
1 cup uncooked kidney beans, soaked overnight and drained

In a large kettle, brown turkey in oil. Add remaining ingredients. Simmer 1 to 2 hours until beans are tender. If chili needs to be thickened, dissolve 2 tablespoons cornstarch in 1/4 cup water. Add to chili and simmer 15 minutes. Serves 4.

(Serving = 1 lean protein; 1 starchy carbohydrate)
NUTRIENTS: 431 calories; 49.5 grams of protein; 6.4 grams of fat; 44.2 grams of carbohydrates; 547 mg of sodium; 1484 mg of potassium; and 90 mg of calcium.

Spicy Turkey Loaf

½ cup finely chopped onion

½ cup finely chopped celery

1 clove garlic, pressed

1 tbsp. safflower oil

1¼ lbs. ground turkey breast, skin removed

½ cup old-fashioned oats

One 8-oz. can tomato sauce

½ cup vegetable juice

1 egg white

1 tsp. red wine vinegar

1 tsp. chili powder

½ tsp. salt-free herb seasoning

Preheat oven to 350 degrees. In a medium skillet, sauté onion, celery, and garlic in oil until tender. In a mixing bowl, combine vegetables, turkey, and remaining ingredients. Mix well. Press into 8" x 4" x 3" loaf pan. Bake 1 hour. Serves 4.

(Serving = 1 lean protein)
NUTRIENTS: 284 calories; 39.0 grams of protein; 6.3 grams of fat; 18.3 grams of carbohydrates; 524 mg of sodium; 884 mg of potassium; and 44 mg of calcium.

Turkey Tortilla Casserole

1 lb. ground turkey breast, skin removed

1 cup chopped onion

1 clove garlic, pressed

3 cups Enchilada Sauce (page 383)

2 cups cooked pinto beans

1 tsp. salt-free herb seasoning

2 tsp. chili powder

¼ tsp. ground cumin

12 corn tortillas

¼ cup chopped green onion

1 tbsp. chopped fresh cilantro

Crumble turkey into a large, microwaveable dish. Microwave, uncovered, 5 minutes. Stir frequently. Add onion and garlic. Microwave 3 minutes. Stir in Enchilada Sauce, beans, herb seasoning, chili powder, and cumin. Microwave 3 minutes. Cut tortillas into thin strands. Stir into turkey mixture. Microwave 4 to 6 minutes until bubbly. Garnish with green onion and cilantro. Serves 4.

(Serving = 1 lean protein; 1 starchy carbohydrate)
NUTRIENTS: 513 calories; 42.0 grams of protein; 4.2 grams of fat; 80.7 grams of carbohydrates; 368 mg of sodium; 1710 mg of potassium; and 287 mg of calcium.

Turkey Topped Potatoes

1 cup chopped onion

1 cup chopped green pepper

1 clove garlic, pressed

½ cup chicken broth, defatted

1 lb. ground turkey breast, skin removed

2 cups chopped tomatoes

One 8-oz. can tomato sauce

1 tbsp. oat flour

1 tsp. dried oregano

1 tsp. salt-free herb seasoning

½ tsp. ground cumin

¼ tsp. black pepper

4 hot baked potatoes

In a large skillet, simmer onion, green pepper, and garlic in broth until tender. Add turkey. Cook turkey, stirring to keep crumbly. Combine tomatoes, tomato sauce, flour, and seasonings. Add to turkey mixture. Simmer, uncovered, 20 minutes. Stir frequently. Serve over baked potatoes. Serves 4.

(Serving = 1 lean protein; 1 starchy carbohydrate; 1 lean, fibrous vegetable)
NUTRIENTS: 312 calories; 34.2 grams of protein; 2.3 grams of fat; 38.0 grams of carbohydrates; 588 mg of sodium; 1496 mg of potassium; and 52 mg of calcium.

Turkey and Green Bean Casserole

1 lb. ground turkey breast, skin removed

¼ cup water

1 medium onion, sliced and separated into rings

1 green pepper, cut into rings

One 4-oz. can mushrooms, drained

One 14½-oz. can tomatoes, chopped

1 tbsp. low-salt soy sauce

1 tsp. salt-free herb seasoning

1 tsp. dried celery flakes

½ tsp. dried summer savory

¼ tsp. black pepper

2 cups frozen French-style green beans

2 tbsp. oat flour

1½ cups oat flour

1 tsp. baking powder

½ tsp. dry mustard

2 egg whites, beaten

1 tbsp. safflower oil

½ cup milk

Preheat oven to 400 degrees. In a large skillet, brown turkey in water. Add onion, green pepper, mushrooms, tomatoes, soy sauce, seasonings, and green beans. Cover. Simmer 15 minutes, stirring occasionally. Sprinkle 2 tablespoons flour over turkey mixture. Stir. Pour into 2½-quart casserole. In a mixing bowl, combine 1½ cups flour, baking powder, and dry mustard. Add remaining ingredients. Stir until moistened. Drop by table-spoonfuls onto turkey mixture. Bake 25 to 30 minutes until browned. Serves 4.

(Serving = 1 lean protein; ¼ starchy carbohydrate; 1 lean, fibrous vegetable)
NUTRIENTS: 420 calories; 41.2 grams of protein; 9.0 grams of fat; 45.6 grams of carbohydrates; 531 mg of sodium; 1122 mg of potassium; and 112 mg of calcium.

Turkey Vegetable Lasagna

1 cup chopped onion

2 cloves garlic, pressed

½ cup water

1 lb. ground turkey breast, skin removed

1 tbsp. safflower oil

One 14½-oz. can tomatoes, chopped

One 8-oz. can tomato sauce

One 4-oz. can mushrooms, drained

¼ cup chicken broth, defatted

1 tsp. dried oregano

1 tsp. dried basil

1 tsp. salt-free herb seasoning

¼ tsp. black pepper

¼ cup chopped fresh parsley

1 cup dry-curd cottage cheese

3 cups sliced zucchini

2 tbsp. oat flour

In a large skillet, sauté onion and garlic in water until tender.
Add turkey and oil. Brown turkey, stirring to keep crumbly.
Add tomatoes, tomato sauce, mushrooms, broth, and seasonings. Simmer, uncovered, 30 to 40 minutes until thickened.
Preheat oven to 350 degrees. Spray an 8" x 11" x 2" baking dish
with nonstick cooking spray. Combine parsley and cottage
cheese. Place half of zucchini in baking dish. Sprinkle with 1
tablespoon oat flour. Top with half of cottage cheese mixture,
then half of turkey sauce. Repeat layers. Bake 30 minutes.
Serves 4.

(Serving = 1 lean protein; 1 lean, fibrous vegetable)
NUTRIENTS: 293 calories; 35.5 grams of protein; 6.0 grams of fat; 26.3
grams of carbohydrates; 1195 mg of sodium; 1307 mg of potassium; and
81 mg of calcium.

Italian Turkey Patties

⅓ cup finely chopped onion

1 clove garlic, finely chopped

One 4-oz. can mushrooms, drained and chopped

¼ cup water

1 lb. ground turkey breast, skin removed

⅓ cup oat bran

1 tsp. dried oregano

½ tsp. dried basil

3 tbsp. tomato paste

1 egg white

1 tsp. Worcestershire sauce

In a small skillet, sauté onion, garlic, and mushrooms in water until tender. In a mixing bowl, combine remaining ingredients. Add onion mixture. Mix well. Shape into 8 patties. Spray a large skillet with nonstick cooking spray. Cook patties 2 to 3 minutes on each side until browned. Serves 4.

(Serving = 1 lean protein)
NUTRIENTS: 180 calories; 31.3 grams of protein; 1.9 grams of fat; 8.9 grams of carbohydrates; 214 mg of sodium; 607 mg of potassium; and 15 mg of calcium.

Turkey Burgers Florentine

1 cup frozen chopped spinach, thawed and drained

1 lb. ground turkey breast, skin removed

¼ cup oat bran

1 tbsp. instant minced onion flakes

1 tsp. salt-free herb seasoning

½ tsp. dried tarragon

¼ tsp. black pepper

1 egg white

One 8-oz. can tomato sauce

1 cup water

1 tsp. no-salt-added, beef-flavored instant bouillon

One 4-oz. can mushrooms, drained

2 tbsp. chopped fresh parsley

2 tbsp. cornstarch

2 tbsp. red wine vinegar

4 cups hot cooked brown rice

Squeeze water from thawed spinach. In a mixing bowl, combine spinach, turkey, oat bran, onion flakes, herb seasoning, tarragon, pepper, and egg white. Mix well. Form into 8 patties. Spray a large skillet with nonstick cooking spray. Cook patties 2 to 3 minutes on each side until browned. Remove to a serving dish. In a medium saucepan, combine tomato sauce, water, bouillon, mushrooms, and parsley. Dissolve cornstarch in vinegar. Add to saucepan. Heat and stir until thickened. Pour over turkey burgers. Serve over rice. Serves 4.

(Serving = 1 lean protein; 1 starchy carbohydrate; ¼ lean, fibrous vegetable)
NUTRIENTS: 416 calories; 37.4 grams of protein; 3.2 grams of fat; 60.1 grams of carbohydrates; 1107 mg of sodium; 1011 mg of potassium; and 100 mg of calcium.

Picante Turkey Patties

¼ cup finely minced onion

1 tbsp. finely minced cilantro

¼ cup water

1 lb. ground turkey breast, skin removed

⅓ cup oat bran

1 tsp. salt-free herb seasoning

½ tsp. ground cumin

½ tsp. chili powder

¼ tsp. black pepper

3 tbsp. picante sauce

1 egg white

In a small skillet, cook onion and cilantro in water until tender. In a mixing bowl, combine remaining ingredients. Add onion mixture. Mix well. Form into 8 patties. Spray a large skillet with nonstick cooking spray. Cook patties 2 to 3 minutes on each side until browned. Serves 4.

(Serving = 1 lean protein)
NUTRIENTS: 167 calories; 30.3 grams of protein; 1.9 grams of fat; 6.4 grams of carbohydrates; 132 mg of sodium; 450 mg of potassium; and 6 mg of calcium.

Gourmet Turkey Burgers

⅓ cup finely chopped onion

1 clove garlic, finely chopped

¼ cup water

1 lb. ground turkey breast, skin removed

¼ cup oat bran

1 tsp. salt-free herb seasoning
½ tsp. dried parsley flakes
¼ tsp. black pepper
3 tbsp. tomato paste
1 egg white
dash Tabasco sauce

In a small skillet, cook onion and garlic in water until tender. In a mixing bowl, combine remaining ingredients. Add onion mixture. Mix well. Form into 8 patties. Spray a large skillet with nonstick cooking spray. Cook patties 2 to 3 minutes on each side until browned. Serves 4.

(Serving = 1 lean protein)
NUTRIENTS: 168 calories; 30.4 grams of protein; 1.8 grams of fat; 7.0 grams of carbohydrates; 77 mg of sodium; 530 mg of potassium; and 13 mg of calcium.

Holiday Turkey Patties

⅓ cup finely chopped onion
⅓ cup finely chopped green pepper
¼ cup water
1 lb. ground turkey breast, skin removed
¼ cup oat bran
1 tsp. dried celery flakes
½ tsp. ground sage
¼ tsp. dried marjoram
¼ tsp. dried thyme
¼ tsp. black pepper
1 tsp. Worcestershire sauce
1 egg white

In a small skillet, cook onion and green pepper in water until tender. In a mixing bowl, combine remaining ingredients. Add onion mixture. Mix well. Form into 8 patties. Spray a large skillet with nonstick cooking spray. Cook patties 2 to 3 minutes on each side until browned. Serves 4.

(Serving = 1 lean protein)
NUTRIENTS: 160 calories; 30.0 grams of protein; 1.8 grams of fat; 5.0 grams of carbohydrates; 73 mg of sodium; 439 mg of potassium; and 5 mg of calcium.

Hunan Turkey Nuggets

1 lb. ground turkey breast, skin removed
⅓ cup oat bran
1 tbsp. instant minced onion flakes
1 tsp. dried celery flakes
¼ tsp. garlic powder
¼ tsp. ground ginger
1 tbsp. low-salt soy sauce
1 egg white
1 cup thinly sliced mushrooms
1 cup thinly sliced onion
½ cup thinly sliced celery
1 cup vegetable juice
1 cup water
2 tsp. no-salt-added beef-flavored instant bouillon
1 tsp. grated fresh ginger root
2 tbsp. cornstarch
¼ cup water

Preheat oven to 400 degrees. In a mixing bowl, combine
turkey, oat bran, onion flakes, celery flakes, garlic powder,
ground ginger, soy sauce, and egg white. Mix well. Form
mixture into 1-inch balls. Spray a shallow baking pan with
nonstick cooking spray. Place turkey balls in pan. Bake 15 to 18
minutes until done. In a large skillet, combine mushrooms,
onion, celery, vegetable juice, water, bouillon, and ginger root.
Bring to a boil. Reduce heat. Simmer until onion is tender.
Dissolve cornstarch in water. Add to skillet. Heat and stir
until thickened. Add cooked turkey balls. Simmer 5 minutes.
Serves 4.

(Serving = 1 lean protein; ½ lean, fibrous vegetable)
NUTRIENTS: 201 calories; 31.8 grams of protein; 2.4 grams of fat; 15.3
grams of carbohydrates; 420 mg of sodium; 659 mg of potassium; and 40
mg of calcium.

Herbed Turkey Nuggets

1 lb. ground turkey breast, skin removed
⅓ cup oat bran
1 tsp. dried parsley flakes
½ tsp. dried marjoram
¼ tsp. dried thyme
½ tsp. paprika
¼ tsp. black pepper
1 egg white
1 cup thinly sliced celery
1 cup thinly sliced carrots
¼ cup chopped green onion
1 clove garlic, pressed

2 cups chicken broth, defatted

2 tbsp. cornstarch

2 tbsp. water

Preheat oven to 400 degrees. In a mixing bowl, combine turkey, oat bran, seasonings, and egg white. Mix well. Form into 1-inch balls. Spray a shallow baking pan with nonstick cooking spray. Place turkey balls in pan. Bake 15 to 18 minutes until done. In a large skillet, combine celery, carrots, green onion, garlic, and broth. Bring to a boil. Reduce heat. Cover. Simmer 10 to 12 minutes until vegetables are tender. Dissolve cornstarch in water. Add to skillet. Heat and stir until thickened. Add cooked turkey balls. Simmer 5 minutes. Serves 4.

(Serving = 1 lean protein; ½ lean, fibrous vegetable)
NUTRIENTS: 192 calories; 31.4 grams of protein; 2.5 grams of fat; 11.4 grams of carbohydrates; 858 mg of sodium; 610 mg of potassium; and 33 mg of calcium.

Creole Turkey Sausage

1 lb. ground turkey breast, skin removed

1 tbsp. Italian herb seasoning

½ tsp. ground coriander

1 tsp. paprika

¼ tsp. black pepper

⅛ tsp. cayenne pepper

½ tsp. ground cumin

½ tsp. garlic powder

1 tsp. instant minced onion flakes

¼ cup oat bran

1 tsp. Kitchen Bouquet

¼ cup chicken broth, defatted

1 egg white

In a large bowl, combine all ingredients. Mix well. Refrigerate 1 hour. Form into small patties. Spray a large skillet with nonstick cooking spray. Cook patties over medium heat until lightly browned on both sides. Serves 4.

Note: This recipe freezes well. You may want to double or triple this recipe and freeze for later use.

(Serving = 1 lean protein)
NUTRIENTS: 171 calories; 30.8 grams of protein; 2.2 grams of fat; 6.9 grams of carbohydrates; 165 mg of sodium; 433 mg of potassium; and 2 mg of calcium.

Savory Turkey Hash

½ cup chopped onion

¼ cup chopped green pepper

¼ cup celery

¼ cup chicken broth, defatted

3 cups julienned cooked turkey breast

2 cups diced cooked new potatoes

½ cup evaporated skimmed milk

1 tbsp. Worcestershire sauce

1 tsp. salt-free herb seasoning

1 tsp. paprika

⅛ tsp. crushed red pepper flakes

2 tbsp. chopped fresh parsley

In a large skillet, cook onion, green pepper, and celery in broth until tender. Stir in turkey and potatoes. Combine remaining ingredients. Add to skillet. Stir. Press flat. Cover. Cook 5 to 7 minutes until hash is hot. Uncover. Brown hash. Turn. Brown other side. Serves 4.

(Serving = 1 lean protein; ½ starchy carbohydrate; ¼ lean, fibrous vegetable)
NUTRIENTS: 218 calories; 32.3 grams of protein; 1.6 grams of fat; 18.0 grams of carbohydrates; 199 mg of sodium; 751 mg of potassium; and 106 mg of calcium.

Chicken Divan

4 cups broccoli florets, cooked
3 cups julienned cooked chicken breast
¼ cup prepared butter-flavored mix
¼ cup oat flour
One 14½-oz. can chicken broth, defatted
½ cup nonfat yogurt
1 tbsp. lemon juice
1 tsp. Worcestershire sauce
1 tsp. curry powder
1 tsp. salt-free herb seasoning
¼ tsp. white pepper
2 tsp. cheese-flavored sprinkles

Preheat oven to 350 degrees. Place broccoli in 8" x 11" x 2" baking dish. Arrange chicken on top. In a medium saucepan, combine prepared butter mix and flour. Add broth. Heat and stir until thickened. Remove from heat. Stir in yogurt, lemon juice, Worcestershire sauce, curry, herb seasoning, and pepper. Pour sauce over chicken and broccoli. Bake 25 to 30 minutes until heated thoroughly. Garnish with cheese sprinkles. Serves 4.

(Serving = 1 lean protein; 1 lean, fibrous vegetable)
NUTRIENTS: 203 calories; 28.3 grams of protein; 4.5 grams of fat; 13.4 grams of carbohydrates; 466 mg of sodium; 556 mg of potassium; and 106 mg of calcium.

Skillet Chicken and Vegetables

1 lb. boneless chicken breasts
2 tbsp. low-salt soy sauce
2 tsp. grated fresh ginger root
½ cup chopped green onion
1 clove garlic, pressed
1 tbsp. safflower oil
1 cup sliced mushrooms
2 cups julienned zucchini
1 cup cauliflower florets
½ cup chicken broth, defatted
2 tsp. cornstarch

Cut chicken breasts into long, thin strips. In a bowl, combine chicken, soy sauce, and ginger root. Set aside. In a large skillet, sauté green onion and garlic in oil until tender. Add mushrooms, zucchini, and cauliflower. Cook and stir until vegetables are just tender. Add chicken mixture. Cook and stir until chicken is no longer pink. Dissolve cornstarch in broth. Add to skillet. Cook and stir until thickened. Serves 4.

(Serving = 1 lean protein; 1 lean, fibrous vegetable)
NUTRIENTS: 181 calories; 21.5 grams of protein; 6.7 grams of fat; 10.9 grams of carbohydrates; 772 mg of sodium; 349 mg of potassium; and 44 mg of calcium.

Chinese Chicken and Broccoli

2 cups sliced mushrooms
½ cup chopped green onion
2 cups chicken broth, defatted
3 cups julienned cooked chicken breast
3 cups broccoli florets
2 tbsp. low-salt soy sauce
2 tsp. grated fresh ginger root
1 tsp. dried summer savory
2 tsp. lemon juice
2 tbsp. cornstarch
2 tbsp. water

In a large skillet, simmer mushrooms and green onion in broth until tender. Add chicken, broccoli, soy sauce, ginger root, and summer savory. Bring to a boil. Reduce heat. Cover. Simmer 15 minutes until broccoli is tender. Stir in lemon juice. Dissolve cornstarch in water. Add to chicken and vegetables. Heat and stir until thickened. Serves 4.

(Serving = 1 lean protein; 1 lean, fibrous vegetable)
NUTRIENTS: 193 calories; 27.4 grams of protein; 4.7 grams of fat; 13.7 grams of carbohydrates; 1116 mg of sodium; 478 mg of potassium; and 82 mg of calcium.

Company Beans and Chicken

1 cup navy beans, soaked overnight and drained

2 cups water

2 cups chicken broth, defatted

1 clove garlic, pressed

1 cup chopped onion

1 cup sliced celery

1 cup sliced carrots

One 14½-oz. can tomatoes, chopped

1 bay leaf

2 tsp. salt-free herb seasoning

½ tsp. ground sage

1 tbsp. dried parsley flakes

¼ tsp. black pepper

2 tbsp. cider vinegar

1 tsp. paprika

3 cups julienned cooked chicken breast

In a large stock pot, combine navy beans, water, and broth. Add remaining ingredients, except chicken. Bring to a boil. Reduce heat. Cover. Simmer 1½ to 2 hours until beans are tender. Add chicken. Simmer 15 minutes. Serves 4.

(Serving = 1 lean protein; 1 starchy carbohydrate; 1 lean, fibrous vegetable)
NUTRIENTS: 377 calories; 37.3 grams of protein; 4.8 grams of fat; 47.4 grams of carbohydrates; 986 mg of sodium; 1289 mg of potassium; and 138 mg of calcium.

Parsleyed Turkey and Rice

½ cup chopped green onion

1 cup chopped celery

1 clove garlic, pressed

2 cups chicken broth, defatted

3 cups julienned cooked turkey breast

2 tbsp. chopped pimientos

One 4-oz. can mushrooms, drained

3 cups cooked brown rice

2 tbsp. dried parsley flakes

1 tsp. dried basil

½ tsp. salt-free herb seasoning

2 tbsp. cornstarch

¼ cup water

In a large skillet, cook green onion, celery, and garlic in broth. Add turkey, pimientos, mushrooms, rice, and seasonings. Bring to a boil. Reduce heat. Cover. Simmer 10 minutes. Dissolve cornstarch in water. Add to turkey mixture. Heat and stir until thickened. Serves 4.

(Serving = 1 lean protein; 1 starchy carbohydrate; ½ lean, fibrous vegetable)
NUTRIENTS: 408 calories; 42.7 grams of protein; 6.0 grams of fat; 45.7 grams of carbohydrates; 1402 mg of sodium; 763 mg of potassium; and 52 mg of calcium.

Paella

1 whole chicken breast, split, skinned, and boned

1 cup sliced onion

2 cloves garlic, pressed

2 tbsp. safflower oil

2 cups water

2 cups chicken broth, defatted

1 cup uncooked brown rice

1 tbsp. paprika

½ tsp. black pepper

½ tsp. cayenne pepper

½ tsp. salt-free herb seasoning

1 tbsp. dried parsley flakes

One 14-oz. can tomatoes, chopped

½ lb. shrimp, peeled and deveined

1½ cups frozen peas, thawed

2 tbsp. chopped pimientos

Cut chicken into long, thin strips. In a Dutch oven, sauté
chicken, onion, and garlic in oil until chicken is lightly
browned. Drain oil from Dutch oven. Add water, broth, rice,
seasonings, and tomatoes. Bring to a boil. Reduce heat. Cover.
Simmer 45 minutes. Stir in shrimp, peas, and pimientos.
Simmer 10 minutes or until shrimp turn opaque. Add additional
water as needed. Serves 4.

(Serving = 1 lean protein; ¾ starchy carbohydrate)
NUTRIENTS: 336 calories; 30.3 grams of protein; 10.2 grams of fat;
30.6 grams of carbohydrates; 1181 mg of sodium; 659 mg of potassium;
and 123 mg of calcium.

Chicken Stir Fry

3 cups julienned cooked chicken breast

2 cups chicken broth, defatted

One 6-oz. pkg. frozen snowpeas

¼ cup chopped green onion

2 tbsp. chopped pimientos

2 tbsp. low-salt soy sauce

2 tsp. red wine vinegar

1 tsp. grated fresh ginger root

¼ tsp. garlic powder

½ tsp. paprika

2 tbsp. cornstarch

¼ cup water

4 cups cooked brown rice

In a large skillet, combine all ingredients except cornstarch, water, and rice. Bring to a boil, stirring occasionally. Reduce heat. Cover. Simmer 10 to 15 minutes until snowpeas are tender. Dissolve cornstarch in water. Add to chicken mixture. Heat and stir until thickened. Serve over hot cooked rice. Serves 4.

(Serving = 1 lean protein; 1 starchy carbohydrate; ½ lean, fibrous vegetable)
NUTRIENTS: 398 calories; 29.3 grams of protein; 5.7 grams of fat; 60.1 grams of carbohydrates; 1621 mg of sodium; 328 mg of potassium; and 51 mg of calcium.

Mandarin Chicken

1 cup sliced celery

One 8-oz. can water chestnuts, drained and sliced thin

2 cups chicken broth, defatted

3 cups julienned cooked chicken breast

3 tbsp. low-salt soy sauce

1 tsp. dried vegetable flakes

2 tsp. grated fresh ginger root

½ tsp. orange peel

2 tbsp. cornstarch

¼ cup water

In a large skillet, cook celery and water chestnuts in broth until celery is tender. Add chicken, soy sauce, vegetable flakes, ginger root, and orange peel. Bring to a boil. Reduce heat. Cover. Simmer 15 minutes. Dissolve cornstarch in water. Add to chicken mixture. Heat and stir until thickened. Serves 4.

(Serving = 1 lean protein; ½ lean, fibrous vegetable)
NUTRIENTS: 172 calories; 23.7 grams of protein; 4.9 grams of fat; 11.4 grams of carbohydrates; 1397 mg of sodium; 284 mg of potassium; and 55 mg of calcium.

Skillet Turkey Supreme

1 cup thinly sliced onion

1 clove garlic, pressed

1 cup sliced celery

2 cups chicken broth, defatted

3 cups julienned cooked turkey breast

1 cup chopped tomatoes

2 cups sliced zucchini

One 8-oz. can tomato sauce

½ tsp. salt-free herb seasoning

1 tsp. paprika

½ tsp. dried basil

2 tsp. dried vegetable flakes

2 tbsp. cornstarch

¼ cup water

In a large skillet, cook onion, garlic, and celery in broth until tender. Add turkey, tomatoes, zucchini, tomato sauce, and seasonings. Bring to a boil. Reduce heat. Cover. Simmer 15 minutes until zucchini is tender. Dissolve cornstarch in water. Add to turkey mixture. Heat and stir until thickened. Serves 4.

(Serving = 1 lean protein; 1 lean, fibrous vegetable)
NUTRIENTS: 292 calories; 40.9 grams of protein; 5.4 grams of fat; 22.6 grams of carbohydrates; 1484 mg of sodium; 1210 mg of potassium; and 75 mg of calcium.

Turkey Papriash

1 cup thinly sliced onion

2 cloves garlic, pressed

1 cup thinly sliced celery

2 cups vegetable juice

2 tbsp. cornstarch

2 tbsp. water

3 cups julienned cooked turkey breast

2 tbsp. paprika

½ tsp. salt-free herb seasoning

¼ tsp. black pepper

½ cup nonfat yogurt, optional

4 cups cooked brown rice

In a large skillet, cook onion, garlic, and celery in vegetable juice until tender. Dissolve cornstarch in water. Stir into vegetables. Add turkey, paprika, herb seasoning, and pepper. Heat and stir until bubbly. Reduce heat. Simmer 10 minutes. Add yogurt. Heat and simmer 2 minutes. Serve over hot cooked rice. Serves 4.

(Serving = 1 lean protein; 1 starchy carbohydrate))
NUTRIENTS: 492 calories; 44.4 grams of protein; 6.1 grams of fat; 64.2 grams of carbohydrates; 1029 mg of sodium; 1052 mg of potassium; and 104 mg of calcium.

Hickory Smoked Turkey

2 tbsp. cornstarch
2 tbsp. low-salt soy sauce
1 tsp. hickory liquid smoke
1 tbsp. cider vinegar
1 cup chicken broth, defatted
3 cups julienned cooked turkey breast

Combine cornstarch and soy sauce. Pour into a medium skillet. Add liquid smoke, vinegar, and chicken broth. Heat and stir until thickened. Add turkey. Simmer 6 to 8 minutes until thoroughly heated. Serves 4.

Note: This recipe freezes well. You may want to double or triple this recipe and package into single or multiple servings. Freeze for later use.

(Serving = 1 lean protein)
NUTRIENTS: 220 calories; 38.1 grams of protein; 5.6 grams of fat; 5.3

grams of carbohydrates; 764 mg of sodium; 505 mg of potassium; and 20 mg of calcium.

Spicy Indian Turkey

1 cup thinly sliced onion
2 cloves garlic, pressed
2 cups chicken broth, defatted
3 cups julienned cooked turkey breast
1 tsp. grated fresh ginger root
½ tsp. ground cloves
¼ tsp. ground cardamon
½ tsp. cinnamon
¼ tsp. black pepper
1 tsp. salt-free herb seasoning
1 tbsp. cornstarch
¼ cup water

In a large skillet, cook onion and garlic in broth until tender. Add turkey, ginger root, and seasonings. Bring to a boil. Reduce heat. Cover. Simmer for 15 minutes. Dissolve cornstarch in water. Add to turkey mixture. Heat and stir until thickened. Serves 4.

(Serving = 1 lean protein)
NUTRIENTS: 231 calories; 38.5 grams of protein; 5.0 grams of fat; 6.9 grams of carbohydrates; 839 mg of sodium; 545 mg of potassium; and 28 mg of calcium.

Southwestern Turkey

2 tbsp. cornstarch
⅔ cup picante sauce
One 4-oz. can chopped green chilies
1 cup chicken broth, defatted
3 cups julienned cooked turkey breast

In a medium skillet, combine cornstarch and picante sauce. Add green chilies and chicken broth. Cook and stir until thickened. Add turkey. Simmer 6 to 8 minutes until thoroughly heated. Serves 4.

Note: This recipe freezes well. You may want to double or triple this recipe and package into single or multiple servings. Freeze for later use.

(Serving = 1 lean protein)
NUTRIENTS: 230 calories; 38.0 grams of protein; 4.9 grams of fat; 8.6 grams of carbohydrates; 584 mg of sodium; 515 mg of potassium; and 20 mg of calcium.

Spicy Chicken and Bean Enchiladas

2 cups Refried Frijoles (page 190)
1½ cups shredded, cooked chicken
1 cup chunky picante sauce
1/3 cup chopped green onion
One 4-oz. can chopped green chilies
2 tbsp. chopped fresh cilantro
1 tsp. chili powder
½ tsp. ground cumin
½ tsp. garlic powder

dash Tabasco sauce

12 corn tortillas, room temperature

2 cups Enchilada Sauce (page 383)

Preheat oven to 350 degrees. In a large bowl, combine all
ingredients except tortillas and Enchilada Sauce. Soften tortillas
by microwaving 20 seconds. Place ⅓ cup filling on each tortilla.
Roll up. Place seam side down in 9" x 13" x 2" baking dish.
Pour Enchilada Sauce over tortillas. Cover. Bake 15 to 20
minutes. Serves 4.

(Serving = ½ lean protein; 1 starchy carbohydrate)
*NUTRIENTS: 452 calories; 27.0 grams of protein; 5.9 grams of fat; 76.6
grams of carbohydrates; 630 mg of sodium; 1094 mg of potassium; and
220 mg of calcium.*

Spinach Enchiladas

2 cups frozen spinach, thawed and drained

½ cup chopped onion

1 cup dry-curd cottage cheese

1 egg white

¼ cup picante sauce

1 tbsp. chopped fresh cilantro

½ tsp. chili powder

1 cup diced, cooked chicken

12 corn tortillas, room temperature

2 cups Enchilada Sauce (page 383)

Preheat oven to 350 degrees. In a mixing bowl, combine
spinach, onion, cottage cheese, egg white, picante sauce,

cilantro, seasonings, and chicken. Soften tortillas by microwaving for 20 seconds. Place ¼ cup filling on each tortilla. Roll up. Place seam side down in 8" x 11" x 2" baking dish. Pour Enchilada Sauce over tortillas. Cover. Bake 20 to 25 minutes. Serves 4.

(Serving = ½ lean protein; ½ starchy carbohydrate; ½ lean, fibrous vegetable)
NUTRIENTS: 340 calories; 21.9 grams of protein; 5.1 grams of fat; 56.3 grams of carbohydrates; 479 mg of sodium; 1030 mg of potassium; and 294 mg of calcium.

Green Chicken Enchiladas

3 cups shredded, cooked chicken
½ cup chopped onion
½ cup picante sauce
½ tsp. paprika
¼ tsp. ground cumin
12 corn tortillas, room temperature
¼ cup prepared butter-flavored mix
¼ cup oat flour
2 cups chicken broth, defatted
½ cup nonfat yogurt
One 4-oz. can chopped green chilies
1 tbsp. chopped canned jalapenos
1 recipe Spicy Salsa (page 389)

Preheat oven to 350 degrees. In a bowl, combine chicken, onion, picante sauce, paprika, and cumin. Soften tortillas by microwaving 20 seconds. Place ¼ cup filling on each tortilla.

Roll up. Place seam side down in 9" x 13" x 2" baking dish. In a saucepan, combine prepared butter mix and oat flour. Add broth. Cook, stirring constantly, until thickened. Stir in yogurt, chilies, and jalapenos. Pour over tortillas. Cover. Bake 20 to 25 minutes. Serve with Spicy Salsa. Serves 4.

(Serving = 1 lean protein; ½ starchy carbohydrate; ½ lean, fibrous vegetable)
NUTRIENTS: 423 calories; 32.4 grams of protein; 8.2 grams of fat; 56.7 grams of carbohydrates; 1176 mg of sodium; 652 mg of potassium; and 207 mg of calcium.

_____

Classic Chicken Enchiladas

¾ cup dry-curd cottage cheese
⅓ cup skim milk
1 tbsp. safflower oil
2 tsp. lemon juice
1 tsp. salt-free herb seasoning
½ tsp. ground cumin
3 cups shredded, cooked chicken
½ cup sliced green onion
One 4-oz. can chopped green chilies
12 corn tortillas, room temperature
2 cups Enchilada Sauce (page 383)

Preheat oven to 350 degrees. In a blender, combine cottage cheese, milk, oil, lemon juice, herb seasoning, and cumin. Blend until smooth. In a large bowl, combine blender mixture, chicken, green onion, and green chilies. Soften tortillas by microwaving 20 seconds. Place ⅓ cup chicken filling on each tortilla. Roll up. Place seam side down in 8" x 11" x 2" baking dish. Pour Enchilada Sauce over tortillas. Cover. Bake 15 to 20 minutes. Serves 4.

(Serving = 1 lean protein; ½ starchy carbohydrate)
NUTRIENTS: 427 calories; 32.8 grams of protein; 10.1 grams of fat; 53.6 grams of carbohydrates; 350 mg of sodium; 782 mg of potassium; and 212 mg of calcium.

8

CHAPTER EIGHT ❧ Starchy Carbohydrates

Helpful Hints

Refer to the chart Using Herbs and Spices (page 14)
to try new combinations of spices.

Potatoes will discolor if cut or peeled too far ahead
of time. Cold lemon water will help slow the
discoloration.

Store potatoes and onions at room temperature,
but not together. Onions shorten the shelf life of
potatoes.

Store brown rice in the refrigerator to increase shelf life.

Mix left-over lentils, barley, or rice with tomato sauce for a
quick pilaf. Serve hot or cold.

Rice should be added to boiling water. Avoid stirring as this
results in clumping.

Rice can be flavored by cooking with one teaspoon of flavored
vinegar, a clove of garlic, an onion wedge, or a sprig of mint.

One cup of dried beans yields about 3 cups of cooked beans.

Legumes are the fruit or seeds from pod-bearing plants, known
as "beans" and "peas."

Beans, lentils, and peas need to be boiled before being eaten.
They contain toxins called lectins which can cause stomach
cramps, nausea, and diarrhea. Peas and lentils are low in lectins;

most beans are high. Boiling destroys lectins; lower temperatures do not. Bring lentils and peas to a brief boil before cooking with low heat. Boil these beans for 10 minutes before reducing heat: black beans, great northern beans, kidney beans, lima beans, navy beans, pink beans, pinto beans, red beans, and soy beans. If unsure of what beans are being used, cook 10 minutes.

Soak dry beans before cooking. After washing beans, completely cover the beans with water and soak overnight. To quick-soak the beans, bring the soaking water and beans to a boil. Boil 2 minutes. Cover. Let stand 1 hour. Drain and cook beans in fresh water.

The skins of potatoes and sweet potatoes should be eaten to increase fiber.

Pierce potatoes 3 or 4 times before baking. This ventilates them and prevents them from exploding.

Winter squash is easier to peel if cooked first.

When buying peas, choose full pods. Store peas unshelled in the refrigerator.

Cooked grains freeze well. Defrost in the microwave or in boiling water.

Grains make excellent fillers for turkey loaves.

Zesty Barley

3 cups chicken broth, defatted

One 14½-oz. can tomatoes, chopped

½ cup chopped onion

½ cup chopped green pepper

1 clove garlic, pressed

1 cup uncooked barley

1 tsp. dried parsley flakes

½ tsp. dried basil

½ tsp. dried oregano

2 tbsp. prepared butter-flavored mix

In a large saucepan, combine broth, tomatoes, onion, green pepper, and garlic. Bring to a boil. Stir in barley, parsley, basil, and oregano. Reduce heat. Cover. Simmer 45 to 55 minutes until barley is tender and broth is absorbed. Stir occasionally while cooking. If barley looks dry, add water as necessary. Stir in prepared butter mix and serve. Serves 4.

(Serving = 1 starchy carbohydrate; ½ lean, fibrous vegetable)
NUTRIENTS: 96 calories; 7.9 grams of protein; 1.6 grams of fat; 44.2 grams of carbohydrates; 1257 mg of sodium; 429 mg of potassium; and 35 mg of calcium.

Barley Mushroom Pilaf

3 cups chicken broth, defatted

2 cups sliced mushrooms

½ cup chopped onion

1 cup uncooked barley

2 tsp. Worcestershire sauce

½ tsp. dried thyme

¼ tsp. black pepper

2 tbsp. chopped pimientos

In a large saucepan, combine broth, mushrooms, and onions. Bring to a boil. Stir in barley, Worcestershire sauce, celery flakes, thyme, and pepper. Reduce heat. Cover. Simmer 45 to 55 minutes until barley is tender and broth is absorbed. Stir occasionally while cooking. Add water as needed. Garnish with pimientos. Serves 4.

(Serving = 1 starchy carbohydrate; ¼ lean, fibrous vegetable)
NUTRIENTS: 85 calories; 7.8 grams of protein; 1.5 grams of fat;
41.5 grams of carbohydrates; 1119 mg of sodium; 179 mg of potassium;
and 39 mg of calcium.

Cuban Black Beans

1 lb. dry black beans, soaked overnight and drained

5 cups chicken broth, defatted

1 cup chopped onion

¼ cup chopped celery

2 cloves garlic, pressed

1 bay leaf

1 tbsp. dried vegetable flakes

1 tsp. dried summer savory

1 tsp. dried lemon peel

1 tsp. ground cumin

¼ tsp. crushed red pepper flakes

1 tsp. hickory liquid smoke

1 tsp. bacon-flavored sprinkles

In a large saucepan, combine drained beans, broth, onion, celery, garlic, and bay leaf. Bring to a boil. Cook 10 minutes. Reduce heat. Add seasonings and liquid smoke. Cover. Simmer 45 to 60 minutes until beans are tender. Remove bay leaf. Stir in bacon sprinkles. Serves 8.

Note: Black beans are wonderful served over rice. For added flavor, top with a little red wine vinegar and chopped green onions.

(Serving = 1 starchy carbohydrate)
NUTRIENTS: 217 calories; 14.0 grams of protein; 1.7 grams of fat; 38.1 grams of carbohydrates; 1133 mg of sodium; 648 mg of potassium; and 95 mg of calcium.

Rum-Baked Black Beans

1 lb. dried black beans
5 cups water
1 cup chopped onion
1 cup chopped celery
½ cup chopped carrots
2 cloves garlic, pressed
1 bay leaf
2 tbsp. chopped pimientos
1 tsp. dried thyme
1 tsp. salt-free herb seasoning
2 tsp. dried parsley flakes
¼ tsp. black pepper
1 tsp. rum extract
1 tsp. orange extract

Preheat oven to 325 degrees. In a large saucepan, combine
drained beans, water, onion, celery, carrots, garlic, and bay
leaf. Bring to a boil. Cook for 10 minutes. Reduce heat. Add
remaining ingredients. Stir to combine. Transfer to a large
casserole dish. Cover. Bake for 1½ to 2 hours until beans are
tender. Remove bay leaf. Serves 8.

(Serving = 1 starchy carbohydrate)
NUTRIENTS: 207 calories; 13.2 grams of protein; 0.9 grams of fat;
38.1 grams of carbohydrates; 35 mg of sodium; 685 mg of potassium; and
90 mg of calcium.

Confetti Beans and Corn

1 onion, thinly sliced
1 green pepper, cut into strips
1 red pepper, cut into strips
¾ cup chicken broth, defatted
2 cups cooked black beans
2 cups frozen corn, thawed
1 tbsp. low-salt soy sauce
1 tsp. Worcestershire sauce
¼ tsp. garlic powder
½ tsp. dried thyme

In a large skillet, simmer onions and peppers in broth until
tender. Add remaining ingredients. Cover. Simmer 5 to 7
minutes until corn is cooked. Serves 4.

(Serving = 1 starchy carbohydrate; 1 lean, fibrous vegetable)
NUTRIENTS: 402 calories; 24.9 grams of protein; 2.4 grams of fat;

75.1 grams of carbohydrate; 252 mg of sodium; 519 mg of potassium; and 36 mg of calcium.

Southwestern Vegetables

1½ cups cooked garbanzo beans
2 cups frozen corn
2 cups frozen French-style green beans
½ cup water
One 4-oz. can chopped green chilies
One 14½-oz. can tomatoes, chopped
1 tbsp. instant minced onion flakes
1 tsp. chili powder

In a large microwaveable dish, combine all ingredients. Cover. Microwave on high 8 to 12 minutes until tender. Stir occasionally. Serves 4.

(Serving = 1 starchy carbohydrate; ½ lean, fibrous vegetable)
NUTRIENTS: 364 calories; 19.4 grams of protein; 4.3 grams of fat; 67.5 grams of carbohydrates; 162 mg of sodium; 1044 mg of potassium; and 156 mg of calcium.

Sweet Garbanzos

½ cup chopped onion
1 clove garlic, pressed
¼ cup water
2 cups cooked garbanzo beans
1 cup diced sweet potatoes
1 cup chopped tomatoes

½ tsp. salt-free herb seasoning

2 tsp. chopped fresh parsley

¼ tsp. dried orange peel

½ tsp. bacon-flavored sprinkles

In a medium skillet, cook onion and garlic in water for 3 minutes. Add remaining ingredients. Bring to a boil. Reduce heat. Cover. Simmer 15 to 20 minutes until sweet potatoes are tender. Serves 4.

(Serving = 1 starchy carbohydrate)
NUTRIENTS: 435 calories; 22.4 grams of protein; 5.0 grams of fat; 77.9 grams of carbohydrates; 53 mg of sodium; 1061 mg of potassium; and 172 mg of calcium.

Zesty Limas

3 cups frozen lima beans

¼ cup chopped onion

1 cup chopped tomatoes

1 tsp. dried parsley flakes

½ tsp. dried marjoram

½ tsp. garlic powder

In a medium-sized, microwaveable dish, combine all ingredients. Cover. Microwave on high 8 to 10 minutes until tender. Stir occasionally. Serves 4.

(Serving = 1 starchy carbohydrate)
NUTRIENTS: 209 calories; 11.3 grams of protein; 0.9 grams of fat; 40.3 grams of carbohydrates; 189 mg of sodium; 852 mg of potassium; and 56 mg of calcium.

Spicy Succotash

2 cups frozen lima beans

2 cups frozen corn

¼ cup chopped green onion

2 tbsp. prepared butter-flavored mix

1 cup chopped tomatoes

½ tsp. salt-free herb seasoning

⅛ tsp. black pepper

1 tsp. dried vegetables flakes

One 4-oz. can chopped green chilies

2 tbsp. chopped fresh cilantro

In a medium sized, microwaveable dish, combine all ingredients except cilantro. Cover. Microwave on high 8 to 10 minutes. Serves 4.

(Serving = 1 starchy carbohydrate)

NUTRIENTS: 195 calories; 9.5 grams of protein; 1.0 grams of fat; 40.1 grams of carbohydrates; 129 mg of sodium; 713 mg of potassium; and 45 mg of calcium.

Refried Frijoles

1 lb. dry pinto beans, soaked overnight and drained

6 cups water

1½ cups finely chopped onion

3 cloves garlic, pressed

½ cup finely chopped green pepper

3 tbsp. prepared butter-flavored mix

1 tsp. salt-free herb seasoning

1 tsp. ground cumin

1 tsp. dried cilantro

¼ tsp. black pepper

In a large stock pot, combine drained beans and water. Bring to a boil and cook for 10 minutes. Reduce heat. Cover. Simmer 1½ to 2 hours until beans are tender. In a large skillet, sauté onion, garlic, and green pepper in prepared butter mix until tender. Stir in seasonings. Drain beans, reserving ½ cup liquid. Mash beans and reserved liquid. Add beans to vegetables. Increase heat to medium high. Cook 10 to 15 minutes, stirring frequently, until liquid is absorbed. Serves 8.

(Serving = 1 starchy carbohydrate)
NUTRIENTS: 211 calories; 13.5 grams of protein; 0.7 grams of fat; 39.2 grams of carbohydrates; 9 mg of sodium; 618 mg of potassium; and 85 mg of calcium.

Cajun Red Beans and Rice

1 lb. dry red beans, soaked overnight and drained
6 cups water
2 cups chopped onion
2 cloves garlic, pressed
1 cup chopped green pepper
¼ tsp. dried oregano
2 tsp. chili powder
1 tsp. cayenne pepper
2 tsp. salt-free herb seasoning
½ tsp. black pepper
2 tbsp. dried parsley flakes
One 8-oz. can tomato sauce
1 tbsp. Worcestershire sauce
3 cups cooked brown rice
2 tsp. bacon-flavored sprinkles

In a large stock pot, combine drained beans, water, onion, and garlic. Bring to a boil and cook for 10 minutes. Reduce heat. Simmer for 1 hour. Add remaining ingredients except rice. Simmer for 1 to2 hours until beans are tender and liquid is thickened. Serve over rice.Top with bacon sprinkles. Serves 8.

(Serving = 1½ starchy carbohydrate; ¼ lean, fibrous vegetable)
NUTRIENTS: 306 calories; 15.6 grams of protein; 1.4 grams of fat;
59.5 grams of carbohydrates; 375 mg of sodium; 816 mg of potassium;
and 94 mg of calcium.

Spanish Baked Beans

1 lb. dry red kidney beans, soaked overnight and drained
1 cup chopped onion
1 clove garlic, pressed
1 tbsp. hickory liquid smoke
1 tsp. dry mustard
One 8-oz. can tomato sauce
One 14½-oz. can tomatoes, chopped
One 2-oz. jar pimientos
½ cup chopped green pepper
2 tsp. bacon-flavored sprinkles
2 tsp. dried vegetable flakes
1 tsp. salt-free herb seasoning
¼ tsp. cayenne pepper

In a large stock pot, combine drained beans, onion, garlic, liquid smoke, dry mustard, tomato sauce, and tomatoes. Add enough water to cover. Bring to a boil and cook for 10 minutes. Reduce heat. Cover. Simmer 1 hour. Preheat oven to 300 degrees. Add remaining ingredients. Pour bean mixture into a heavy casserole dish. Bake 1 to 2 hours until beans are tender, stirring occasionally. Add additional water as needed. Serves 8.

(Serving = 1 starchy carbohydrate)
NUTRIENTS: 228 calories; 14.2 grams of protein; 1.1 grams of fat; 42.5 grams of carbohydrates; 243 mg of sodium; 837 mg of potassium; and 83 mg of calcium.

Hickory Smoked Pinto Beans

1 lb. dry pinto beans, soaked overnight and drained
5 cups water
1 cup chopped onion
2 cloves garlic, pressed
One 14½-oz. can tomatoes, chopped
¼ tsp. crushed red pepper flakes
2 tsp. chili powder
2 tsp. salt-free herb seasoning
2 tsp. bacon-flavored sprinkles
2 tsp. hickory liquid smoke
1 tsp. onion powder

In a large stock pot, combine drained beans, water, onion, and garlic. Bring to a boil and cook for 10 minutes. Reduce heat. Add remaining ingredients. Cover. Simmer 1½ to 2 hours until beans are tender. Add water as needed. Serves 8.

(Serving = 1 starchy carbohydrate)
NUTRIENTS: 217 calories; 13.8 grams of protein; 0.8 grams of fat; 40.3 grams of carbohydrates; 76 mg of sodium; 705 mg of potassium; and 85 mg of calcium.

Southwestern Pintos

1 lb. dry pinto beans, soaked overnight and drained

5 cups water

1 cup chopped onion

One 14½-oz. can tomatoes, chopped

1 tsp. salt-free herb seasoning

2 tsp. chili powder

½ tsp. ground cumin

½ tsp. garlic powder

One 4-oz. can chopped green chilies

2 tbsp. chopped fresh cilantro

1 tbsp. lime juice

In a large stock pot, combine drained beans, water, and onion.
Bring to a boil and cook for 10 minutes. Reduce heat. Add
tomatoes, herb seasoning, chili powder, cumin, and garlic
powder. Cover. Simmer 1 to 1½ hours until beans are tender.
Add green chilies, cilantro, and lime juice. Simmer uncovered
for 30 minutes. Serves 8.

(Serving = 1 starchy carbohydrate)
NUTRIENTS: 220 calories; 13.9 grams of protein; 0.8 grams of fat;
41.0 grams of carbohydrates; 76 mg of sodium; 705 mg of potassium; and
87 mg of calcium.

Frosty Weather Lentil Casserole

1½ cups dry lentils

3 cups water

1 cup chopped onion

1 clove garlic, pressed

1½ cups grated carrots

½ cup chopped green pepper

One 14½-oz. can tomatoes, chopped

¼ cup chicken broth, defatted

1 tsp. salt-free herb seasoning

¼ tsp. black pepper

½ tsp. dried marjoram

½ tsp. dried thyme

In a large saucepan, combine lentils and water. Bring to a boil. Reduce heat. Cover. Simmer for 30 minutes. In a medium skillet, simmer onion, garlic, carrots, green pepper, tomatoes, and broth until tender. Stir in seasonings. Preheat oven to 350 degrees. Spray a 2-quart casserole with nonstick cooking spray. Drain lentils. Combine lentils and vegetables. Stir to mix. Pour into casserole. Cover. Bake for 1 hour. Serves 4.

(Serving = 1 starchy carbohydrate; 1 lean, fibrous vegetable)
NUTRIENTS: 314 calories; 20.9 grams of protein; 1.2 grams of fat;
57.9 grams of carbohydrates; 276 mg of sodium; 1035 mg of potassium;
and 97 mg of calcium.

Seasoned Black-Eyed Peas

¼ cup chopped onion

¼ cup sliced celery

¼ cup chopped green pepper

·1 cup chicken broth, defatted

3 cups frozen black-eyed peas

1 cup chopped tomatoes

½ tsp. salt-free herb seasoning

⅛ tsp. black pepper

⅛ tsp. garlic powder

1 tsp. bacon-flavored sprinkles

In a medium saucepan, sauté onion, celery, and green pepper in broth until tender. Add remaining ingredients. Bring to a boil. Reduce heat. Cover. Simmer 30 to 40 minutes until peas are tender. Serves 4.

(Serving = 1 starchy carbohydrate; ¼ lean, fibrous vegetable)
NUTRIENTS: 170 calories; 11.2 grams of protein; 0.9 grams of fat; 31.5 grams of carbohydrates; 388 mg of sodium; 557 mg of potassium; and 41 mg of calcium.

Black-Eyed Peas and Rice

2 cups dry black-eyed peas, soaked overnight and drained

4 cups water

1½ cups chopped onion

3 cloves garlic, pressed

1 tsp. dried thyme

1 tsp. dry mustard

1 tbsp. Worcestershire sauce

2 bay leaves

¼ tsp. black pepper

1 tsp. salt-free herb seasoning

¾ cup uncooked brown rice

1 cup chicken broth, defatted

In a large stock pot, combine drained peas, water, onion, garlic, thyme, dry mustard, Worcestershire sauce, and bay leaves.

Bring to a boil. Reduce heat. Cover and simmer 30 minutes. Add remaining ingredients. Cover. Simmer 45 minutes. Remove bay leaves before serving. Serves 8.

(Serving = 1 starchy carbohydrate)
NUTRIENTS: 84 calories; 4.4 grams of protein; 0.4 grams of fat; 16.3 grams of carbohydrates; 240 mg of sodium; 191 mg of potassium; and 22 mg of calcium.

Savory Bulgur

3 cups chicken broth, defatted
¼ cup chopped green onion
1 clove garlic, pressed
1½ cups uncooked bulgur
1 bay leaf
½ tsp. dried summer savory
½ tsp. ground sage
1 tsp. dried vegetable flakes
2 tbsp. prepared butter-flavored mix
1 tbsp. chopped fresh parsley

In a large saucepan, combine broth, onion, and garlic. Bring to a boil. Stir in bulgur, bay leaf, savory, sage, and vegetable flakes. Reduce heat. Cover. Simmer 15 minutes until liquid is absorbed. Stir in prepared butter mix and parsley. Serves 4.

(Serving = 1 starchy carbohydrate)
NUTRIENTS: 246 calories; 8.3 grams of protein; 1.8 grams of fat; 50.3 grams of carbohydrates; 1114 mg of sodium; 181 mg of potassium; and 32 mg of calcium.

Bulgur Pilaf

1½ cups bulgur

3 cups chicken broth, defatted

⅓ cup chopped green onion

1 tsp. dried basil

½ tsp. dried mint flakes

½ tsp. dried lemon peel

¼ tsp. almond extract

2 tbsp. chopped fresh parsley

In a medium saucepan, combine all ingredients, except parsley. Bring to a boil. Reduce heat. Cover. Simmer 15 to 20 minutes. Add parsley. Toss to mix. Serve immediately. Serves 4.

(Serving = 1 starchy carbohydrate)
NUTRIENTS: 246 calories; 8.3 grams of protein; 1.8 grams of fat; 50.3 grams of carbohydrates; 1114 mg of sodium; 181 mg of potassium; and 32 mg of calcium.

Smoked Swiss Chard

1 lb. Swiss chard

1 cup finely chopped onion

1 clove garlic, pressed

½ cup chicken broth, defatted

2 tbsp. prepared butter-flavored mix

½ tsp. hickory liquid smoke

1 tsp. salt-free herb seasoning

¼ tsp. crushed red pepper flakes

1 tsp. bacon-flavored sprinkles

Thoroughly rinse chard. Remove stems. Cut into thin strips. Set aside. In a large saucepan, simmer onion and garlic in broth until tender. Add prepared butter mix, liquid smoke, herb seasoning, pepper flakes, and chard. Stir to combine. Cover. Cook 6 to 10 minutes until chard is wilted and tender. Garnish with bacon sprinkles. Serves 4.

(Serving = 1 starchy carbohydrate)
NUTRIENTS: 45 calories; 3.3 grams of protein; 0.5 grams of fat; 8.7 grams of carbohydrates; 343 mg of sodium; 643 mg of potassium; and 105 mg of calcium.

Chard With Mustard Greens

½ lb. Swiss chard
½ lb. mustard greens
1 medium red onion, thinly sliced
½ cup chicken broth, defatted
1 tsp. salt-free herb seasoning
1 tbsp. low-salt soy sauce

Thoroughly wash chard and greens. Coarsely chop leaves and tender stems. Discard any tough stems. In a large skillet, cook onions in broth for 3 minutes. Add chard, greens, herb season-ing, and soy sauce. Cover. Steam over low heat 15 to 20 minutes until greens are tender. Serves 4.

Note: Any combination of greens may be substituted for the mustard greens. Alternatives include kale, dandelion greens, turnip greens, and collard greens.

(Serving = 1 starchy carbohydrate)
NUTRIENTS: 40 calories; 3.2 grams of protein; 1.0 grams of fat;
7.0 grams of carbohydrates; 427 mg of sodium; 495 mg of potassium; and
131 mg of calcium.

_____

Corn With Zucchini

4 cups frozen corn
2 cups sliced zucchini
½ cup sliced onion
1 cup chopped tomatoes
¼ cup water
¼ tsp. garlic powder
½ tsp. dried oregano

In a medium-sized, microwaveable dish, combine all ingredients. Cover. Microwave on high 6 to 8 minutes until tender. Stir once. Serves 4.

(Serving = 1 starchy carbohydrate; ½ lean, fibrous vegetable)
NUTRIENTS: 117 calories; 4.2 grams of protein; 0.8 grams of fat;
28.2 grams of carbohydrates; 287 mg of sodium; 431 mg of potassium;
and 23 mg of calcium.

_____

Corn With Cilantro

4 cups frozen corn
¼ cup chopped green onion
¼ cup water
One 4-oz. can chopped green chilies

⅛ tsp. dried cumin

¼ tsp. dried cilantro

In a medium-sized, microwaveable dish, combine all ingredients. Cover. Microwave on high 6 to 8 minutes until tender.
Stir once. Serves 4.

(Serving = 1 starchy carbohydrate)
NUTRIENTS: 98 calories; 3.5 grams of protein; 0.7 grams of fat;
23.5 grams of carbohydrates; 5 mg of sodium; 209 mg of potassium; and
11 mg of calcium.

Pimiento Corn With Green Beans

2 cups frozen French-style green beans

½ cup water

4 cups frozen corn

2 tbsp. chopped pimiento

1 tsp. dried parsley flakes

¼ tsp. salt-free herb seasoning

¼ tsp. dried basil

In a medium-sized, microwaveable dish, combine green beans
and water. Cover. Microwave on high 4 minutes. Add remaining ingredients. Stir and cover. Continue cooking 5 to 7
minutes until tender. Serves 2.

(Serving = 1 starchy carbohydrate; ½ lean, fibrous vegetable)
NUTRIENTS: 226 calories; 8.8 grams of protein; 1.8 grams of fat;
53.9 grams of carbohydrates; 14 mg of sodium; 627 mg of potassium; and
76 mg of calcium.

Festive Corn

¼ cup chopped onion

¼ cup chopped green pepper

4 cups frozen corn

½ cup chopped tomatoes

¼ cup water

¼ tsp. salt-free herb seasoning

In a medium-sized, microwaveable dish, combine all ingredients. Cover. Microwave on high 6 to 8 minutes until tender. Stir once. Serves 4.

(Serving = 1 starchy carbohydrate; ¼ lean, fibrous vegetable)
NUTRIENTS: 99 calories; 3.6 grams of protein; 0.8 grams of fat;
23.5 grams of carbohydrates; 6 mg of sodium; 282 mg of potassium; and
10 mg of calcium.

Baked Kasha With Spinach

1 cup dry-curd cottage cheese

6 egg whites

½ cup chicken broth, defatted

2 tsp. instant minced onion flakes

1 tsp. dried basil

1 tsp. dried thyme

¼ tsp. black pepper

3 cups cooked kasha

1½ cups frozen chopped spinach, thawed and drained

One 2-oz. jar pimientos

Preheat oven to 350 degrees. In a blender container, combine cottage cheese, egg whites, broth, onion flakes, basil, thyme, and pepper. Blend until thoroughly mixed. Combine kasha, spinach, and pimientos. Add blended mixture. Stir. Spray a 9" x 13" x 2" baking dish with nonstick cooking spray. Spoon combined ingredients into dish. Bake 40 to 50 minutes until lightly browned. Cut into squares and serve hot. Serves 4.

(Serving = ½ lean protein; 1 starchy carbohydrate; ¼ lean, fibrous vegetable)
NUTRIENTS: 313 calories; 18.9 grams of protein; 2.4 grams of fat; 59.8 grams of carbohydrates; 329 mg of sodium; 659 mg of potassium; and 194 mg of calcium.

Basil Peas With Celery

3 cups frozen peas
1 cup sliced celery
¼ cup sliced green onion
¼ cup water
½ tsp. dried basil
½ tsp. butter-flavored sprinkles

In a medium-sized, microwaveable dish, combine all ingredients. Cover. Microwave on high 6 to 8 minutes until tender. Stir occasionally. Serves 4.

(Serving = 1 starchy carbohydrate)
NUTRIENTS: 99 calories; 6.5 grams of protein; 0.6 grams of fat; 18.0 grams of carbohydrates; 143 mg of sodium; 270 mg of potassium; and 112 mg of calcium.

Peas With Shredded Lettuce

3 cups frozen peas

¼ cup water

½ tsp. onion powder

½ tsp. dried marjoram

2 cups shredded Boston lettuce

In a medium-sized, microwaveable dish, combine all ingredients, except lettuce. Cover. Microwave on high 4 minutes. Top with shredded lettuce. Cover. Cook 2 to 4 minutes until peas are tender. Serves 4.

(Serving = 1 starchy carbohydrate; ¼ lean, fibrous vegetable)
NUTRIENTS: 95 calories; 6.4 grams of protein; 0.6 grams of fat; 16.8 grams of carbohydrates; 113 mg of sodium; 240 mg of potassium; and 109 mg of calcium.

Pea Celebration

3 cups frozen peas

¼ cup chopped green onion

¼ cup water

¼ tsp. salt-free herb seasoning

½ tsp. dried summer savory

One 6-oz. pkg. frozen snow peas

In a medium-sized, microwaveable dish, combine all ingredients except snowpeas. Cover. Microwave on high 4 minutes. Add snow peas. Cover. Microwave 3 to 5 minutes until tender. Serves 4.

(Serving = 1 starchy carbohydrate; ½ lean, fibrous vegetable)
NUTRIENTS: 118 calories; 7.7 grams of protein; 0.6 grams of fat;
22.1 grams of carbohydrates; 111 mg of sodium; 184 mg of potassium;
and 102 mg of calcium.

Peas Oriental

3 cups frozen peas
One 8-oz. can water chestnuts, drained and thinly sliced
¼ cup chicken broth, defatted
½ tsp. dried vegetable flakes
⅛ tsp. black pepper
2 tsp. low-salt soy sauce

In a medium-sized, microwaveable dish, combine all ingredients. Cover. Microwave on high 6 to 8 minutes until tender. Stir occasionally. Serves 4.

(Serving = 1 starchy carbohydrate)
NUTRIENTS: 118 calories; 7.0 grams of protein; 1.5 grams of fat;
21.0 grams of carbohydrates; 628 mg of sodium; 204 mg of potassium;
and 124 mg of calcium.

Minted Peas

3 cups frozen peas
¼ cup water
½ tsp. dried vegetable flakes
2 tsp. dried mint flakes

In a medium-sized, microwaveable dish, combine all ingredients. Cover. Microwave on high 6 to 8 minutes until tender. Stir occasionally. Serves 4.

(Serving = 1 starchy carbohydrate)
NUTRIENTS: 91 calories; 6.1 grams of protein; 0.6 grams of fat; 16.1 grams of carbohydrates; 110 mg of sodium; 168 mg of potassium; and 99 mg of calcium.

Springtime Potatoes

2 lbs. new potatoes
½ cup chicken broth, defatted
3 tbsp. lemon juice
3 tbsp. finely chopped fresh parsley
½ tsp. salt-free herb seasoning
⅛ tsp. white pepper

Scrub potatoes with a brush. Cook unpeeled potatoes in boiling water 15 to 20 minutes until tender. Drain. Combine remaining ingredients. Pour over potatoes. Heat and serve. Serves 4.

(Serving = 1 starchy carbohydrate)
NUTRIENTS: 142 calories; 4.0 grams of protein; 0.3 grams of fat; 31.6 grams of carbohydrates; 191 mg of sodium; 751 mg of potassium; and 15 mg of calcium.

Sautéed New Potatoes

2 lbs. new potatoes
2 tbsp. safflower oil

¼ cup finely chopped green onion

2 tbsp. chopped fresh parsley

½ tsp. garlic powder

½ tsp. salt-free herb seasoning

⅛ tsp. black pepper

Wash and scrub potatoes. Cook unpeeled potatoes in boiling water 15 to 20 minutes until tender. Drain and cool. Cut potatoes into ¼ inch slices. Heat oil in a large, nonstick skillet. Add potatoes. Sprinkle with green onions, parsley, garlic powder, herb seasoning, and pepper. Cook 4 to 5 minutes until potatoes start to brown. Turn. Cook until golden brown. Serves 4.

(Serving = 1 starchy carbohydrate)
NUTRIENTS: 204 calories; 4.0 grams of protein; 7.0 grams of fat; 32.3 grams of carbohydrates; 7 mg of sodium; 764 mg of potassium; and 16 mg of calcium.

Confetti Potatoes

2 lbs. new potatoes

½ cup nonfat yogurt

½ cup chopped cucumber

¼ cup sliced radishes

¼ cup chopped green onion

1 tsp. dried celery flakes

⅛ tsp. garlic powder

Wash and scrub potatoes. Cook unpeeled potatoes in boiling water 15 to 20 minutes until tender. Drain. Cut potatoes into quarters.Combine remaining ingredients. Pour over potatoes. Gently cook over low heat 1 to 2 minutes until heated thoroughly. Do not allow to boil. Serves 4.

Note: This recipe is also excellent served cold. You may want to double this recipe and serve half one day as a hot vegetable and the other half the next day as a cold salad.

(Serving = 1 starchy carbohydrate)
NUTRIENTS: 160 calories; 5.1 grams of protein; 0.7 grams of fat; 34.2 grams of carbohydrates; 22 mg of sodium; 825 mg of potassium; and 53 mg of calcium.

Caraway Potatoes

2 lbs. potatoes
¾ cup water
1 tsp. no-salt-added beef-flavored instant bouillon
1 cup sliced red onion
1 clove garlic, pressed
1 tsp. caraway seeds
2 tsp. dried celery flakes
½ tsp. salt-free herb seasoning
⅛ tsp. black pepper
3 tbsp. prepared butter-flavored mix
2 tbsp. chopped fresh parsley

Preheat oven to 350 degrees. Scrub potatoes with a brush. If large, cut in half. Cook unpeeled potatoes in boiling water 15 to 20 minutes until almost tender. In small skillet, combine water and bouillon. Cook onion parsley. Remove potatoes from water, reserving ½ cup water. Cut potatoes into ¼-inch slices.

Spray a 2-quart casserole with nonstick cooking spray. Arrange potatoes and onion mixture in layers. Pour reserved water over vegetables. Cover. Bake for 30 to 35 minutes until potatoes are tender. Uncover for the last 10 minutes. Serves 4.

(Serving = 1 starchy carbohydrate)
NUTRIENTS: 148 calories; 4.2 grams of protein; 0.2 grams of fat;
33.3 grams of carbohydrates; 8 mg of sodium; 781 mg of potassium; and
19 mg of calcium.

Gourmet Potato Hash

3 cups diced new potatoes
½ cup chopped onion
½ cup chopped green pepper
⅓ cup chicken broth, defatted
1 cup frozen corn, thawed
2 tbsp. prepared butter-flavored mix
1 tsp. dried thyme
½ tsp. dried tarragon
¼ tsp. black pepper
2 tbsp. chopped fresh cilantro
One 2-oz. jar chopped pimientos

Cook potatoes in boiling water 10 to 15 minutes until almost tender. Drain. In a large skillet, cook onion and green pepper in broth for 5 minutes. Add corn, prepared butter mix, thyme, tarragon, and pepper. Cook for 2 minutes. Stir in potatoes and cilantro. Cook over medium heat until bottom turns golden brown. Turn. Cook until golden. Garnish with pimientos. Serves 4.

(Serving = 1 starchy carbohydrate)
NUTRIENTS: 116 calories; 3.7 grams of protein; 0.5 grams of fat;
26.2 grams of carbohydrates; 130 mg of sodium; 436 mg of potassium;
and 17 mg of calcium.

Easy Oven-Fried Potatoes

2 lbs. potatoes
seasonings as desired
    (chili powder, garlic powder, onion powder, salt-free
    herb seasoning, paprika, Italian herb seasoning)

Scrub potatoes with a brush. Boil unpeeled potatoes 15 to 20
minutes until almost tender. Drain and refrigerate. Preheat
oven to 450 degrees. When cool enough to handle, slice
lengthwise into french fries or crosswise into round cottage
fries. Spray a baking sheet with nonstick cooking spray. Spread
potatoes onto sheet. Spray potatoes with nonstick cooking
spray. Season as desired. Bake 15 to 18 minutes until golden
brown. Turn and brown other side. Bake 10 to 15 minutes.
Potatoes should be crispy. Serve plain or with catsup, dip, or
salsa. Serves 4.

(Serving = 1 starchy carbohydrate)
NUTRIENTS: 140 calories; 3.9 grams of protein; 0.2 grams of fat;
31.4 grams of carbohydrates; 6 mg of sodium; 748 mg of potassium; and
13 mg of calcium.

Herbed Potato Skins

4 large baking potatoes
salt-free herb seasoning, garlic powder,
     or onion powder to taste

Preheat oven to 450 degrees. Scrub potatoes with a brush and
dry. Using a paring knife, peel 3/4-inch wide strips of skin
from the potatoes. Peel end-to-end. Remove a thin layer of
potato flesh with each strip. Place peeled potatoes in a bowl of
water and reserve for another use. Spray a baking sheet with
nonstick cooking spray. Arrange potato peels on sheet, skin side
up and in one layer. Spray peels with nonstick cooking spray.
Season as desired. Bake 15 to 20 minutes until potato
skins are crisp and golden. Serve with catsup, dip, or salsa.
Serves 4.

Note: Potato skins may be prepared ahead of time. Reheat at
450 degrees for 5 to 10 minutes.

(Serving = 1 starchy carbohydrate)

Potatoes O'Brien

2 lbs. potatoes
¼ cup chopped onion
¼ cup chopped celery
¼ cup chopped green pepper
½ cup chicken broth, defatted
½ tsp. salt-free herb seasoning
1 tbsp. chopped fresh parsley
2 tsp. bacon-flavored sprinkles

Scrub potatoes. Peel and dice. Cook in boiling water 10 to 15 minutes until almost tender. Drain. In a medium skillet, sauté onion, celery, and green pepper in broth until tender. Add diced potatoes, herb seasoning, and parsley. Cook over medium-high heat until potatoes are brown. Turn potatoes. Brown on other side. Season with bacon sprinkles. Serves 4.

(Serving = 1 starchy carbohydrate)
NUTRIENTS: 148 calories; 4.3 grams of protein; 0.4 grams of fat; 33.7 grams of carbohydrates; 201 mg of sodium; 794 mg of potassium; and 21 mg of calcium.

Baked Potatoes With Savory Toppings

4 uniform baking potatoes

Preheat oven to 400 degrees. Wash and scrub potatoes with a brush. Pierce with a fork. Arrange on oven shelf. Bake 45 to 60 minutes until done. A done potato "gives" when squeezed (use an oven mitt to test). Make a crosswise cut in top of potato. Press ends. Push up and fluff with a fork. Top with selected toppings.

Note: To foil-bake potatoes: scrub, dry, wrap in foil, pierce, and bake. Potatoes can also be baked in a microwave. Cover with plastic wrap (don't use foil). Four potatoes will take15 to 20 minutes.

(Serving = 1 starchy carbohydrate)

Parsley Topping

½ cup nonfat yogurt

1 tbsp. chopped fresh parsley

½ tsp. onion powder

¼ tsp. dried basil

⅛ tsp. black pepper

Combine all ingredients. Spoon on baked potatoes. Serves 4.

(Serving = 1 starchy carbohydrate)
NUTRIENTS: 114 calories; 3.6 grams of protein; 0.6 grams of fat;
22.6 grams of carbohydrates; 18 mg of sodium; 543 mg of potassium; and
43 mg of calcium.

Dill Topping

½ cup nonfat yogurt

½ tsp. mustard

¼ tsp. dried dill weed

½ tsp. onion powder

¼ tsp. garlic powder

Combine all ingredients. Spoon on baked potatoes. Serves 4.

(Serving = 1 starchy carbohydrate)
NUTRIENTS: 114 calories; 3.6 grams of protein; 0.6 grams of fat;
22.6 grams of carbohydrates; 18 mg of sodium; 543 mg of potassium; and
43 mg of calcium.

Chive Topping

½ cup nonfat yogurt
1 tbsp. chopped fresh parsley
1 tbsp. chopped fresh chives
½ tsp. instant minced onion flakes

Combine all ingredients. Spoon on baked potatoes. Serves 4.

(Serving = 1 starchy carbohydrate)
NUTRIENTS: 114 calories; 3.6 grams of protein; 0.6 grams of fat;
22.6 grams of carbohydrates; 18 mg of sodium; 543 mg of potassium; and
43 mg of calcium.

Stuffed Baked Potatoes

4 large baking potatoes

Bake potatoes. When done, cut in half lengthwise. Scoop out
potato pulp. Mix with choice of stuffings. Refill potato shells.
Reheat in oven for 10 minutes.

Note: Potatoes can be prepared and stuffed ahead of time.
Refrigerate until needed. Reheat in 350 degree oven for 15
minutes.

(Serving = 1 starchy carbohydrate)
NUTRIENTS: 114 calories; 3.6 grams of protein; 0.6 grams of fat;
22.6 grams of carbohydrates; 18 mg of sodium; 543 mg of potassium; and
43 mg of calcium.

Chicken and Corn Stuffing

1 cup chopped cooked chicken

⅓ cup cooked corn

1 tbsp. chopped onion

1 tbsp. chopped green pepper

½ tsp. salt-free herb seasoning

⅛ tsp. black pepper

¼ cup nonfat yogurt

2 tbsp. chopped pimientos

Combine all ingredients, except pimientos, with potato pulp from baked potatoes. Refill potato shells. Garnish with pimientos. Reheat and serve. Serves 4.

(Serving = ¼ lean protein; 1 starchy carbohydrate)
NUTRIENTS: 163 calories; 10.9 grams of protein; 1.5 grams of fat; 25.4 grams of carbohydrates; 28 mg of sodium; 595 mg of potassium; and 31 mg of calcium.

Florentine Stuffing

2 cups frozen spinach, thawed

1 cup sliced mushrooms

¾ cup chicken broth, defatted

1 tbsp. cornstarch

¼ cup prepared butter-flavored mix

½ tsp. salt-free herb seasoning

¼ tsp. nutmeg

¼ tsp. dried lemon peel

Press liquid from thawed spinach. In a medium skillet, simmer mushrooms in broth until tender. Dissolve cornstarch in prepared butter mix. Add to mushrooms. Heat and stir until thickened. Stir in spinach and seasonings. Simmer 5 minutes. Stir in potato pulp. Refill potato shells. Reheat and serve. Serves 4.

(Serving = 1 starchy carbohydrate; ½ lean, fibrous vegetable)
NUTRIENTS: 136 calories; 6.3 grams of protein; 0.7 grams of fat; 28.4 grams of carbohydrates; 359 mg of sodium; 840 mg of potassium; and 130 mg of calcium.

Tuna Stuffing

One 7-oz. can water-packed albacore tuna, drained
1 cup chopped tomatoes
1 tsp. instant minced onion flakes
1 tsp. dried celery flakes
¼ tsp. paprika
¼ tsp. black pepper
2 tbsp. red wine vinegar
¼ cup nonfat yogurt

Combine all ingredients with potato pulp from baked potatoes. Refill potato shells. Reheat and serve. Serves 4.

(Serving = ½ lean protein; 1 starchy carbohydrate)
NUTRIENTS: 161 calories; 12.8 grams of protein; 0.7 grams of fat; 24.4 grams of carbohydrates; 25 mg of sodium; 745 mg of potassium; and 35 mg of calcium.

Potatoes Italiano

2 lbs. potatoes
½ cup thinly sliced onion
¼ cup chopped green pepper
¼ cup chopped red pepper
1 clove garlic, pressed
½ cup chicken broth, defatted
½ cup chopped tomatoes
One 8-oz. can tomato sauce
1 tsp. dried oregano
½ tsp. dried basil
¼ tsp. black pepper
2 tbsp. chopped fresh parsley

Scrub potatoes with a brush. Cut into ⅛-inch slices. In a large skillet, simmer potatoes, onion, peppers, and garlic in broth for 8 minutes. Add tomatoes, tomato sauce, oregano, basil, and pepper. Cover. Simmer for 30 minutes until tender. Stir occasionally. Garnish with parsley. Serves 4.

(Serving = 1 starchy carbohydrate; ¼ lean, fibrous vegetable)
NUTRIENTS: 178 calories; 5.5 grams of protein; 0.6 grams of fat; 39.8 grams of carbohydrates; 527 mg of sodium; 1113 mg of potassium; and 44 mg of calcium.

Scalloped Potatoes

2 lbs. potatoes
1 clove garlic, pressed
1 cup thinly sliced onion
½ tsp. salt-free herb seasoning

¼ tsp. black pepper

1 cup skim milk

¼ cup prepared butter-flavored mix

½ tsp. dried thyme

1 bay leaf

1 tbsp. chopped fresh parsley

Preheat oven to 325 degrees. Peel potatoes. Cut into thin slices.
Spray a 2-quart casserole dish or a 9-inch deep flan dish with
nonstick cooking spray. Rub garlic all over the dish. Arrange the
potatoes and onion in layers. Season each layer with herb
seasoning and pepper. Combine milk, prepared butter mix,
thyme, and bay leaf. Pour over potatoes. Bake uncovered for 1
to 1½ hours until potatoes are tender and browned. Milk
should be absorbed during cooking. Garnish with parsley.
Serves 4.

(Serving = 1 starchy carbohydrate)
NUTRIENTS: 178 calories; 6.5 grams of protein; 0.3 grams of fat;
38.2 grams of carbohydrates; 42 mg of sodium; 916 mg of potassium; and
100 mg of calcium.

Mashed Potatoes

2 lbs. potatoes

1 bay leaf

2 tsp. dried celery flakes

1 clove garlic, pressed

1 tsp. cornstarch

1 tbsp. nonfat yogurt

⅛ tsp. black pepper

¼ tsp. salt-free herb seasoning

Wash and scrub potatoes. Cut into quarters. Cook potatoes, bay leaf, celery flakes, and garlic in boiling water until potatoes are tender. With a slotted spoon, transfer potatoes to a large bowl. Reserve potato water. Combine cornstarch with ¼ cup potato water. Add to potatoes. Mash potatoes, adding more potato water if needed. Stir in yogurt and seasonings. Serves 4.

(Serving = 1 starchy carbohydrate)
NUTRIENTS: 143 calories; 4.0 grams of protein; 0.3 grams of fat; 32.4 grams of carbohydrates; 7 mg of sodium; 753 mg of potassium; and 17 mg of calcium.

Wintertime Oven-Roasted Potatoes

2 lbs. potatoes
1 tbsp. safflower oil
1 tsp. dried oregano
¼ tsp. garlic powder
½ tsp. paprika
¼ tsp. cayenne pepper

Preheat oven to 425 degrees. Line a shallow baking pan with aluminum foil. Scrub potatoes and dry. Cut unpeeled potatoes into quarters. Place in a mixing bowl. Combine oil and seasonings. Pour over potatoes. Toss until well coated. Arrange potatoes on pan in a single layer. Bake 30 minutes. Turn potatoes. Continue to bake 12 to 15 minutes until potatoes are well browned. Serves 4.

(Serving = 1 starchy carbohydrate)
NUTRIENTS: 170 calories; 3.9 grams of protein; 3.6 grams of fat;
31.4 grams of carbohydrates; 6 mg of sodium; 748 mg of potassium; and
13 mg of calcium.

Potatoes Viniagrette

2 lbs. potatoes
¼ cup sliced celery
2 tbsp. chopped green onion
3 tbsp. tarragon vinegar
3 tbsp. prepared butter-flavored mix
1 tsp. dried parsley flakes
½ tsp. onion powder
⅛ tsp. black pepper

Wash and scrub potatoes. Cut into quarters. Cook in boiling
water 15 to 18 minutes until tender. Drain potatoes. Combine
remaining ingredients. Pour over drained potatoes. Toss gently
and serve. Serves 4.

Note: This recipe is also excellent served cold. You may want
to double this recipe and serve half today as a hot vegetable and
serve the other half tomorrow as a cold salad.

(Serving = 1 starchy carbohydrate)
NUTRIENTS: 143 calories; 4.0 grams of protein; 0.2 grams of fat;
32.8 grams of carbohydrates; 14 mg of sodium; 77.2 mg of potassium;
and 17 mg of calcium.

Seasoned Brown Rice

6⅔ cups water
4 tsp. instant minced onion flakes
½ tsp. garlic powder
2 tsp. dried marjoram
¼ tsp. black pepper
2⅔ cups brown rice

In a large saucepan, combine water and seasonings. Bring to a boil. Add rice. Reduce heat. Cover. Simmer 45 to 50 minutes until liquid is absorbed. Serves 8.

Variation 1: For seasonings use 1½ teaspoons dried dill weed, 1½ teaspoons paprika, ½ teaspoon dry mustard, 1 teaspoon salt-free herb seasoning, and ¼ teaspoon black pepper.

Variation 2: For seasonings use 2 tablespoons low-salt soy sauce, 1 tablespoon instant minced onion flakes, and ⅛ teaspoon crushed red pepper flakes.

Variation 3: For seasonings use 2 teaspoons dried celery flakes, 1 teaspoon ground sage, 1 teaspoon dried thyme, 1 teaspoon garlic powder, and ¼ teaspoon black pepper.

(Serving = 1 starchy carbohydrate)
NUTRIENTS: 234 calories; 4.9 grams of protein; 1.2 grams of fat; 50.5 grams of carbohydrates; 5 mg of sodium; 140 mg of potassium; and 21 mg of calcium.

Brown Rice Ratatouille

½ cup chopped onion
1 clove garlic, pressed

1 cup chicken broth, defatted

1 cup chopped tomatoes

One 8-oz. can tomato sauce

1 small eggplant, peeled and diced

1 cup frozen green beans

1 tbsp. dried parsley flakes

2 tsp. Italian herb seasoning

4 cups cooked brown rice

In a large skillet, cook onion and garlic in broth until tender. Add tomatoes, tomato sauce, eggplant, green beans, parsley, and Italian herb seasoning. Cover. Simmer 15 minutes until eggplant and beans are tender. Add rice. Simmer 5 to 7 minutes until thoroughly heated. Serves 4.

(Serving = 1 starchy carbohydrate; 1 lean, fibrous vegetable)
NUTRIENTS: 292 calories; 7.9 grams of protein; 1.9 grams of fat; 62.7 grams of carbohydrates; 1237 mg of sodium; 712 mg of potassium; and 79 mg of calcium.

_____

Brown Rice and Spinach Pilaf

1 lb. fresh spinach

½ cup chopped onion

1 cup chicken broth, defatted

4 cups cooked brown rice

¼ cup chopped fresh parsley

2 tsp. dried mint flakes

½ tsp. salt-free herb seasoning

⅛ tsp. black pepper

Wash spinach thoroughly and drain. In a large skillet, cook onion in broth until tender. Add remaining ingredients. Simmer 8 to 10 minutes until spinach is wilted. Stir occasionally. Serves 4.

(Serving = 1 starchy carbohydrate; ½ lean, fibrous vegetable)
NUTRIENTS: 268 calories; 9.1 grams of protein; 1.8 grams of fat; 55.2 grams of carbohydrates; 984 mg of sodium; 731 mg of potassium; and 145 mg of calcium.

Gourmet Rice Casserole

2 cups sliced mushrooms
¼ cup chopped green onion
¼ cup prepared butter-flavored mix
½ tsp. dried thyme
½ tsp. dried marjoram
¼ tsp. black pepper
2 tsp. bacon-flavored mix
1⅓ cups uncooked brown rice
3½ cups water
4 tsp. no-salt-added, beef-flavored instant bouillon
1 tbsp. instant minced onion flakes

Preheat oven to 350 degrees. In a medium frying pan, sauté mushrooms and green onion in prepared butter mix until tender. Add thyme, marjoram, pepper, bacon sprinkles, and rice. Stir until well mixed. Spray a 2½-quart casserole with nonstick cooking spray. Pour rice mixture into casserole. Combine water, bouillon, and onion flakes. Bring to a boil. Pour over rice mixture. Stir to mix. Cover. Bake for 1 hour.

Uncover during last 15 minutes of baking. Serves 4.

(Serving = 1 starchy carbohydrate)
NUTRIENTS: 248 calories; 6.0 grams of protein; 1.3 grams of fat;
53.0 grams of carbohydrates; 6 mg of sodium; 156 mg of potassium; and
35 mg of calcium.

_____

Brown Rice With Sprouts

¼ cup chopped green onion
2 tsp. grated fresh ginger root
1 cup chicken broth, defatted
4 cups cooked brown rice
¼ tsp. garlic powder
One 16-oz. can bean sprouts, drained
1 cup alfalfa sprouts
2 tbsp. low-salt soy sauce

In a large skillet, cook onion and ginger root in broth for 3
minutes. Add remaining ingredients. Simmer 6 to 10 minutes
until thoroughly heated. Stir occasionally. Serves 4.

(Serving = 1 starchy carbohydrate; ½ lean, fibrous vegetable)
NUTRIENTS: 272 calories; 10.0 grams of protein; 3.1 grams of fat;
51.8 grams of carbohydrates; 1208 mg of sodium; 26.2 mg of potassium;
and 73 mg of calcium.

_____

Brown Rice Supreme

½ cup julienned carrots
½ cup julienned zucchini

1 tbsp. grated fresh ginger root

1 cup chicken broth, defatted

4 cups cooked brown rice

¼ tsp. garlic powder

½ tsp. dried lemon peel

1 tbsp. lemon juice

½ tsp. nutmeg

2 tbsp. chopped fresh parsley

In a large skillet, simmer carrots, zucchini, and ginger root in broth until tender. Add remaining ingredients, except parsley. Simmer 6 to 8 minutes until thoroughly heated. Stir occasionally. Garnish with parsley. Serves 4.

(Serving = 1 starchy carbohydrate; ¼ lean, fibrous vegetable)
NUTRIENTS: 239 calories; 5.4 grams of protein; 1.5 grams of fat; 50.8 grams of carbohydrates; 976 mg of sodium; 231 mg of potassium; and 36 mg of calcium.

Brown Rice With Mushrooms

½ cup sliced green onion

½ cup sliced celery

1 cup sliced mushrooms

½ cup chicken broth, defatted

4 cups cooked brown rice

2 tbsp. prepared butter-flavored mix

1 tbsp. low-salt soy sauce

½ tsp. dried marjoram

In a large skillet, simmer green onions, celery, and mushrooms in broth until tender. Add remaining ingredients. Simmer 6 to 8 minutes, until thoroughly heated. Stir occasionally. Serves 4.

(Serving = 1 starchy carbohydrate; ¼ lean, fibrous vegetable)
NUTRIENTS: 244 calories; 6.0 grams of protein; 1.8 grams of fat;
52.6 grams of carbohydrates; 882 mg of sodium; 216 mg of potassium;
and 49 mg of calcium.

Southwestern Brown Rice

1⅓ cups uncooked brown rice
2 tsp. instant minced onion flakes
½ tsp. garlic powder
3⅓ cups chicken broth, defatted
One 14⅓-oz. can tomatoes, chopped
One 4-oz. can chopped green chilies
1 tbsp. lemon juice
2 tbsp. chopped fresh cilantro

In a medium saucepan, combine all ingredients except cilantro. Bring to a boil. Reduce heat. Cover. Simmer 45 minutes until liquid is absorbed. Garnish with cilantro. Serves 4.

(Serving = 1 starchy carbohydrate)
NUTRIENTS: 280 calories; 7.3 grams of protein; 2.3 grams of fat;
57.8 grams of carbohydrates; 1379 mg of sodium; 389 mg of potassium;
and 43 mg of calcium.

Green Pepper Rice

½ cup chopped green pepper
½ cup chopped green onion
½ cup chopped celery
1 cup chicken broth, defatted
4 cups cooked brown rice
⅓ cup chopped fresh parsley
½ tsp. salt-free herb seasoning
⅛ tsp. black pepper

In a large skillet, simmer green pepper, green onion, and celery in broth until tender. Add remaining ingredients. Simmer 6 to 8 minutes until heated. Stir occasionally. Serves 4.

(Serving = 1 starchy carbohydrate; ¼ lean, fibrous vegetable)
NUTRIENTS: 243 calories; 5.7 grams of protein; 1.5 grams of fat; 52.8 grams of carbohydrates; 921 mg of sodium; 261 mg of potassium; and 48 mg of calcium.

Easy Spanish Rice

1⅓ cups uncooked brown rice
3⅓ cups chicken broth, defatted
1 tbsp. instant minced onion flakes
½ tsp. garlic powder
1 tbsp. chili powder
2 tsp. dried vegetable flakes
¼ tsp. black pepper
One 14½-oz. can tomatoes, chopped

In a medium saucepan, combine all ingredients. Bring to a boil. Reduce heat. Cover and simmer 45 minutes until liquid is absorbed. Serves 4.

(Serving = 1 starchy carbohydrate)
NUTRIENTS: 274 calories; 7.1 grams of protein; 2.3 grams of fat; 56.2 grams of carbohydrates; 1379 mg of sodium; 389 mg of potassium; and 40 mg of calcium.

Holiday Wild Rice

2 cups sliced mushrooms
½ cup sliced green onion
2 tbsp. prepared butter-flavored mix
⅓ cup dry white wine
1 tsp. ground sage
¼ tsp. black pepper
1 tbsp. Worcestershire sauce
4 cups cooked wild rice
2 tbsp. chopped fresh parsley

In a large skillet, combine mushrooms, green onion, prepared butter mix, wine, and sage. Simmer until tender. Add remaining ingredients. Simmer 5 minutes until thoroughly heated. Serves 4.

(Serving = 1 starchy carbohydrate)
NUTRIENTS: 600 calories; 23.9 grams of protein; 1.2 grams of fat; 125.2 grams of carbohydrates; 14 mg of sodium; 403 mg of potassium; and 48 mg of calcium.

Italian Brown Rice

½ cup chopped green pepper
½ cup chopped onion
1 cup chicken broth, defatted
4 cups cooked brown rice
One 14½-oz. can tomatoes, chopped
½ tsp. dried oregano
½ tsp. dried basil
½ tsp. garlic powder

In a large skillet, simmer green pepper and onion in broth until tender. Add remaining ingredients. Simmer 6 to 8 minutes until thoroughly heated. Stir occasionally. Serves 4.

(Serving = 1 starchy carbohydrate; ½ lean, fibrous vegetable)
NUTRIENTS: 261 calories; 6.5 grams of protein; 1.6 grams of fat;
55.0 grams of carbohydrates; 1040 mg of sodium; 421 mg of potassium;
and 39 mg of calcium.

Stuffed Squash

2 acorn squash
1 cup sliced celery
1 cup chopped onion
Two 4-oz. cans mushrooms, drained
2 tbsp. prepared butter-flavored mix
1 tsp. dried parsley flakes
¼ tsp. nutmeg
½ tsp. salt-free herb seasoning
½ tsp. dried marjoram
1 tsp. cheese-flavored sprinkles

Preheat oven to 375 degrees. Wash squash. Cut in half lengthwise. Remove seeds and stringy membrane. Place cut side
down in a shallow baking pan. Add water to a depth of ¼ -inch.
Bake 30 to 40 minutes until squash is tender. In a medium
skillet, sauté celery, onion, and mushrooms in prepared butter
mix until tender. Add seasonings. Remove squash from oven.
Turn cut side up. Fill halves with vegetable mixture. Top with
cheese sprinkles. Return to oven. Bake 10 minutes. Serves 4.

(Serving = 1 starchy carbohydrate; ½ lean, fibrous vegetable)
NUTRIENTS: 118 calories; 5.1 grams of protein; 0.3 grams of fat;
28.2 grams of carbohydrates; 312 mg of sodium; 1035 mg of potassium;
and 86 mg of calcium.

Spaghetti Squash Italiano

1 medium spaghetti squash
4 cups Spaghetti Sauce (page 388)

Preheat oven to 350 degrees. Wash squash. Pierce and bake 1
to 1½ hours until soft. Remove squash from oven and cool
slightly. Cut in half lengthwise. Remove seeds and stringy
membrane. Scoop out the pulp with a fork. The pulp resembles
strands of spaghetti. Serve with Spaghetti Sauce. Serves 4.

(Serving = 1 starchy carbohydrate)
NUTRIENTS: 43 calories; 1.5 grams of protein; 0.1 grams of fat;
10.9 grams of carbohydrates; 1 mg of sodium; 375 mg of potassium; and
31 mg of calcium. (Does not include Spaghetti Sauce.)

Spaghetti Squash Florentine

4 cups cooked spaghetti squash

2 cups frozen chopped spinach, thawed and drained

One 4-oz. can mushrooms, drained

¼ cup prepared butter-flavored mix

½ cup nonfat yogurt

1 tbsp. cheese-flavored sprinkles

1 tsp. salt-free herb seasoning

1 tsp. dried chervil

¼ tsp. garlic powder

¼ tsp. black pepper

Preheat oven to 350 degrees. In a large bowl, combine all ingredients. Toss until well blended. Spray a 2-quart casserole with nonstick cooking spray. Turn mixture into casserole. Cover. Bake for 30 minutes. Serves 4.

(Serving = 1 starchy carbohydrate; ½ lean, fibrous vegetable)
NUTRIENTS: 68 calories; 6.0 grams of protein; 0.9 grams of fat;
11.6 grams of carbohydrates; 229 mg of sodium; 703 mg of potassium;
and 143 mg of calcium.

Sunshine Squash

4 cups cooked butternut squash

¼ cup prepared butter-flavored mix

1 tsp. orange extract

1 tsp. vanilla extract

½ tsp. dried orange peel

½ tsp. cinnamon

¼ tsp. ground ginger

4 egg whites

Preheat oven to 350 degrees. In a blender, combine squash, prepared butter mix, orange extract, vanilla, orange peel, cinnamon, and ginger. Blend until smooth. Beat egg whites until stiff. Fold squash into egg whites. Spray a 2-quart casserole with nonstick cooking spray. Turn mixture into casserole. Bake 45 to 50 minutes until set. Serve immediately. Serves 4.

(Serving = 1 starchy carbohydrate)
NUTRIENTS: 42 calories; 6.3 grams of protein; 0.2 grams of fat; 25.8 grams of carbohydrates; 50 mg of sodium; 881 mg of potassium; and 74 mg of calcium.

Oatmeal Squash Dressing

5 cups water
2 cups old-fashioned oatmeal
1 cup oat bran
3 cups cooked butternut squash
2 egg whites
¼ cup prepared butter-flavored mix
2 Granny Smith apples, grated
1 tsp. ground sage
½ tsp. cinnamon
¼ tsp. nutmeg
¼ cup chopped Garbanzo Nuts (page 371)

Preheat oven to 350 degrees. In a medium saucepan, bring water to a boil. Stir in oatmeal and oat bran. Cook 5 minutes. Stir occasionally. Remove from heat. Add squash, egg whites, prepared butter mix, apple, sage, cinnamon, and nutmeg. Beat with an electric mixer for 3 minutes until well blended. Stir in

Garbanzo Nuts. Spray a 9" x 13" x 2" baking dish with non-stick cooking spray. Pour mixture into dish. Bake for 1 hour. Serves 6.

(Serving = 1 starchy carbohydrate)
NUTRIENTS: 250 calories; 11.6 grams of protein; 4.1 grams of fat; 56.7 grams of carbohydrates; 23 mg of sodium; 745 mg of potassium; and 70 mg of calcium.

Sautéed Sweet Potatoes

2 lbs. sweet potatoes
1 cup sliced red onion
¼ cup chicken broth, defatted
1 tsp. dried vegetable flakes
¼ tsp. cinnamon
⅛ tsp. nutmeg

Wash sweet potatoes. Boil unpeeled sweet potatoes 20 to 25 minutes until just tender. Drain, peel, and dice. In a medium skillet, cook onion in broth until tender. Add sweet potatoes and remaining ingredients. Cook and stir until sweet potatoes are lightly browned. Serves 4.

(Serving = 1 starchy carbohydrate)
NUTRIENTS: 227 calories; 3.8 grams of protein; 0.8 grams of fat; 52.1 grams of carbohydrates; 115 mg of sodium; 514 mg of potassium; and 71 mg of calcium.

Sweet Potato Medley

½ cup chopped onion

1 cup sliced celery

1 cup chicken broth, defatted

1 cup sliced carrots

3 cups diced sweet potatoes

2 tsp. dried vegetable flakes

2 cups diced zucchini

½ tsp. dried orange peel

In a large skillet, simmer onion and celery in broth 2 to 3 minutes. Add carrots, sweet potatoes, and vegetable flakes. Cover. Cook 8 to 10 minutes until carrots and sweet potatoes are almost tender. Add zucchini and orange peel. Cover and cook 6 to 8 minutes until all vegetables are tender. Serves 4.

(Serving = 1 starchy carbohydrate; 1 lean, fibrous vegetable)
NUTRIENTS: 254 calories; 12.1 grams of protein; 1.5 grams of fat; 49.8 grams of carbohydrates; 508 mg of sodium; 821 mg of potassium; and 86 mg of calcium.

Maple Sweet Potatoes

2 lbs. sweet potatoes

½ tsp. cinnamon

¼ tsp. maple flavoring

⅛ tsp. rum extract

¼ cup hot water

Wash sweet potatoes. Boil unpeeled sweet potatoes 20 to 25 minutes until tender. Drain. Peel sweet potatoes. In a large bowl, combine sweet potatoes, cinnamon, maple flavoring, rum extract, and hot water. Beat until light and fluffy. Add additional hot water if required. Serves 4.

(Serving = 1 starchy carbohydrate)
NUTRIENTS: 210 calories; 3.1 grams of protein; 0.8 grams of fat; 48.3 grams of carbohydrates; 19 mg of sodium; 447 mg of potassium; and 59 mg of calcium.

Tropical Yams

2 lbs. yams
⅔ cup water
2 tsp. cornstarch
2 tsp. sugar-free orange-flavored gelatin
⅛ tsp. ground ginger
½ tsp. pineapple extract
¼ tsp. coconut extract

Wash yams. Boil unpeeled yams until tender. Drain and peel. Cut into 1-inch slices. Arrange in a serving dish. Cover and keep warm. In a small saucepan, bring water to a boil. Dissolve cornstarch in 1 tablespoon of water. Stir into boiling water. Cook over medium heat until thickened. Stir constantly. Remove from heat. Stir in gelatin until dissolved. Add remaining ingredients. Pour over yams. Serve immediately. Serves 4.

(Serving = 1 starchy carbohydrate)
NUTRIENTS: 200 calories; 4.1 grams of protein; 0.4 grams of fat; 46.8 grams of carbohydrates; 0 mg of sodium; 1171 mg of potassium; and 39 mg of calcium.

9

¶ Lean, Fibrous Vegetables

Helpful Hints

Refer to the chart Using Herbs and Spices (page 12) to try new combinations of spices.

Replace butter or oil when cooking vegetables with liquids like defatted chicken broth, vegetable broth, or water. Bring liquid to a boil, add vegetables, and stir until tender. Add extra liquid if required.

Use carrots to sweeten foods that call for 1 or 2 tablespoons of sugar or molasses like soups, stews, spaghetti sauce, barbecue sauce, or casseroles. Add diced or shredded carrots to the recipes. For sauces, simmer them with large carrot chunks and remove the chunks before serving.

Sauté vegetables in prepared butter-flavored mix for a great buttery taste.

Pour prepared butter-flavored mix over cooked vegetables or shake on butter sprinkles to give a rich flavor.

Cooking vegetables until just tender-crisp helps retain the best flavor and nutritional value.

Okra is fresh if the pointed tip breaks off easily.

Retain vegetable skins whenever possible to increase fiber.

Use evaporated skimmed milk when recipes call for cream.

Substitute dry-curd cottage cheese for cheeses.

If you do not have a steamer, place a rack in a skillet, wok, or large pot. Add enough water to cover the rack. Heat to boiling. Place food items on a plate. Place plate on rack. Cover. Steam according to recipe instructions.

Crush herbs before adding to recipes. This releases the flavors. Generally use ¼ to ½ teaspoon of dried herbs for each 4 servings.

Add herbs to uncooked foods, such as salad dressings or dips as long as possible before serving. Herbs need time for flavors to "marry."

Seasoning is an expressive art. When testing a new herb, crush some and let it warm in your hand. Sniff it and then taste it. If it seems strong, bitter, or pungent, be cautious.

Herbed Artichoke Hearts

4 cups frozen artichoke hearts
½ cup chicken broth, defatted
2 tbsp. prepared butter-flavored mix
1 tsp. dried parsley flakes
½ tsp. dried tarragon
½ tsp. dry mustard
¼ tsp. garlic powder
2 tsp. cornstarch
1 tbsp. lemon juice

Cook artichoke hearts according to package directions. Drain. In a small saucepan, combine broth, prepared butter mix, and seasonings. Bring to a boil. Dissolve cornstarch in lemon juice. Add to broth. Cook and stir until thickened. Pour over cooked artichoke hearts. Serves 4.

(Serving = 1 lean, fibrous vegetable)
NUTRIENTS: 70 calories; 4.8 grams of protein; 1.0 grams of fat; 14.9 grams of carbohydrates; 266 mg of sodium; 423 mg of potassium; and 34 mg of calcium.

Asparagus Tarragon

2 lbs. asparagus spears
½ cup chopped green pepper
¼ cup chopped green onion
½ cup chicken broth, defatted
½ tsp. dried tarragon
½ tsp. dried parsley flakes
⅛ tsp. black pepper
1 tbsp. chopped pimientos

Rinse asparagus and break off tough root ends. In a medium skillet, cook green pepper and onion in broth for 5 minutes. Add asparagus, tarragon, parsley, and pepper. Cover. Simmer for 5 minutes or until tender. Garnish with pimientos. Serves 4.

(Serving = 1 lean, fibrous vegetable)
NUTRIENTS: 54 calories; 5.4 grams of protein; 0.6 grams of fat; 9.7 grams of carbohydrates; 190 mg of sodium; 456 mg of potassium; and 53 mg of calcium.

Asparagus Oriental

2 lbs. asparagus spears
2 tbsp. chopped onion
2 tbsp. water
1 tbsp. low-salt soy sauce
1 tsp. grated fresh ginger root

Rinse asparagus and break off tough root ends. In a medium-sized, microwaveable dish, combine all ingredients. Cover. Microwave on high 8 to 10 minutes until tender. Serves 4.

(Serving = 1 lean, fibrous vegetable)
NUTRIENTS: 51 calories; 5.3 grams of protein; 0.9 grams of fat; 8.7 grams of carbohydrates; 153 mg of sodium; 440 mg of potassium; and 53 mg of calcium.

Bean Sprouts With Celery

1 cup freeze-dried mushrooms
1 cup chicken broth, defatted
1 cup thinly sliced onion
1 cup sliced celery
1 tbsp. low-salt soy sauce
One 14-oz. can bean sprouts, drained
1 tbsp. cornstarch
2 tbsp. water

Reconstitute freeze-dried mushrooms in chicken broth. In a medium skillet, cook onion and celery in mushroom broth until tender. Add soy sauce and bean sprouts. Dissolve cornstarch in water. Add to vegetables. Heat and stir until broth thickens. Serves 4.

(Serving = 1 lean, fibrous vegetable)
NUTRIENTS: 55 calories; 4.6 grams of protein; 1.4 grams of fat; 9.1 grams of carbohydrates; 557 mg of sodium; 174 mg of potassium; and 60 mg of calcium.

Country Beets and Greens

1½ lbs. small beets, untrimmed
3 tbsp. prepared butter-flavored mix
2 tbsp. lemon juice
½ tsp. salt-free herb seasoning
1 tsp. dried thyme
¼ tsp. dried rosemary, crumbled
⅛ tsp. black pepper

Rinse beets. Cut off leaves and wash thoroughly. Remove ribs and set aside. Leave 1-inch stems on beets. Leave root ends on. Do not peel. Place beets in a large saucepan. Cover with water. Bring to a boil. Reduce heat. Cook 30 to 40 minutes until a knife pierces beet easily. Remove beets from saucepan. Add beet greens to saucepan. Cook for 3 minutes. Drain and cool. Peel beets and julienne. Chop greens. In a medium saucepan, combine beets and greens. Add remaining ingredients. Heat over low heat. Serves 4.

(Serving = 1 lean, fibrous vegetable)
NUTRIENTS: 55 calories; 3.2 grams of protein; 0.4 grams of fat; 12.1 grams of carbohydrates; 12 mg of sodium; 414 mg of potassium; and 95 mg of calcium.

Harvard Beets

⅓ cup chicken broth, defatted

1 tbsp. cornstarch

3 tbsp. cider vinegar

1 tbsp. lemon juice

2 tbsp. prepared butter-flavored mix

½ tsp. salt-free herb seasoning

½ tsp. dried lemon peel

2 lbs. peeled, cooked beets

½ tsp. orange extract

2 packets sugar substitute

In a medium saucepan, combine broth and cornstarch. Add vinegar, lemon juice, prepared butter mix, herb seasoning, and lemon peel. Cook over medium heat and stir until thickened. Add beets and orange extract and heat thoroughly. Remove from heat. Stir in sugar substitute. Serves 4.

(Serving = 1 lean, fibrous vegetable)
NUTRIENTS: 78 calories; 4.4 grams of protein; 0.6 grams of fat; 17.6 grams of carbohydrates; 140 mg of sodium; 565 mg of potassium; and 129 mg of calcium.

Beets L'Orange

2 lbs. beets

1 tsp. cornstarch

⅓ cup chicken broth, defatted

1 tsp. dried orange peel

1 tsp. dried celery flakes

⅛ tsp. cinnamon

Trim leaves off beets, leaving 1-inch stems. Rinse thoroughly.
Leave root ends on. Do not peel. Place beets in a large saucepan. Cover with water. Bring to a boil. Reduce heat. Cook 40
to 60 minutes until knife pierces beets easily. Drain. Cover with
cold water. Peel and slice beets. Dissolve cornstarch in broth. In
a medium saucepan, combine broth, orange peel, celery flakes,
and cinnamon. Heat and stir until thickened. Add sliced beets
and heat. Serves 4.

(Serving = 1 lean, fibrous vegetable)
NUTRIENTS: 76 calories; 4.4 grams of protein; 0.6 grams of fat;
17.0 grams of carbohydrates; 140 mg of sodium; 554 mg of potassium;
and 128 mg of calcium.

Bok Choy Oriental

1 lb. bok choy
⅓ cup chicken broth, defatted
¼ tsp. garlic powder
1 tbsp. low-salt soy sauce
½ tsp. salt-free herb seasoning

Rinse bok choy. Cut into thin shreds. In a large skillet, heat
broth. Add remaining ingredients. Cover and steam over low
heat 8 to 10 minutes. Serves 4.

(Serving = 1 lean, fibrous vegetable)
NUTRIENTS: 21 calories; 1.7 grams of protein; 0.6 grams of fat;
3.6 grams of carbohydrates; 300 mg of sodium; 306 mg of potassium; and
54 mg of calcium.

Easy Broccoli

4 cups broccoli florets
¼ cup chicken broth, defatted
1 tsp. dried chervil
1 tsp. dried vegetable flakes
½ tsp. salt-free herb seasoning
⅛ tsp. black pepper

In a medium-sized, microwaveable dish, combine all ingredients. Cover. Microwave on high for 8 to 10 minutes. Stir after 4 minutes. Serves 4.

(Serving = 1 lean, fibrous vegetable)
NUTRIENTS: 49 calories; 5.5 grams of protein; 0.5 grams of fat;
9.0 grams of carbohydrates; 115 mg of sodium; 575 mg of potassium; and
156 mg of calcium.

Broccoli Quiche

4 cups frozen chopped broccoli
½ cup chopped onion
1 clove garlic, pressed
¼ cup water
4 egg whites
¼ cup skim milk
½ cup dry-curd cottage cheese
1 tbsp. oat flour
1 tsp. butter flavoring
½ tsp. dried dill weed
½ tsp. salt-free herb seasoning

¼ tsp. paprika

1 tsp. cheese-flavored sprinkles

Preheat oven to 350 degrees. In a medium-sized, microwaveable dish, combine broccoli, onion, garlic, and water. Cover. Microwave on high 4 minutes. Spray a 9-inch quiche pan with nonstick cooking spray. Pour broccoli into pan. Beat egg whites until frothy. Add milk, cottage cheese, flour, and seasonings, except cheese sprinkles. Beat until blended. Pour over broccoli. Bake 45 to 55 minutes until set. Garnish with cheese sprinkles. Serves 4.

(Serving = ¼ lean protein; 1 lean, fibrous vegetable)
NUTRIENTS: 87 calories; 11.2 grams of protein; 0.7 grams of fat; 12.2 grams of carbohydrates; 94 mg of sodium; 529 mg of potassium; and 146 mg of calcium.

Broccoli and Carrots Cayenne

2 cups broccoli florets

2 cups thinly sliced carrots

¼ cup sliced green onion

½ cup chicken broth, defatted

½ tsp. salt-free herb seasoning

¼ tsp. cayenne pepper

2 tbsp. nonfat yogurt

In a medium-sized, microwaveable dish, combine all ingredients, except yogurt. Cover. Microwave on high 8 to 10 minutes. Stir after 4 minutes. Garnish with nonfat yogurt. Microwave 1 minute. Serves 4.

(Serving = 1 lean, fibrous vegetable)
NUTRIENTS: 54 calories; 3.4 grams of protein; 0.6 grams of fat;
10.4 grams of carbohydrates; 231 mg of sodium; 373 mg of potassium;
and 66 mg of calcium.

Best Broccoli Sauté

4 cups broccoli florets
1 cup sliced mushrooms
¼ cup chicken broth, defatted
¼ tsp. garlic powder
½ tsp. salt-free herb seasoning
½ tsp. dried marjoram

In a medium skillet, combine all ingredients. Bring to a boil.
Reduce heat. Cover. Simmer 5 to 7 minutes until vegetables are
tender. Serves 4.

(Serving = 1 lean, fibrous vegetable)
NUTRIENTS: 47 calories; 4.9 grams of protein; 0.4 grams of fat;
8.3 grams of carbohydrates; 124 mg of sodium; 354 mg of potassium; and
67 mg of calcium.

Broccoflower with Pepper

4 cups broccoflower florets
1 green pepper, cut into thin strips
½ cup chicken broth, defatted
One 2-oz. jar chopped pimientos
1 tsp. grated fresh ginger root
½ tsp. salt-free herb seasoning

Combine all ingredients in a medium-sized, microwaveable dish. Cover. Microwave on high 8 to 10 minutes until tender. Stir occasionally. Serves 4.

(Serving = 1 lean, fibrous vegetable)
NUTRIENTS: 49 calories; 4.2 grams of protein; 0.6 grams of fat; 9.1 grams of carbohydrates; 211 mg of sodium; 380 mg of potassium; and 46 mg of calcium.

Vegetables Canton

1 cup sliced onion
1 tbsp. grated fresh ginger root
½ cup chicken broth, defatted
3 cups broccoli florets
3 cups coarsely chopped fresh spinach
1 cup sliced celery
2 tbsp. low-salt soy sauce
One 6-oz. pkg. frozen snowpeas, thawed

In a large skillet, simmer onion and ginger root in broth until tender. Add remaining ingredients except snowpeas. Cover and steam over low heat 8 to 10 minutes. Add snowpeas. Cover and steam 3 to 5 minutes until vegetables are tender. Serves 4.

(Serving = 1½ lean, fibrous vegetable)
NUTRIENTS: 92 calories; 7.6 grams of protein; 1.7 grams of fat; 16.7 grams of carbohydrates; 574 mg of sodium; 646 mg of potassium; and 110 mg of calcium.

Broccoli Italiano

4 cups frozen chopped broccoli
One 14½-oz. can tomatoes, chopped
⅛ tsp. garlic powder
1 tsp. Italian herb seasoning
⅛ tsp. black pepper

In a medium-sized, microwaveable dish, combine all ingredients. Cover. Microwave on high 8 to 10 minutes. Stir after 4 minutes. Serves 4.

(Serving = 1 lean, fibrous vegetable)
NUTRIENTS: 76 calories; 6.7 grams of protein; 0.8 grams of fat; 14.3 grams of carbohydrates; 179 mg of sodium; 677 mg of potassium; and 116 mg of calcium.

Lively Lemon Broccoli

4 cups broccoli florets
¼ cup chicken broth, defatted
½ tsp. salt-free herb seasoning
¼ tsp. ground ginger
½ tsp. dried lemon peel
1 tbsp. lemon juice
1 tbsp. prepared butter-flavored mix

In a microwaveable dish, combine broccoli, broth, herb seasoning, ginger and lemon peel. Cover. Microwave on high 8 to 10 minutes. Stir after 4 minutes. Combine lemon juice and prepared butter mix. Pour over broccoli. Toss gently. Serves 4.

(Serving = 1 lean, fibrous vegetable)
NUTRIENTS: 42 calories; 4.5 grams of protein; 0.4 grams of fat;
7.5 grams of carbohydrates; 124 mg of sodium; 354 mg of potassium;
and 57 mg of calcium.

Holiday Brussels Sprouts

4 cups Brussels sprouts
½ cup chicken broth, defatted
½ tsp. ground sage
¼ tsp. ground nutmeg
One 8-oz. can water chestnuts, drained and thinly sliced
2 tbsp. prepared butter-flavored mix

Wash sprouts and remove any loose or yellowed leaves. Cut off ends and trim as necessary. With the tip of a sharp knife, make a cross-cut ¼-inch deep in the base of each sprout. In a medium saucepan, combine sprouts, broth, sage, and nutmeg. Bring to a boil. Reduce heat. Cover and simmer for 8 minutes. Add water chestnuts. Cover and simmer 6 to 8 minutes until sprouts are just tender. Drain. Pour prepared butter mix over vegetables. Toss gently. Serves 4.

(Serving = 1 lean, fibrous vegetable)
NUTRIENTS: 90 calories; 7.9 grams of protein; 0.8 grams of fat;
17.4 grams of carbohydrates; 332 mg of sodium; 590 mg of potassium;
and 72 mg of calcium.

Creamed Brussels Sprouts

4 cups Brussels sprouts
¼ cup chopped onion
1 clove garlic, pressed
¼ cup chicken broth, defatted
1 tbsp. prepared butter-flavored mix
1 tbsp. oat flour
½ cup skim milk
1 tsp. cheese-flavored sprinkles
1 tsp. dried dill weed
¼ tsp. paprika
⅛ tsp. white pepper

In a medium-sized, microwaveable dish, combine sprouts, onion, garlic, and broth. Cover. Microwave on high 11 to 13 minutes until just tender. Meanwhile, prepare sauce. In a small saucepan, combine prepared butter mix and flour. Slowly stir in milk while cooking over medium heat. Stir constantly until sauce is thickened. Stir in cheese sprinkles, dill weed, paprika, and pepper. Remove from heat. Pour over sprouts. Microwave, uncovered, 1 to 2 minutes until sauce is bubbly. Serves 4.

(Serving = 1 lean, fibrous vegetable)
NUTRIENTS: 96 calories; 9.3 grams of protein; 1.0 grams of fat; 17.2 grams of carbohydrates; 131 mg of sodium; 667 mg of potassium; and 96 mg of calcium.

Oriental Cabbage

½ cup chopped onion
1 clove garlic, pressed

1 tsp. grated fresh ginger root

½ cup water

½ tsp. salt-free, beef-flavored instant bouillon

¼ tsp. garlic powder

1 tbsp. low-salt soy sauce

6 cups shredded cabbage

In a medium skillet, simmer onion, garlic, and ginger root in water for 3 minutes. Stir in bouillon, garlic powder, and soy sauce. Add cabbage. Cover. Cook over low heat 15 to 20 minutes until tender. Stir occasionally while cooking. Serves 4.

(Serving = 1 lean, fibrous vegetable)
NUTRIENTS: 47 calories; 2.5 grams of protein; 0.7 grams of fat; 10.0 grams of carbohydrates; 182 mg of sodium; 399 mg of potassium; and 83 mg of calcium.

Cabbage Dijonnaise

5 cups shredded cabbage

1 cup thinly sliced onion

1 cup chopped tomatoes

¼ cup chicken broth, defatted

2 tsp. Dijon mustard

2 tbsp. chopped fresh parsley

½ tsp. salt-free herb seasoning

⅛ tsp. black pepper

In a medium-sized, microwaveable bowl, combine cabbage, onion, and tomatoes. Combine remaining ingredients and pour

over vegetables. Cover. Microwave on high 8 to 10 minutes.
Stir occasionally. Serves 4.

(Serving = 1 lean, fibrous vegetable)
NUTRIENTS: 60 calories; 2.9 grams of protein; 0.5 grams of fat;
13.2 grams of carbohydrates; 123 mg of sodium; 490 mg of potassium;
and 77 mg of calcium.

Pennsylvania Red Cabbage

5 cups shredded red cabbage
2 Granny Smith apples, unpeeled and diced
¼ cup cider vinegar
¼ cup chicken broth, defatted
½ tsp. allspice
½ tsp. bacon-flavored sprinkles
3 packets sugar substitute

In a medium skillet, combine all ingredients except bacon
sprinkles and sugar substitute. Cover. Cook over low heat 15 to
20 minutes until tender. Stir occasionally while cooking. Add
bacon sprinkles and sugar substitute. Toss and serve. Serves 4.

(Serving = 1 lean, fibrous vegetable)
NUTRIENTS: 82 calories; 2.8 grams of protein; 0.6 grams of fat;
20.1 grams of carbohydrates; 126 mg of sodium; 431 mg of potassium;
and 60 mg of calcium.

Gourmet Cabbage

½ cup chicken broth, defatted
5 cups shredded cabbage
1 cup shredded carrots
¼ cup sliced green onion
½ tsp. dried dill weed
⅛ tsp. black pepper
⅛ tsp. dry mustard
1 tsp. butter-flavored sprinkles

In a medium-sized, microwaveable dish, combine all ingredients except butter sprinkles. Cover. Microwave on high 8 to 10 minutes. Stir occasionally. Garnish with butter sprinkles. Toss gently. Serves 4.

(Serving = 1 lean, fibrous vegetable)
NUTRIENTS: 48 calories; 2.3 grams of protein; 0.5 grams of fat; 10.5 grams of carbohydrates; 224 mg of sodium; 394 mg of potassium; and 78 mg of calcium.

Caraway Cabbage

6 cups shredded cabbage
⅓ cup chicken broth, defatted
½ tsp. salt-free herb seasoning
⅛ tsp. black pepper
1 tsp. caraway seeds
1 tsp. butter-flavored sprinkles

In a medium-sized, microwaveable dish, combine all ingredients except butter sprinkles. Cover. Microwave on high 8 to 10 minutes. Stir occasionally. Garnish with butter sprinkles. Toss gently. Serves 4.

(Serving = 1 lean, fibrous vegetable)
NUTRIENTS: 38 calories; 2.1 grams of protein; 0.4 grams of fat; 8.2 grams of carbohydrates; 154 mg of sodium; 352 mg of potassium; and 75 mg of calcium.

Parsleyed Carrots

3 cups thinly sliced carrots
1 cup sliced celery
¼ cup sliced green onion
½ cup chicken broth, defatted
½ tsp. salt-free herb seasoning
⅛ tsp. black pepper
2 tbsp. chopped fresh parsley

In a medium-sized, microwaveable dish, combine all ingredients except parsley. Cover. Microwave on high 8 to 10 minutes until tender. Stir occasionally. Sprinkle with parsley. Serves 4.

(Serving = 1 lean, fibrous vegetable)
NUTRIENTS: 46 calories; 1.6 grams of protein; 0.4 grams of fat; 10.1 grams of carbohydrates; 255 mg of sodium; 355 mg of potassium; and 52 mg of calcium.

Dilled Carrots

4 cups thinly sliced carrots
½ cup chicken broth, defatted

1 tsp. dried vegetable flakes

½ tsp. dried dill weed

¼ tsp. salt-free herb seasoning

2 tbsp. prepared butter-flavored mix

In a medium-sized, microwaveable dish, combine all ingredients except prepared butter mix. Cover. Microwave on high 10 to 12 minutes until tender. Stir occasionally. Pour prepared butter mix over carrots and toss gently. Serves 4.

(Serving = 1 lean, fibrous vegetable)
NUTRIENTS: 49 calories; 1.5 grams of protein; 0.5 grams of fat; 10.8 grams of carbohydrates; 235 mg of sodium; 336 mg of potassium; and 52 mg of calcium.

Sunshine Carrots

4 cups thinly sliced carrots

½ cup water

2 tsp. grated fresh ginger root

½ tsp. cinnamon

½ tsp. dried orange peel

1 tsp. orange extract

In a medium-sized, microwaveable dish, combine all ingredients. Cover. Microwave on high 10 to 12 minutes until tender. Stir occasionally. Serves 4.

(Serving = 1 lean, fibrous vegetable)
NUTRIENTS: 47 calories; 1.4 grams of protein; 0.3 grams of fat; 10.7 grams of carbohydrates; 50 mg of sodium; 333 mg of potassium; and 50 mg of calcium.

Citrus Carrots

4 cups thinly sliced carrots

½ cup water

½ tsp. salt-free herb seasoning

⅛ tsp. nutmeg

½ tsp. dried marjoram

1 tbsp. lemon juice

1 tbsp. chopped fresh parsley

1 tbsp. prepared butter-flavored mix

In a medium-sized, microwaveable dish, combine carrots, water, herb seasoning, nutmeg, and marjoram. Cover. Microwave on high 10 to 12 minutes. Stir occasionally. Combine lemon juice, parsley, and prepared butter mix. Pour over carrots. Toss gently. Serves 4.

(Serving = 1 lean, fibrous vegetable)
NUTRIENTS: 47 calories; 1.4 grams of protein; 0.3 grams of fat; 10.7 grams of carbohydrates; 50 mg of sodium; 333 mg of potassium; and 50 mg of calcium.

Minted Carrots

4 cups thinly sliced carrots

½ cup water

1 tsp. dried vegetable flakes

2 tsp. dried mint flakes

In a medium-sized, microwaveable dish, combine all ingredients. Cover. Microwave on high 10 to 12 minutes until tender. Stir occasionally. Serves 4.

(Serving = 1 lean, fibrous vegetable)
NUTRIENTS: 47 calories; 1.4 grams of protein; 0.3 grams of fat;
10.7 grams of carbohydrates; 50 mg of sodium; 333 mg of potassium; and
50 mg of calcium.

Holiday Cauliflower

4 cups frozen cauliflower
½ cup chicken broth, defatted
½ cup chopped celery
¼ cup chopped onion
One 4-oz. can mushrooms, drained
½ tsp. salt-free herb seasoning
½ tsp. ground sage
¼ tsp. dried thyme
2 tbsp. prepared butter-flavored mix
1 tbsp. chopped fresh parsley

In a medium-sized, microwaveable dish, combine all ingredients except prepared butter mix and parsley. Cover. Microwave on high 8 to 10 minutes until tender. Pour prepared butter mix over cauliflower. Toss gently. Garnish with parsley. Serves 4.

(Serving = 1 lean, fibrous vegetable)
NUTRIENTS: 51 calories; 4.1 grams of protein; 0.5 grams of fat;
11.4 grams of carbohydrates; 632 mg of sodium; 787 mg of potassium;
and 67 mg of calcium.

Cauliflower Supreme

3 cups cauliflower florets

1 cup thinly sliced carrots

1 small red onion, sliced and separated into rings

½ cup chicken broth, defatted

½ tsp. dried dill weed

⅛ tsp. black pepper

½ tsp. salt-free herb seasoning

¼ tsp. dried lemon peel

⅛ tsp. dry mustard

2 tbsp. prepared butter-flavored mix

In a medium-sized, microwaveable dish, combine all ingredients, except prepared butter mix. Cover. Microwave on high 8 to 10 minutes. Stir occasionally. Pour prepared butter mix over vegetables. Toss gently. Serves 4.

(Serving = 1 lean, fibrous vegetable)
NUTRIENTS: 43 calories; 2.7 grams of protein; 0.3 grams of fat;
8.5 grams of carbohydrates; 210 mg of sodium; 341 mg of potassium; and
39 mg of calcium.

Cauliflower Country Style

4 cups cauliflower florets

1 cup sliced celery

¼ cup sliced green onion

½ cup chicken broth, defatted

½ tsp. dried basil

¼ tsp. salt-free herb seasoning

½ tsp. paprika

½ cup chopped tomatoes
½ tsp. bacon-flavored sprinkles

In a medium-sized, microwaveable dish, combine cauliflower, celery, onion, broth, basil, herb seasoning, and paprika. Cover. Microwave on high 8 minutes. Stir occasionally. Add tomatoes and bacon sprinkles. Toss gently. Microwave 1 to 2 minutes. Serves 4.

(Serving = 1 lean, fibrous vegetable)
NUTRIENTS: 44 calories; 3.4 grams of protein; 0.5 grams of fat; 8.4 grams of carbohydrates; 232 mg of sodium; 465 mg of potassium; and 41 mg of calcium.

Minted Cauliflower

4 cups cauliflower florets
½ cup chicken broth, defatted
1 tsp. dried vegetable flakes
2 tsp. dried mint flakes
⅛ tsp. dried lemon peel

In a medium-sized, microwaveable dish, combine all ingredients. Cover. Microwave on high 10 to 12 minutes until tender. Stir occasionally. Serves 4.

(Serving = 1 lean, fibrous vegetable)
NUTRIENTS: 30 calories; 2.7 grams of protein; 0.4 grams of fat; 5.2 grams of carbohydrates; 199 mg of sodium; 298 mg of potassium; and 27 mg of calcium.

Glazed Celery

4 cups sliced celery and leaves
1 cup chicken broth, defatted
1 tbsp. lemon juice
½ tsp. salt-free herb seasoning
¼ tsp. dried tarragon
1 tbsp. cornstarch
2 tbsp. water
2 tbsp. chopped pimientos

Combine celery, broth, lemon juice, herb seasoning, and tarragon in a medium skillet. Cover and simmer over low heat 10 to 12 minutes until almost tender. Dissolve cornstarch in water. Add to celery. Cook and stir until thickened. Garnish with pimientos. Serves 4.

(Serving = 1 lean, fibrous vegetable)
NUTRIENTS: 24 calories; 1.2 grams of protein; 0.4 grams of fat; 5.1 grams of carbohydrates; 497 mg of sodium; 347 mg of potassium; and 43 mg of calcium.

Ratatouille

1 medium green pepper, thinly sliced
1 medium onion, thinly sliced
2 cloves garlic, pressed
1 medium eggplant, peeled and cubed
2 medium zucchini, sliced
One 14½-oz. can tomatoes, chopped
¼ cup chicken broth, defatted
½ tsp. dried basil

1 tsp. salt-free herb seasoning

⅛ tsp. black pepper

2 tbsp. chopped fresh parsley

Coat a heavy skillet with nonstick cooking spray. Sauté green pepper, onion, and garlic until slightly cooked. Stir constantly. If vegetables begin to stick, add 2 tablespoons of water as needed. Add all remaining ingredients except parsley. Cover. Simmer over low heat for 15 minutes. Stir in parsley and cook 5 to 10 minutes until vegetables are tender. Serves 4.

(Serving = 1 lean, fibrous vegetable)
NUTRIENTS: 79 calories; 3.4 grams of protein; 0.6 grams of fat; 17.8 grams of carbohydrates; 611 mg of sodium; 704 mg of potassium; amd 39 mg of calcium.

Elegant Eggplant

1 medium eggplant

1 stalk celery, chopped

1 shredded carrot

1 cup chopped onion

¼ cup chicken broth, defatted

One 4-oz. can mushrooms, drained

¼ tsp. garlic powder

1 tsp. Italian herb seasoning

¼ tsp. dried oregano

1 cup tomatoes, chopped

1 cup Spaghetti Sauce (page 388)

Preheat oven to 350 degrees. Slice eggplant into ½-inch slices
and peel. Sprinkle cut surfaces with salt. Let stand ½ hour. In a
medium skillet, sauté celery, carrot, and onion in broth until
tender. Add mushrooms, garlic powder, Italian seasoning,
oregano, and tomatoes. Simmer 5 minutes. Rinse and drain
slices. Spray a 9" x 13" x 2" baking dish with nonstick cooking
spray. Arrange eggplant in dish. Spoon cooked vegetables on
top of eggplant slices. Top with Spaghetti Sauce. Bake 30 to 40
minutes until eggplant is tender. Serves 4.

(Serving = 1 lean, fibrous vegetable)
NUTRIENTS: 92 calories; 2.9 grams of protein; 2.3 grams of fat;
18.1 grams of carbohydrates; 585 mg of sodium; 600 mg of potassium;
and 44 mg of calcium.

Spicy Mixed Greens

1 lb. collard greens
1 lb. mustard greens
1 tbsp. grated fresh ginger root
½ cup chicken broth, defatted
1 tsp. dried basil
½ tsp. garlic powder
¼ tsp. crushed red pepper flakes
1 tsp. salt-free herb seasoning

Wash and clean greens. Coarsely chop leaves and tender stems.
Discard any tough stems. In a large skillet, combine all ingredients. Cover. Steam over low heat 15 to 20 minutes until
tender. Serves 4.

Note: Any combination of greens may be used including dandelion greens, turnip greens, or kale.

(Serving = 1 lean, fibrous vegetable)
NUTRIENTS: 83 calories; 7.7 grams of protein; 1.5 grams of fat; 14.7 grams of carbohydrates; 271 mg of sodium; 886 mg of potassium; and 440 mg of calcium.

Home-Style Green Bean Casserole

4 cups frozen cut green beans
¼ cup water
½ cup chopped onion
One 4-oz. can mushrooms
1 cup skim milk
2 tbsp. oat flour
1 tsp. butter-flavored sprinkles
1 tbsp. cheese-flavored sprinkles
1 tsp. salt-free herb seasoning

Preheat oven to 350 degrees. In a medium-sized, micro-waveable dish, combine beans, water, and onion. Cover. Microwave on high for 6 minutes. Drain. Spray an 8" x 11" x 2" baking dish with nonstick cooking spray. Spoon beans into dish. Combine all remaining ingredients. Stir until well blended. Pour over beans. Bake 30 to 40 minutes until beans are tender. Serves 4.

(Serving = 1 lean, fibrous vegetable)
NUTRIENTS: 104 calories; 6.7 grams of protein; 0.9 grams of fat; 20.4 grams of carbohydrates; 177 mg of sodium; 471 mg of potassium; and 148 mg of calcium.

Oriental Green Beans

1 lb. green beans
1 cup sliced celery
¼ cup chopped green onion
½ cup water
1 tbsp. low-salt soy sauce
⅛ tsp. garlic powder
1 tsp. dried vegetable flakes

Wash and trim beans. Cut into 1-inch pieces. In a medium-sized, microwaveable dish, combine all ingredients. Cover. Microwave on high 10 to 12 minutes until tender. Stir occasionally. Serves 4.

(Serving = 1 lean, fibrous vegetable)
NUTRIENTS: 48 calories; 2.8 grams of protein; 0.7 grams of fat; 10.0 grams of carbohydrates; 190 mg of sodium; 394 mg of potassium; and 80 mg of calcium.

Green Beans Italiano

4 cups frozen cut green beans
½ cup chopped onion
1 cup chopped tomatoes
⅓ cup water
½ tsp. Italian herb seasoning
½ tsp. dried oregano
¼ tsp. salt-free herb seasoning

In a medium-sized, microwaveable dish, combine all ingredients. Cover. Microwave on high 10 to 12 minutes until tender. Stir occasionally. Serves 4.

(Serving = 1 lean, fibrous vegetable)
NUTRIENTS: 64 calories; 3.3 grams of protein; 0.4 grams of fat;
14.7 grams of carbohydrates; 9 mg of sodium; 407 mg of potassium; and
74 mg of calcium.

Herbed Green Beans

4 cups frozen cut green beans
½ cup water
¼ tsp. dry mustard
½ tsp. dried celery flakes
1 tsp. salt-free herb seasoning
¼ tsp. dried rosemary, crumbled
1 tsp. butter-flavored sprinkles

In a medium-sized, microwaveable dish, combine all ingredients, except butter sprinkles. Cover. Microwave on high 10 to 12 minutes until tender. Stir occasionally. Garnish with butter sprinkles. Serves 4.

(Serving = 1 lean, fibrous vegetable)
NUTRIENTS: 44 calories; 2.4 grams of protein; 0.3 grams of fat;
10.2 grams of carbohydrates; 6 mg of sodium; 243 mg of potassium; and
65 mg of calcium.

Savory Green Beans

4 cups frozen French-style green beans
¼ cup chopped green onion
¼ cup chopped pimientos
½ cup water

1 tsp. dried summer savory

¼ tsp. dried thyme

¼ tsp. salt-free herb seasoning

In a medium-sized, microwaveable dish, combine all ingredients. Cover. Microwave on high 10 to 12 minutes until tender.
Stir occasionally. Serves 4.

(Serving = 1 lean, fibrous vegetable)
NUTRIENTS: 54 calories; 2.8 grams of protein; 0.4 grams of fat;
12.6 grams of carbohydrates; 7 mg of sodium; 260 mg of potassium; and
69 mg of calcium.

Country Green Beans

1 lb. green beans

½ cup chopped onion

1 cup sliced mushrooms

½ cup chicken broth, defatted

1 tsp. hickory liquid smoke

1 tbsp. prepared butter-flavored mix

1 tsp. bacon-flavored sprinkles

Wash and trim beans. Cut into 1-inch pieces. In a medium-
sized, microwaveable dish, combine beans, onion, mushrooms,
broth, and liquid smoke. Cover. Microwave on high 10 to 12
minutes until tender. Stir occasionally. Combine prepared
butter mix and bacon sprinkles. Pour over beans. Serves 4.

(Serving = 1 lean, fibrous vegetable)
NUTRIENTS: 60 calories; 3.4 grams of protein; 0.4 grams of fat;

12.8 grams of carbohydrates; 197 mg of sodium; 345 mg of potassium; and 87 mg of calcium.

Peppers Supreme

2 medium green peppers, cut into strips
2 cups sliced celery
1 cup chopped tomatoes
½ cup chopped green onion
2 tsp. grated fresh ginger root
½ cup chicken broth, defatted
1 tbsp. cornstarch
2 tbsp. low-salt soy sauce

In a medium skillet, simmer peppers, celery, tomatoes, onion, and ginger root in broth until tender. Dissolve cornstarch in soy sauce. Add to vegetables. Cook and stir until thickened. Serves 4.

(Serving = 1 lean, fibrous vegetable)
NUTRIENTS: 50 calories; 2.5 grams of protein; 1.3 grams of fat; 9.8 grams of carbohydrates; 558 mg of sodium; 477 mg of potassium; and 42 mg of calcium.

Fiesta Peppers

2 medium red peppers, cut into strips
2 medium green peppers, cut into strips
1 onion, thinly sliced
2 tomatoes, chopped
½ cup chicken broth, defatted

½ tsp. ground cumin

1 tsp. dried oregano

½ tsp. salt-free herb seasoning

⅓ cup nonfat yogurt

1 tbsp. chopped fresh cilantro

1 tsp. bacon-flavored sprinkles

In a medium skillet, combine peppers, onion, tomatoes, broth, cumin, oregano, and herb seasoning. Cook vegetables 6 to 8 minutes until tender. Remove from heat. Drain if necessary. Combine nonfat yogurt, cilantro, and bacon sprinkles. Stir into vegetables. Serves 4.

(Serving = 1 lean, fibrous vegetable)
NUTRIENTS: 68 calories; 3.4 grams of protein; 0.9 grams of fat; 14.1 grams of carbohydrates; 217 mg of sodium; 540 mg of potassium; and 53 mg of calcium.

Southern Kale

2 lbs. kale

½ cup chopped onion

1 clove garlic, pressed

½ cup chicken broth, defatted

1 tsp. salt-free herb seasoning

¼ tsp. black pepper

⅛ tsp. ground cloves

1 tsp. bacon-flavored sprinkles

Wash kale thoroughly. Strip leaves from the tough mid-ribs. Tear leaves into small pieces. In a large skillet, cook onion and garlic in broth for 3 minutes. Add kale, herb seasoning, pepper, and cloves. Cover. Cook over low heat 15 to 20 minutes until tender. Stir occasionally while cooking. Garnish with bacon sprinkles. Serves 4.

(Serving = 1 lean, fibrous vegetable)
NUTRIENTS: 131 calories; 14.1 grams of protein; 2.0 grams of fat; 22.5 grams of carbohydrates; 358 mg of sodium; 894 mg of potassium; and 573 mg of calcium.

Creamed Kale

2 lbs. kale
1 cup chopped red pepper
½ cup chicken broth, defatted
1 tsp. dried celery flakes
½ tsp. onion powder
½ tsp. salt-free herb seasoning
¼ tsp. black pepper
2 tbsp. prepared butter-flavored mix
2 tbsp. oat flour
1 cup skim milk
1 tsp. cheese-flavored sprinkles

Wash kale thoroughly. Strip leaves from the tough mid-ribs. Tear leaves into small pieces. In a large skillet, combine kale, red peppers, broth, celery flakes, onion powder, herb seasoning, and pepper. Cover. Cook over low heat for 15 to 20 minutes until tender. Drain if necessary. In a small saucepan, combine prepared butter mix and flour. Slowly stir in milk while cooking over medium heat. Stir constantly until sauce is

thickened. Stir in cheese sprinkles. Pour sauce over kale. Mix
well and serve hot. Serves 4.

(Serving = 1 lean, fibrous vegetable)
NUTRIENTS: 177 calories; 17.5 grams of protein; 2.6 grams of fat;
29.7 grams of carbohydrates; 392 mg of sodium; 1062 mg of potassium;
and 646 mg of calcium.

Sautéed Mushrooms

2 lbs. mushrooms
2 tsp. salt-free herb seasoning
2 tsp. Worcestershire sauce
2 tbsp. low-salt soy sauce
¼ cup prepared butter-flavored mix

Wash mushrooms and remove stems. In a large skillet, combine
all ingredients. Cover. Cook over low heat 8 to 10 minutes
until tender. Serves 4.

(Serving = 1 lean, fibrous vegetable)
NUTRIENTS: 64 calories; 6.1 grams of protein; 0.7 grams of fat;
10.0 grams of carbohydrates; 34 mg of sodium; 940 mg of potassium; and
14 mg of calcium.

Okra Gumbo

3 cups sliced okra -
½ cup chopped onion
½ cup chopped green pepper
½ cup chicken broth, defatted

1 cup chopped tomatoes

½ tsp. dried marjoram

¼ tsp. garlic powder

½ tsp. salt-free herb seasoning

⅛ tsp. black pepper

In a medium saucepan, cook okra in a small amount of boiling water for 10 minutes. Drain and rinse. In a medium skillet combine onion, pepper, and broth. Simmer until tender. Add okra, tomatoes, and seasonings. Cook 3 to 5 minutes until heated. Serves 4.

(Serving = 1 lean, fibrous vegetable)
NUTRIENTS: 54 calories; 3.0 grams of protein; 0.5 grams of fat; 10.8 grams of carbohydrates; 192 mg of sodium; 375 mg of potassium; and 81 mg of calcium.

Chinese Vegetable Medley

1 cup sliced celery

1 clove garlic, pressed

½ cup chicken broth, defatted

One 14-oz. can bean sprouts, drained

Two 6-oz. pkg. frozen snowpeas, thawed

One 8-oz. can bamboo shoots, sliced

One 4-oz. can mushrooms, drained

2 tbsp. low-salt soy sauce

1 tbsp. cornstarch

3 green onions, sliced

In a medium skillet, sauté celery and garlic in broth until tender. Add bean sprouts, snowpeas, bamboo shoots, and mushrooms. Sauté 5 to 7 minutes until snowpeas are tender. Combine soy sauce and cornstarch. Add to vegetables. Heat and stir until thickened. Garnish with onion. Serves 4.

(Serving = 1 lean, fibrous vegetable)
NUTRIENTS: 97 calories; 7.8 grams of protein; 1.9 grams of fat; 17.9 grams of carbohydrates; 656 mg of sodium; 255 mg of potassium; and 52 mg of calcium.

Garlic Spinach

2 lbs. fresh spinach (2 bunches or packages)
2 cloves garlic, pressed
2 medium tomatoes, wedge cut
½ tsp. salt-free herb seasoning
⅛ tsp. black pepper
½ tsp. dried chervil

Wash spinach thoroughly and drain. Remove and discard stems. Tear large leaves into small pieces. In a large skillet, combine all ingredients. Cover. Simmer 10 to 15 minutes until spinach is wilted. Stir occasionally. Serves 4.

(Serving = 1 lean, fibrous vegetable)
NUTRIENTS: 76 calories; 8.1 grams of protein; 0.8 grams of fat; 14.0 grams of carbohydrates; 163 mg of sodium; 1250 mg of potassium; and 221 mg of calcium.

Scalloped Spinach and Broccoli

2 cups frozen chopped broccoli

2 tbsp. water

3 cups frozen chopped spinach, thawed

One 4-oz. can mushrooms, drained

½ cup chopped onion

1 cup skim milk

4 egg whites

3 tbsp. oat flour

1 tsp. salt-free herb seasoning

½ tsp. dried oregano

¼ tsp. garlic powder

⅛ tsp. black pepper

Preheat oven to 350 degrees. In a small covered casserole, microwave broccoli and water on high for 5 minutes. Drain. Press liquid from thawed spinach. In a large mixing bowl, combine spinach, broccoli, mushrooms, and onion. In a small mixing bowl, combine remaining ingredients. Beat until well blended. Pour over vegetables. Stir until combined. Spray an 8" x 11" x 2" baking dish with nonstick cooking spray. Pour vegetable mixture into dish. Bake for 40 to 50 minutes until center is set. Serves 4.

(Serving = ¼ lean protein; 1 lean, fibrous vegetable)
NUTRIENTS: 152 calories; 15.8 grams of protein; 1.6 grams of fat;
23.3 grams of carbohydrates; 356 mg of sodium; 1009 mg of potassium;
and 302 mg of calcium.

Spinach Souffle

2 tbsp. prepared butter-flavored mix

2 tbsp. oat flour

½ cup skim milk

3 cups frozen chopped spinach, thawed

1 tsp. instant minced onion flakes

1 tsp. Worcestershire sauce

1 tbsp. cheese-flavored sprinkles

¼ tsp. nutmeg

¼ tsp. black pepper

6 egg whites

Preheat oven to 350 degrees. In a small saucepan, combine prepared butter mix and flour. Slowly stir in milk and heat until thickened. Remove from heat and set aside. Press liquid from thawed spinach. Place spinach, minced onion, Worcestershire sauce, cheese sprinkles, nutmeg, and pepper in a blender. Blend until spinach is pureed. Beat egg whites until stiff. Gently fold in pureed spinach. Pour mixture into an ungreased 2-quart casserole. Bake 35 to 40 minutes until a knife inserted in the center comes out clean. Serve immediately. Serves 4.

(Serving = ½ lean protein; ½ lean, fibrous vegetable)
NUTRIENTS: 96 calories; 12.2 grams of protein; 1.0 grams of fat; 12.1 grams of carbohydrates; 205 mg of sodium; 645 mg of potassium; and 203 mg of calcium.

Spinach Oriental

3 cups frozen chopped spinach

One 6-oz. pkg. frozen snowpeas

2 tsp. grated fresh ginger root
1 tbsp. low-salt soy sauce
1 tbsp. lemon juice
⅛ tsp. garlic powder

In a large skillet, combine all ingredients. Cover. Simmer 10 to 15 minutes until snowpeas are tender. Stir occasionally. Serves 4.

(Serving = 1 lean, fibrous vegetable)
NUTRIENTS: 63 calories; 6.5 grams of protein; 1.4 grams of fat; 10.9 grams of carbohydrates; 416 mg of sodium; 531 mg of potassium; and 168 mg of calcium.

Spicy Spinach Sauté

1½ lbs. fresh spinach (1½ bunches or packages)
2 cups sliced mushrooms
½ tsp. onion powder
¼ tsp. garlic powder
1 tsp. salt-free herb seasoning
⅛ tsp. crushed red pepper flakes
2 tbsp. prepared butter-flavored mix

Wash spinach thoroughly and drain. Remove and discard stems. Tear large leaves into small pieces. In a large skillet, combine all ingredients. Cover. Simmer 10 to 15 minutes until spinach is wilted and mushrooms are tender. Stir occasionally. Serves 4.

(Serving = 1 lean, fibrous vegetable)
NUTRIENTS: 69 calories; 8.2 grams of protein; 0.8 grams of fat;

11.3 grams of carbohydrates; 161 mg of sodium; 1067 mg of potassium; and 222 mg of calcium.

Wilted Spinach and Sprouts

1½ lbs. fresh spinach (1½ bunches or packages)

2 cups sliced mushrooms

½ tsp. onion powder

½ tsp. dried rosemary, crumbled

1 tsp. dried vegetable flakes

⅛ tsp. black pepper

1 cup alfalfa sprouts

1 tbsp. lemon juice

Wash spinach thoroughly and drain. Remove and discard stems. Tear large leaves into small pieces. In a large skillet, combine spinach, mushrooms, onion powder, rosemary, vegetable flakes, and pepper. Cover. Simmer 10 to 15 minutes until spinach is wilted. Add alfalfa sprouts and lemon juice. Remove from heat. Toss and serve. Serves 4.

(Serving = ¼ lean, fibrous vegetable)
NUTRIENTS: 81 calories; 9.8 grams of protein; 1.1 grams of fat; 12.6 grams of carbohydrates; 161 mg of sodium; 1067 mg of potassium; and 234 mg of calcium.

Country-Style Spinach

2 lbs. fresh spinach (2 bunches or packages)

¼ cup chopped green onion

½ tsp. salt-free herb seasoning

1 tsp. dried parsley flakes

½ tsp. dried marjoram

¼ cup nonfat yogurt

1 tsp. bacon-flavored sprinkles

Wash spinach thoroughly and drain. Remove and discard stems. Tear large leaves into small pieces. In a large skillet, combine spinach, onion, herb seasoning, parsley, and marjoram. Cover. Simmer 10 to 15 minutes until spinach is wilted. Drain any excess liquid. Combine yogurt and bacon sprinkles. Stir into spinach. Heat 1 to 2 minutes. Do not boil. Serves 4.

(Serving = 1 lean, fibrous vegetable)
NUTRIENTS: 70 calories; 7.9 grams of protein; 0.9 grams of fat; 11.4 grams of carbohydrates; 169 mg of sodium; 1104 mg of potassium; and 231 mg of calcium.

Italian Stuffed Tomatoes

4 medium tomatoes

¼ cup chopped onion

1 cup shredded zucchini

2 cups sliced mushrooms

¼ tsp. dried oregano

1 tbsp. chopped fresh parsley

⅛ tsp. garlic powder

1 egg white

1 tbsp. Toasted Oats (page 379)

Cut tomatoes in half, crosswise. Scoop out the center, leaving a shell about ¼ inch thick. In a medium skillet, combine tomato pulp, onion, zucchini, and mushrooms. Cover. Cook 6 to 8 minutes. Remove skillet from heat. Drain. Add oregano, parsley, garlic powder, and egg white. Mix well. Stuff tomato halves. Place stuffed tomatoes in a shallow microwaveable dish. Sprinkle with Toasted Oats. Microwave, uncovered, 5 to 6 minutes until tomatoes are soft. Serves 4.

(Serving = 1 lean, fibrous vegetable)
NUTRIENTS: 74 calories; 4.6 grams of protein; 0.7 grams of fat; 15.9 grams of carbohydrates; 158 mg of sodium; 510 mg of potassium; and 40 mg of calcium.

Turnips O'Brien

3 tbsp. finely chopped green pepper
3 tbsp. finely chopped green onion
3 tbsp. finely chopped celery
¼ cup chicken broth, defatted
4 cups shredded, peeled turnips
½ tsp. salt-free herb seasoning
¼ tsp. paprika
⅛ tsp. white pepper
2 tbsp. prepared butter-flavored mix
1 tbsp. chopped fresh parsley

In a medium skillet, simmer pepper, onion, and celery in broth for 5 minutes. Add turnips, herb seasoning, paprika, and pepper. Cover. Simmer 8 to 10 minutes until turnips are tender. Stir in prepared butter mix and parsley. Serves 4.

(Serving = 1 lean, fibrous vegetable)
NUTRIENTS: 34 calories; 3.3 grams of protein; 0.4 grams of fat;
6.7 grams of carbohydrates; 110 mg of sodium; 474 mg of potassium; and
251 mg of calcium.

Baked Yellow Squash

4 cups sliced yellow squash
¼ cup chicken broth, defatted
2 egg whites
2 tbsp. oat flour
1 tsp. baking powder
2 tbsp. instant minced onion flakes
½ tsp. salt-free herb seasoning
½ tsp. dried basil
¼ tsp. black pepper
2 tbsp. prepared butter-flavored mix
1 tbsp. cheese-flavored sprinkles
¼ cup Toasted Oats (page 379)

Preheat oven to 350 degrees. In a medium-sized, microwaveable bowl, combine squash and broth. Microwave on high
6 to 8 minutes until tender. Mash. Beat egg whites. Stir in
squash and remaining ingredients except Toasted Oats. Spray a
2-quart casserole with nonstick cooking spray. Pour squash
mixture into casserole. Bake for 30 minutes. Sprinkle with
Toasted Oats. Serves 4.

(Serving = 1 lean, fibrous vegetable)
NUTRIENTS: 110 calories; 7.0 grams of protein; 1.7 grams of fat;
19.2 grams of carbohydrates; 118 mg of sodium; 366 mg of potassium;
and 3 mg of calcium.

Squash Pudding Supreme

2 cups diced zucchini

2 cups diced yellow squash

4 egg whites

½ cup evaporated skimmed milk

1 tsp. baking powder

2 tbsp. oat flour

½ tsp. cinnamon

¼ tsp. ground ginger

⅛ tsp. ground cloves

¼ tsp. nutmeg

1 tsp. vanilla extract

Preheat oven to 350 degrees. Combine all ingredients in a blender or food processor. Blend until smooth. Spray a 9" x 13" x 2" baking dish with nonstick cooking spray. Pour mixture into dish. Bake for 35 to 40 minutes until set. Serves 4.

(Serving = ¼ lean, fibrous vegetable)
NUTRIENTS: 100 calories; 8.7 grams of protein; 0.7 grams of fat; 16.3 grams of carbohydrates; 366 mg of sodium; 515 mg of potassium; and 108 mg of calcium.

Yellow Squash Medley

¼ cup sliced green onion

1 clove garlic, pressed

½ cup sliced celery

½ cup sliced carrots

½ cup sliced green pepper

½ cup chicken broth, defatted

3 cups sliced yellow squash

2 tbsp. low-salt soy sauce

½ tsp. salt-free herb seasoning

½ tsp. dried marjoram

In a medium skillet, simmer onion, garlic, celery, carrots, and pepper in broth until tender. Add remaining ingredients. Cover. Cook 5 to 7 minutes until squash is tender. Serves 4.

(Serving = 1 lean, fibrous vegetable)
NUTRIENTS: 35 calories; 1.8 grams of protein; 0.3 grams of fat; 9.0 grams of carbohydrates; 210 mg of sodium; 312 mg of potassium; and 17 mg of calcium.

Zucchini With Mushrooms

3 cups sliced zucchini

2 cups sliced mushrooms

½ cup sliced celery

½ cup chopped onion

½ cup chicken broth, defatted

½ tsp. dried thyme

⅛ tsp. black pepper

In a medium-sized, microwaveable dish, combine all ingredients. Microwave on high 6 to 8 minutes until tender. Stir occasionally. Serves 4.

(Serving = 1 lean, fibrous vegetable)
NUTRIENTS: 54 calories; 2.7 grams of protein; 0.4 grams of fat;

13.3 grams of carbohydrates; 625 mg of sodium; 378 mg of potassium; and 42 mg of calcium.

Southwestern Zucchini

4 cups sliced zucchini
1 onion, sliced and separated into rings
1 green pepper, cut into strips
1 cup chopped tomatoes
¼ cup picante sauce
¼ tsp. garlic powder
¼ tsp. chili powder

In a medium skillet, combine all ingredients. Cover. Simmer over low heat 6 to 8 minutes until vegetables are tender. Stir occasionally. Serves 4.

(Serving = 1½ lean, fibrous vegetable)
NUTRIENTS: 55 calories; 2.2 grams of protein; 0.4 grams of fat; 12.5 grams of carbohydrates; 368 mg of sodium; 458 mg of potassium; and 28 mg of calcium.

Confetti Squash

2 cups sliced zucchini
2 cups sliced yellow squash
½ cup sliced onion
3 tbsp. water
½ tsp. dried basil
½ tsp. salt-free herb seasoning
1 tbsp. lemon juice

2 tbsp. chopped fresh parsley

One 2-oz. jar chopped pimientos

In a medium-sized, microwaveable dish, combine squash, onion, water, basil, and herb seasoning. Cover. Microwave on high 6 to 8 minutes until tender. Stir occasionally. Stir in lemon juice. Garnish with parsley and pimientos. Serves 4.

(Serving = 1 lean, fibrous vegetable)
NUTRIENTS: 48 calories; 2.0 grams of protein; 0.3 grams of fat; 11.3 grams of carbohydrates; 284 mg of sodium; 371 mg of potassium; and 20 mg of calcium.

Zucchini Italiano

4 cups sliced zucchini

½ cup sliced onion

1 cup chopped tomatoes

2 tbsp. water

2 tsp. dried parsley flakes

½ tsp. Italian herb seasoning

⅛ tsp. black pepper

In a medium-sized, microwaveable dish, combine all ingredients. Cover. Microwave on high 6 to 8 minutes until tender. Stir occasionally. Serves 4.

(Serving = 1 lean, fibrous vegetable)
NUTRIENTS: 42 calories; 1.7 grams of protein; 0.2 grams of fat; 9.7 grams of carbohydrates; 284 mg of sodium; 370 mg of potassium; and 22 mg of calcium.

Dilled Zucchini

4 cups sliced zucchini

¼ cup water

1 tbsp. instant minced onion flakes

2 tsp. dried parsley flakes

½ tsp. dried dill weed

1 tbsp. lemon juice

In a medium-sized, microwaveable dish, combine all ingredients, except lemon juice. Cover. Microwave on high 6 to 8 minutes until zucchini is tender. Stir occasionally. Drain. Stir in lemon juice. Serves 4.

(Serving = 1 lean, fibrous vegetable)
NUTRIENTS: 21 calories; 0.8 grams of protein; 0.1 grams of fat; 5.2 grams of carbohydrates; 281 mg of sodium; 206 mg of potassium; and 13 mg of calcium.

Herbed Zucchini

4 cups sliced zucchini

¼ cup water

1 tsp. dried oregano

½ tsp. dried parsley flakes

½ tsp. dried basil

In a medium-sized, microwaveable dish, combine all ingredients. Cover. Microwave on high 6 to 8 minutes until zucchini is tender. Stir occasionally. Serves 4.

(Serving = 1 lean, fibrous vegetable)

NUTRIENTS: 21 calories; 0.8 grams of protein; 0.1 grams of fat;
5.2 grams of carbohydrates; 281 mg of sodium; 206 mg of potassium; and
13 mg of calcium.

10

¶ *Soups*

Helpful Hints

Use oat bran to thicken soups.

Refer to the chart Using Herbs and Spices (page 12) to try new combinations of spices.

Defat chicken broth by chilling for several hours and then separating the congealed fat from the top of the liquid. Strain through several layers of cheesecloth to remove any remaining fat.

Remove all fat from the top of canned chicken broth.

Fat can be removed from a liquid by pouring the liquid through a coffee filter.

Choose low-sodium canned broths. Choose no-salt-added bouillons.

Add leftover grains to most soups. Beans add protein and fiber.

Use butter sprinkles or prepared butter-flavored mix to achieve that buttery taste.

Use skim milk when making cream soups.

Garnish soups with cheese sprinkles or bacon sprinkles.

Use flavored vinegars in soups to enhance flavor.

Shrimp and Chicken Chowder

6 cups chicken broth, defatted

½ cup chopped onion

½ cup chopped green pepper

1 cup sliced celery

One 14½-oz. can stewed tomatoes

One 4-oz. can chopped green chilies

3 cups frozen corn

½ tsp. garlic powder

¼ tsp. dried thyme

½ tsp. dried basil

½ tsp. cayenne pepper

¼ tsp. black pepper

1 tsp. dried parsley flakes

1½ cups chopped, cooked chicken breasts

8 oz. shrimp, peeled and deveined

In a medium stock pot, combine all ingredients except chicken and shrimp. Bring to a boil. Reduce heat. Cover and simmer 45 minutes. Add chicken. Cook 15 minutes. Add shrimp. Cook 10 minutes until shrimp turn opaque. Serves 4.

(Serving = 1 lean protein; 1 starchy carbohydrate; ½ lean, fibrous vegetable)
NUTRIENTS: 317 calories; 29.6 grams of protein; 4.9 grams of fat; 44.0 grams of carbohydrates; 2508 mg of sodium; 892 mg of potassium; and 96 mg of calcium.

Basic Chicken Broth

8 cups water
3 lbs. chicken breasts, skinned
1 onion, wedge cut
2 stalks celery, cut into chunks
1 carrot, cut into chunks
1 tsp. dried parsley flakes
1 bay leaf
¼ tsp. black pepper

In a large stock pot, combine all ingredients. Bring to a boil. Reduce heat. Cover. Simmer 1½ to 2 hours until chicken is tender. Remove chicken. Save for later use. Strain broth. Refrigerate until fat congeals on top. Skim off fat and discard. Strain broth through several thicknesses of cheesecloth to remove any remaining fat. Refrigerate or freeze broth.

Note: Freeze broth in ice cube trays or muffin pans. When frozen, put broth cubes in a freezer bag. Use in recipes that call for small amounts of chicken broth. Makes 8 cups.

Tortilla Chicken Rice Soup

1⅓ cups uncooked brown rice
4 cups chicken broth, defatted
4 cups water
1 cup chopped onion
One 28-oz. can tomatoes, chopped
One 4-oz. can chopped green chilies
3 cups chopped, cooked chicken breasts
½ tsp. garlic powder
1 tbsp. chili powder

2 tsp. ground cumin

2 tsp. dried cilantro

¼ tsp. black pepper

2 tbsp. lime juice

3 corn tortillas

¼ cup chopped green onion

½ cup chopped tomatoes

In a large stock pot, combine brown rice, broth, water, and onion. Bring to a boil. Reduce heat. Cover and simmer 45 minutes. Add canned tomatoes, green chilies, chicken, and seasonings. Cover. Simmer 30 to 45 minutes until rice is tender. Stir in lime juice. Cut tortillas into thin strips. Ladle soup into serving bowls. Top with tortilla strips, green onion, and tomatoes. Serves 4.

(Serving = 1 lean protein; ½ lean, fibrous vegetable)
NUTRIENTS: 501 calories; 32.9 grams of protein; 6.6 grams of fat; 78.1 grams of carbohydrates; 1857 mg of sodium; 944 mg of potassium; and 108 mg of calcium.

Chicken Vegetable Soup

3 cups shredded, cooked chicken breasts

4 cups chicken broth, defatted

2 cups vegetable juice

One 14½-oz. can tomatoes, chopped

1 cup green beans

1 cup chopped celery

1 cup shredded red cabbage

1 cup freeze-dried mushrooms

One 4-oz. jar chopped pimientos

1 bay leaf

2 tbsp. instant minced onion flakes

1 tbsp. dried parsley flakes

1 tsp. dried oregano

¼ tsp. cayenne pepper

½ tsp. salt-free herb seasoning

1 tsp. paprika

In a large stock pot, combine all ingredients. Bring to a boil.
Reduce heat. Cover. Simmer 45 to 55 minutes until green
beans are tender. Discard bay leaf. Serves 4.

(Serving = 1 lean protein; 1 lean, fibrous vegetable)
*NUTRIENTS: 230 calories; 27.0 grams of protein; 4.8 grams of fat; 20.2
grams of carbohydrates; 2067 mg of sodium; 865 mg of potassium; and 99
mg of calcium.*

Chicken and Potato Soup Florentine

6 cups chicken broth, defatted

1½ cups shredded, cooked chicken breasts

1 cup chopped onion

2 cups diced potatoes

1 cup frozen peas

1 lb. fresh spinach (1 bunch or package)

½ cup chopped fresh parsley

1 tbsp. dried vegetable flakes

½ tsp. garlic powder

¼ tsp. white pepper

¼ tsp. dried lemon peel

In a large stock pot, combine all ingredients. Bring to a boil. Reduce heat. Cover and simmer 45 to 55 minutes until tender. Serves 4.

(Serving = ½ lean protein; 1 starchy carbohydrate; ½ lean, fibrous vegetable)
NUTRIENTS: 227 calories; 21.0 grams of protein; 3.8 grams of fat; 29.6 grams of carbohydrates; 2378 mg of sodium; 1120 mg of potassium; and 198 mg of calcium.

Oriental Chicken Soup

6 cups chicken broth, defatted
2 cups shredded, cooked chicken breasts
½ cup chopped green onion
1 cup freeze-dried mushrooms
2 cups frozen chopped spinach
1 cup frozen snowpeas
1 tbsp. low-salt soy sauce
1 tsp. grated fresh ginger root
¼ tsp. white pepper
1 tsp. dried vegetable flakes
1 tsp. dried parsley flakes
3 egg whites
4 slices lemon for garnish

In a large saucepan, combine all ingredients except egg whites and lemon. Bring to a boil. Reduce heat. Cover and simmer 15 minutes. Slowly add egg whites. Stir constantly until egg whites are set. Simmer 5 minutes. Garnish with lemon slices. Serves 4.

(Serving = 1 lean protein; 1 lean, fibrous vegetable)
NUTRIENTS: 208 calories; 26.1 grams of protein; 4.6 grams of fat; 19.0
grams of carbohydrates; 2524 mg of sodium; 544 mg of potassium; and
158 mg of calcium.

Smoked Turkey and Bean Soup

1 lb. dry pinto beans, soaked overnight and drained
6 cups water
2 cups chicken broth, defatted
2 cups vegetable juice
2 bay leaves
2 lbs. ground turkey breast, skin removed
1 cup chopped onion
2 cloves garlic, pressed
1 cup sliced green pepper
1 cup sliced celery
1 cup sliced carrots
One 14½-oz. can tomatoes, chopped
1 tsp. black pepper
1 tsp. cayenne pepper
½ tsp. ground cumin
½ tsp. ground ginger
1 tbsp. dried vegetable flakes
2 tsp. salt-free herb seasoning
1 tsp. hickory liquid smoke

In a large stock pot, combine drained beans, water, broth,
vegetable juice, and bay leaves. Bring to a boil and boil for 10
minutes. Reduce heat. Cover and simmer 1 hour. Spray a
medium skillet with nonstick cooking spray. Brown turkey.

Add turkey and remaining ingredients to stock pot. Cover.
Simmer 45 to 55 minutes until beans are tender. Serves 8.

*(Serving = 1 lean protein; 1 starchy carbohydrate; ½ lean, fibrous
vegetable)*
*NUTRIENTS: 377 calories; 42.8 grams of protein; 2.5 grams of fat; 45.6
grams of carbohydrates; 707 mg of sodium; 1312 mg of potassium; and
110 mg of calcium.*

Sicilian Turkey and Pea Soup

1 lb. ground turkey breast, skin removed
1 lb. dry split peas
2 qts. water
1 cup chopped onion
2 cloves garlic, pressed
2 cups sliced carrots
2 cups sliced celery
1 cup diced potatoes
1 tbsp. dried vegetable flakes
1 tsp. salt-free herb seasoning
1½ tsp. Italian herb seasoning
1 tsp. dried oregano
½ tsp. ground cumin
½ tsp. black pepper
½ tsp. cayenne pepper
1 tsp. onion powder

In a large stock pot sprayed with nonstick cooking spray, brown
ground turkey. Add remaining ingredients. Bring to a boil.
Reduce heat. Cover. Simmer 1 to 2 hours until peas are very
soft. Serves 4.

(Serving = 1 lean protein; 2 starchy carbohydrates; 1 lean, fibrous vegetable)
NUTRIENTS: *603 calories; 57.9 grams of protein; 2.7 grams of fat; 88.6 grams of carbohydrates; 196 mg of sodium; 1934 mg of potassium; and 96 mg of calcium.*

Spicy Rice and Vegetable Chowder

1⅓ cups uncooked brown rice
4 cups chicken broth, defatted
One 28-oz. can tomatoes, chopped
Two 6-oz. cans tomato paste
6 cups water
1 cup chopped onion
1 bay leaf
½ tsp. garlic powder
2 tsp. salt-free herb seasoning
¼ tsp. black pepper
1 tsp. dried basil
1 tsp. paprika
3 cups shredded cabbage
1 cup sliced carrots
2 cups sliced celery
1 cup chopped green pepper
One 4-oz. can chopped green chilies

In a large stock pot, combine rice, broth, tomatoes, tomato paste, water, onion, and seasonings. Bring to a boil. Reduce heat. Cover and simmer 45 minutes. Add remaining ingredients. Bring to a boil. Reduce heat. Cover. Simmer 30 to 45 minutes until vegetables are tender. Discard bay leaf. Serves 8.

(Serving = ½ starchy carbohydrate; 1 lean, fibrous vegetable)
NUTRIENTS: 236 calories; 7.8 grams of protein; 1.8 grams of fat; 50.1
grams of carbohydrates; 955 mg of sodium; 1139 mg of potassium; and
112 mg of calcium.

Old-Fashioned Minestrone

1 cup dry garbanzo beans, soaked overnight and drained
1 cup dry kidney beans, soaked overnight and drained
2 qts. water
1 cup chopped onion
2 cloves garlic, pressed
1 cup sliced celery
1 cup frozen green beans
1 cup sliced zucchini
1 cup frozen chopped spinach
One 28-oz. can tomatoes, chopped
1 tbsp. dried vegetable flakes
2 tsp. Italian herb seasoning
¼ tsp. dried marjoram
⅛ tsp. dried thyme
⅛ tsp. dried rosemary, crumbled
½ tsp. salt-free herb seasoning

In a large stock pot, combine drained beans and water. Bring to
a boil and boil for 10 minutes. Reduce heat. Cover and simmer
1 hour. Add remaining ingredients. Cover. Simmer 45 to 55
minutes until beans and vegetables are tender. Serves 8.

(Serving = 1 starchy carbohydrate; ¾ lean, fibrous vegetable)
NUTRIENTS: 236 calories; 14.2 grams of protein; 2.0 grams of fat; 43.2

grams of carbohydrates; 254 mg of sodium; 947 mg of potassium; and 123 mg of calcium.

Hearty Vegetable Bean Soup

1 lb. dry kidney beans, soaked overnight and drained

2 qts. water

2 cups chicken broth, defatted

2 cups sliced celery

1 cup chopped onion

1 cup chopped green pepper

1 cup cubed potatoes

2 cups frozen corn

One 8-oz. can tomato sauce

One 28-oz. can tomatoes, chopped

1 tbsp. chili powder

1 tsp. ground cumin

½ tsp. garlic powder

1 tbsp. dried vegetable flakes

¼ tsp. black pepper

1 ½ tsp. salt-free herb seasoning

In a large stock pot, combine drained beans and water. Bring to a boil for 10 minutes. Reduce heat. Cover and simmer 1 hour. Add remaining ingredients. Cover. Simmer 45 to 55 minutes until beans and vegetables are tender. Serves 8.

(Serving = 1 ½ starchy carbohydrate; ½ lean, fibrous vegetable)
NUTRIENTS: 174 calories; 9.5 grams of protein; 1.1 grams of fat; 34.3 grams of carbohydrates; 645 mg of sodium; 785 mg of potassium; and 67 mg of calcium.

Savory Lima Bean Soup

1 lb. dry lima beans, soaked overnight and drained

2 qts. water

1 bay leaf

1 cup sliced celery

1 cup sliced carrots

1 cup chopped onion

1 cup frozen green beans

One 28-oz. can tomatoes, chopped

1 tsp. salt-free herb seasoning

1 tbsp. dried vegetable flakes

1 tsp. dried basil

1 tsp. dried oregano

¼ tsp. black pepper

¼ tsp. garlic powder

2 tbsp. cider vinegar

In a large stock pot, combine drained beans, water, and bay leaf. Bring to a boil and boil for 10 minutes. Reduce heat. Cover and simmer 45 minutes. Add remaining ingredients. Cover. Simmer 45 to 55 minutes until beans and vegetables are tender. Discard bay leaf. Serves 8.

(Serving = 1 starchy carbohydrate; ¾ lean, fibrous vegetable)
NUTRIENTS: 239 calories; 13.5 grams of protein; 1.2 grams of fat; 45.8 grams of carbohydrates; 164 mg of sodium; 1243 mg of potassium; and 72 mg of calcium.

Classic Navy Bean Soup

1 lb. dry navy beans, soaked overnight and drained

2 qts. water

1 bay leaf

1 cup chopped onion

1 cup sliced carrots

1 cup sliced celery

One 8-oz. can tomato sauce

One 28-oz. can tomatoes, chopped

1 tsp. dried parsley flakes

1 tsp. dried summer savory

2 tsp. salt-free herb seasoning

¼ tsp. black pepper

1 tsp. hickory liquid smoke

2 tsp. cider vinegar

In a large stock pot, combine drained beans, water, and bay leaf. Bring to a boil and boil for 10 minutes. Reduce heat. Cover and simmer 1 hour. Add remaining ingredients. Cover. Simmer 2 to 3 hours until beans are tender. Add additional water if necessary. Discard bay leaf. Serves 8.

(Serving = 1 starchy carbohydrate; ½ lean, fibrous vegetable)
NUTRIENTS: 241 calories; 14.7 grams of protein; 1.3 grams of fat; 45.3 grams of carbohydrates; 338 mg of sodium; 1146 mg of potassium; and 115 mg of calcium.

Cajun White Bean Soup

1 lb. dry navy beans, soaked overnight and drained

4 cups water

4 cups chicken broth, defatted

1 bay leaf

1 cup chopped onion

2 cloves garlic, pressed

1 cup sliced celery

2 tsp. dried vegetable flakes

2 tsp. salt-free herb seasoning

¼ tsp. black pepper

⅛ tsp. cayenne pepper

1 tsp. hickory liquid smoke

2 tsp. cider vinegar

¼ cup chopped green onion for garnish

In a large stock pot, combine drained beans, water, broth, and bay leaf. Bring to a boil and boil for 10 minutes. Reduce heat. Cover and simmer 1 hour. Add remaining ingredients except green onion. Cover. Simmer 2 to 3 hours until beans are tender. Add additional water if necessary. Discard bay leaf. Garnish with green onion. Serves 8.

(Serving = 1 starchy carbohydrate)
NUTRIENTS: 215 calories; 13.8 grams of protein; 1.5 grams of fat; 38.3 grams of carbohydrates; 771 mg of sodium; 775 mg of potassium; and 101 mg of calcium.

Smoky Split Pea Soup

1 lb. dry split peas

7 cups water

1 cup chopped onion

2 cups sliced celery

1 cup sliced carrots

1 bay leaf

1 tbsp. hickory liquid smoke

1 tbsp. dried vegetable flakes

2 tsp. salt-free herb seasoning

½ tsp. dried marjoram

¼ tsp. white pepper

1 tsp. dried parsley flakes

½ tsp. garlic powder

¼ chopped green onion for garnish

In a large stock pot, combine all ingredients, except green onion. Bring to a boil. Reduce heat. Cover and simmer 1 to 2 hours until peas are very soft. Discard bay leaf. Garnish with green onion. Serves 6.

(Serving = 1 starchy carbohydrate; ¾ lean, fibrous vegetable)
NUTRIENTS: 290 calories; 19.3 grams of protein; 0.8 grams of fat; 53.6 grams of carbohydrates; 84 mg of sodium; 901 mg of potassium; and 56 mg of calcium.

Fresh Pea Soup Supreme

2 cups shelled peas

1 cup cubed potatoes

3 cups chopped fresh spinach

½ cup chopped green onion

2 cups shredded Boston lettuce

3 cups chicken broth, defatted

1 tbsp. dried vegetable flakes

¼ tsp. black pepper

½ tsp. dried chervil

2 tsp. salt-free herb seasoning

In a large saucepan, combine all ingredients. Bring to a boil. Reduce heat. Cover. Simmer 15 to 20 minutes until potatoes are tender. Serves 4.

(Serving = 1 starchy carbohydrate; ½ lean, fibrous vegetable)
NUTRIENTS: 128 calories; 7.8 grams of protein; 1.5 grams of fat; 22.5 grams of carbohydrates; 1222 mg of sodium; 583 mg of potassium; and 133 mg of calcium.

Garden Potato Soup

3 cups cubed potatoes

2 cups cut green beans

4 cups chicken broth, defatted

1 bay leaf

2 cups sliced carrots

½ cup chopped green onion

1 tsp. salt-free herb seasoning

½ tsp. garlic powder

¼ tsp. dried thyme

1 tsp. dried celery flakes

½ tsp. dried basil

1 tbsp. fresh mint sprigs for garnish

In a large saucepan, combine potatoes, green beans, chicken broth, and bay leaf. Bring to a boil. Reduce heat. Cover and simmer 10 minutes. Add carrots, green onion, herb seasoning, garlic powder, thyme, celery flakes, and basil. Simmer 20 to 25 minutes until vegetables are tender. Discard bay leaf. Serve and garnish with fresh mint sprigs. Serves 4.

(Serving = 1 starchy carbohydrate; 1 lean, fibrous vegetable)
NUTRIENTS: 160 calories; 5.9 grams of protein; 1.6 grams of fat; 32.9 grams of carbohydrates; 1518 mg of sodium; 804 mg of potassium; and 86 mg of calcium.

Vichyssoise

4 cups sliced potatoes
1 cup sliced leeks, bottom parts only
½ cup chopped onion
½ cup sliced celery
2 cups chicken broth, defatted
2 cups water
½ tsp. salt-free herb seasoning
¼ tsp. white pepper
1 tsp. paprika
½ tsp. dried chervil
¼ tsp. dried rosemary, crumbled
2 tbsp. chopped fresh chives for garnish

In a large saucepan, combine all ingredients except chives. Bring to a boil. Reduce heat. Cover. Simmer 45 minutes until vegetables are tender. Serve hot or cold. Garnish with chives. Serves 4.

(Serving = 1 starchy carbohydrate; ½ lean, fibrous vegetable)
NUTRIENTS: 151 calories; 4.9 grams of protein; 0.8 grams of fat; 34.0 grams of carbohydrates; 769 mg of sodium; 755 mg of potassium; and 40 mg of calcium.

Tomato Corn Chowder

5 cups chopped tomatoes

2 cups chicken broth, defatted

2 cups corn kernels cut from cobs

½ cup water

1 tbsp. dried vegetable flakes

1 tsp. salt-free herb seasoning

½ tsp. dried summer savory

¼ tsp. dried basil

1 bay leaf

⅛ tsp. black pepper

1 tbsp. fresh parsley sprigs for garnish

In a medium saucepan, combine tomatoes and chicken broth. Bring to a boil. Reduce heat. Cover. Cook until tomatoes are very tender. In a large saucepan, combine corn, water, vegetable flakes, herb seasoning, summer savory, basil, bay leaf, and black pepper. Simmer 8 to 10 minutes until corn is almost tender. Put cooked tomatoes through a sieve. Discard skins and seeds. Add tomato liquid to corn mixture. Cover. Simmer 10 to 15 minutes to blend the flavors. Discard bay leaf. Serve garnished with fresh parsley. Serves 4.

(Serving = ½ starchy carbohydrate; 1 lean, fibrous vegetable)
NUTRIENTS: 144 calories; 5.8 grams of protein; 1.8 grams of fat; 30.1 grams of carbohydrates; 941 mg of sodium; 746 mg of potassium; and 29 mg of calcium.

Garden Vegetable Soup

4 cups water

2 cups chicken broth, defatted

1 cup chopped onion

1 cup chopped celery

1 cup sliced carrots

½ cup chopped green pepper

2 cups sliced mushrooms

2 cups shredded cabbage

2 cups broccoli florets

One 28-oz. can tomatoes, chopped

1 tsp. Italian herb seasoning

1 bay leaf

½ tsp. garlic powder

1 tsp. dried oregano

½ tsp. onion powder

½ tsp. dried lemon peel

In a large stock pot, combine all ingredients. Bring to a boil. Reduce heat. Cover and simmer 1 hour until vegetables are tender. Serves 8.

(Serving = 1 lean, fibrous vegetable)
NUTRIENTS: 69 calories; 4.1 grams of protein; 0.7 grams of fat; 13.4 grams of carbohydrates; 548 mg of sodium; 538 mg of potassium; and 65 mg of calcium.

Festive Vegetable Soup

4 cups chicken broth, defatted

2 cups water

½ cup chopped onion

½ cup chopped celery

½ cup chopped carrots

1 cup chopped broccoli florets

2 cups green beans

One 6-oz. can tomato paste

¼ cup picante sauce

1 tbsp. dried parsley flakes

½ tsp. garlic powder

½ tsp. onion powder

¼ tsp. ground cumin

¼ tsp. black pepper

¾ cup sliced yellow squash

¾ cup sliced zucchini

In a large stock pot, combine all ingredients except squash and zucchini. Bring to a boil. Reduce heat. Cover. Simmer 45 minutes. Add squash and zucchini. Cover. Simmer 20 to 30 minutes until vegetables are tender. Serves 8.

(Serving = 1 lean, fibrous vegetable)
NUTRIENTS: 71 calories; 3.5 grams of protein; 0.9 grams of fat; 14.9 grams of carbohydrates; 863 mg of sodium; 541 mg of potassium; and 74 mg of calcium.

Elegant Onion Soup

6 cups thinly sliced onion

2 tbsp. safflower oil

2 qts. water

1 tbsp. no-salt-added, beef-flavored bouillon

1 cup shredded carrots

1 cup shredded zucchini

3 bay leaves

3 whole cloves

1 ½ tsp. salt-free herb seasoning

¼ tsp. black pepper

¼ tsp. dried thyme

½ cup dry white wine

2 tbsp. cornstarch

In a large stock pot, cook onions in oil for 20 to 30 minutes. Stir frequently until onions are lightly browned and glazed. Add remaining ingredients except white wine and cornstarch. Bring to a boil. Reduce heat. Cover and simmer 45 minutes. Mix white wine and cornstarch. Add to soup. Cook until slightly thickened and bubbly. Serves 8.

(Serving = 1 lean, fibrous vegetable)
NUTRIENTS: 106 calories; 2.2 grams of protein; 3.5 grams of fat; 16.9 grams of carbohydrates; 89 mg of sodium; 305 mg of potassium; and 44 mg of calcium.

Tomato Gazpacho

2 cups vegetable juice

½ cup chopped celery

¾ cup chopped cucumber

¾ cup chopped green pepper

½ cup chopped green onion

1 cup chopped tomatoes

2 tbsp. lime juice

¼ tsp. garlic powder

¼ tsp. black pepper

½ tsp. dried oregano

dash Tabasco sauce

In a medium bowl, combine all ingredients. Cover. Refrigerate 6 hours or overnight. Serves 4.

(Serving = 1 lean, fibrous vegetable)
NUTRIENTS: 55 calories; 2.0 grams of protein; 0.2 grams of fat; 12.9 grams of carbohydrates; 379 mg of sodium; 513 mg of potassium; and 36 mg of calcium.

Piquant Tomato Soup

3 cups tomato juice

2 stalks celery, sliced

2 slices onion

1 bay leaf

6 whole cloves

1 tsp. sliced fresh ginger root

½ tsp. paprika

1 cup chicken broth, defatted

1 tsp. low-salt soy sauce

4 slices lemon for garnish

2 tbsp. chopped green onion for garnish

In a medium saucepan, combine tomato juice, celery, onion, bay leaf, cloves, ginger root, and paprika. Bring to a boil. Reduce heat. Cover and simmer 20 minutes. Strain soup and discard seasonings. Return liquid to saucepan. Add chicken broth and soy sauce. Heat through. Garnish with lemon slices and green onion. Serves 4.

(Serving = ½ lean, fibrous vegetable)
NUTRIENTS: 49 calories; 2.5 grams of protein; 0.9 grams of fat; 10.2 grams of carbohydrates; 1061 mg of sodium; 581 mg of potassium; and 56 mg of calcium.

Tomato Soup Florentine

4 cups chicken broth, defatted
Two 28-oz. cans tomatoes, chopped
One 8-oz. can tomato sauce
½ cup sliced green onion
4 cups frozen chopped spinach
1 cup shredded cabbage
1 cup cauliflower florets
½ tsp. garlic powder
½ tsp. onion powder
¼ tsp. cayenne pepper
1 tbsp. dried vegetable flakes
1 tsp. dried oregano
1 tsp. dried basil
1 bay leaf

In a large stock pot, combine all ingredients. Bring to a boil. Reduce heat. Cover. Simmer 30 to 45 minutes until vegetables are tender. Discard bay leaf. Serves 8.

(Serving = 1 lean, fibrous vegetable)
*NUTRIENTS: 99 calories; 6.9 grams of protein; 1.4 grams of fat; 18.2
grams of carbohydrates; 1265 mg of sodium; 1010 mg of potassium; and
149 mg of calcium.*

Oriental Zucchini Soup

6 cups chicken broth, defatted
½ cup chopped green onion
½ cup thinly sliced celery
1 cup sliced bamboo shoots
1 cup sliced mushrooms
1 cup shredded zucchini
2 tsp. dried parsley flakes
½ tsp. salt-free herb seasoning
¼ tsp. white pepper
1 tsp. dried basil
¼ tsp. garlic powder

In a medium saucepan, combine all ingredients. Bring to a boil.
Reduce heat. Cover and simmer 8 to 10 minutes. Serves 4.

(Serving = 1 lean, fibrous vegetable)
*NUTRIENTS: 62 calories; 3.7 grams of protein; 1.8 grams of fat; 10.1
grams of carbohydrates; 2386 mg of sodium; 238 mg of potassium; and 53
mg of calcium.*

11

⅄ Salads

Hints for Salads and Dressings

Use prepared butter-flavored mix to replace vegetable oil in marinades and salad dressings.

Use safflower oil as the oil of choice when recipes call for oil. Use half or quarter amounts, substituting chicken broth or water for the other portion.

Use flavored vinegars on salads and salad dressings to enhance the flavor.

Use Mock Mayo (page 369) in place of mayonnaise.

Use Mock Sour Cream (page 369) or nonfat yogurt in place of sour cream.

Refer to the chart Using Herbs and Spices (page12) to try new combinations of spices.

Use Dijon mustard to enhance the flavor of vinegar-based dressings.

Make cole slaw a day ahead of time using a small amount of salad dressing. Liquid is drawn out of the slaw while marinating.

Smash garlic clove with the flat side of a knife. This loosens the skin for easy removal.

Make tossed salads with a wide variety of vegetables. A good guide is to use a vegetable of every color.

Shrimp-Stuffed Tomatoes

4 large tomatoes

1 lb. cooked medium shrimp, shelled and deveined

One 6-oz. pkg. frozen snowpeas, thawed and drained

2 tbsp. finely chopped onion

¼ cup white wine vinegar

¼ cup dry white wine

½ tsp. dried oregano

¼ tsp. onion powder

¼ tsp. garlic powder

⅛ tsp. black pepper

¼ tsp. paprika

Wash and core tomatoes. Cut each tomato into six wedges, cutting to within ½ inch of the bottom of the tomato. Carefully spread the wedges slightly apart. Cover and chill. In a medium bowl, combine shrimp, snowpeas, and onion. Combine remaining ingredients. Pour over shrimp mixture. Cover. Refrigerate several hours before serving. To serve, drain shrimp mixture and spoon mixture into tomato cups. Serves 4.

(Serving = 1 lean protein; 1 lean, fibrous vegetable)
NUTRIENTS: 176 calories; 23.7 grams of protein; 1.3 grams of fat; 17.1 grams of carbohydrates; 164 mg of sodium; 653 mg of potassium; and 95 mg of calcium.

Louisiana Shrimp Salad

⅓ cup Yogurt Thousand Island Dressing (page 346)

1 lb. cooked medium shrimp, shelled and deveined

1 cup chopped celery

½ cup chopped tomatoes

½ cup chopped onion

2 tbsp. chopped dill pickle

¼ tsp. salt-free herb seasoning

3 hard-boiled egg whites, chopped

Boston lettuce leaves

Prepare Yogurt Thousand Island Dressing according to recipe instructions. In a medium salad bowl, combine shrimp, celery, tomatoes, onion, dill pickle, herb seasoning, and egg whites. Pour dressing over salad and toss. Cover and chill before serving. Serve on lettuce leaves. Serves 4.

(Serving = 1 lean protein; ½ lean, fibrous vegetable)
NUTRIENTS: 135 calories; 24.1 grams of protein; 1.0 grams of fat; 6.1 grams of carbohydrates; 229 mg of sodium; 468 mg of potassium; and 91 mg of calcium.

Tuna Vegetable Toss

½ cup Vegetable French Dressing (page 344)

Two 7-oz. cans water-packed albacore tuna, drained

3 cups cooked peas

1 cup sliced carrots

1 cup chopped cauliflower florets

¼ cup sliced green onion

1 cup chopped tomatoes

Prepare Vegetable French Dressing according to recipe instructions. In a salad bowl, combine remaining ingredients. Pour dressing over salad and toss. Cover and chill thoroughly before serving. Serves 4.

(Serving = 1 lean protein; 1 starchy carbohydrate; 1 lean, fibrous vegetable)
NUTRIENTS: 248 calories; 36.2 grams of protein; 15.6 grams of fat;
7.9 grams of carbohydrates; 359 mg of sodium; 706 mg of potassium; and
74 mg of calcium.

Tuna and Potato Salad

½ cup Lemon Mustard Vinaigrette (page 340)
Two 7-oz. cans water-packed albacore tuna, drained
3 cups cubed, cooked potatoes
1 cup cooked green beans
¼ cup chopped green pepper
¼ cup chopped onion
½ cup shredded carrots

Prepare Lemon Mustard Vinaigrette according to recipe
instructions. In a salad bowl, combine remaining ingredients.
Pour dressing over salad and toss. Cover and chill several hours
before serving. Serves 4.

(Serving = 1 lean protein; 1 starchy carbohydrate; ½ lean, fibrous vegetable)
NUTRIENTS: 228 calories; 31.2 grams of protein; 1.0 grams of fat;
22.8 grams of carbohydrates; 51 mg of sodium; 832 mg of potassium; and
46 mg of calcium.

Fancy Tuna Salad With Asparagus

¼ cup nonfat yogurt
2 tbsp. white wine vinegar
2 tbsp. chicken broth, defatted
1 tsp. instant minced onion flakes

1 tsp. dried parsley flakes

½ tsp. dried lemon peel

⅛ tsp. black pepper

1 tsp. dried vegetable flakes

Two 7-oz. cans water-packed albacore tuna, drained

1 cup alfalfa sprouts

2 cups cooked asparagus

1 cup wedge-cut tomatoes

3 hard-boiled egg whites, quartered

In a small bowl, combine yogurt, vinegar, broth, and seasonings. Chill while preparing rest of salad. Arrange tuna in the center of four salad plates. Top with sprouts. Surround with asparagus, tomatoes, and egg whites. Pour chilled dressing over salad. Serves 4.

(Serving = 1 lean protein; 1 lean, fibrous vegetable)
NUTRIENTS: 185 calories; 34.7 grams of protein; 1.5 grams of fat;
6.2 grams of carbohydrates; 94 mg of sodium; 677 mg of potassium; and
67 mg of calcium.

Garden Tuna Salad

One 7-oz. can water-packed albacore tuna, drained

2 tbsp. nonfat yogurt

¼ cup chopped celery

¼ cup shredded carrots

2 tbsp. finely chopped onion

½ tsp. dried marjoram

2 tbsp. chopped pimientos

1 tbsp. chopped dill pickle

1 tbsp. tomato paste

1 tsp. red wine vinegar

In a salad bowl, combine all ingredients. Cover and chill before serving. Serves 4.

(Serving = 1 lean protein)
NUTRIENTS: 51 calories; 9.6 grams of protein; 0.4 grams of fat; 2.4 grams of carbohydrates; 28 mg of sodium; 146 mg of potassium; and 21 mg of calcium.

South of the Border Salad

1¼ cups water, divided use

½ tsp. Kitchen Bouquet (optional)

1 lb. ground turkey breast, skin removed

1 clove garlic, pressed

¼ cup chopped onion

¼ cup tomato paste

¼ tsp. ground oregano

1 tbsp. chili powder

¾ tsp. dried cumin

1 tsp. paprika

¼ tsp. cayenne pepper

8 cups torn Boston lettuce

1 cup wedge-cut tomatoes

1½ cups cooked kidney beans

¼ cup green onion

⅓ cup Vegetable French Dressing (page 344)

1 recipe Spicy Salsa (page 389)

In a large skillet, combine ½ cup water and Kitchen Bouquet. Brown turkey, garlic, and onion in water mixture. Stir frequently to keep turkey crumbly. Add tomato paste, ¾ cup water, oregano, chili powder, cumin, paprika, and cayenne pepper. Simmer 10 to 15 minutes until thickened. In a large salad bowl, combine lettuce, tomatoes, kidney beans, and green onions. Add turkey mixture and Vegetable French Dressing. Toss. Serve with Spicy Salsa. Serves 4.

(Serving = 1 lean protein; ½ starchy carbohydrate; 1 lean, fibrous vegetable)
NUTRIENTS: 387 calories; 36.6 grams of protein; 16.6 grams of fat; 25.1 grams of carbohydrates; 105 mg of sodium; 1124 mg of potassium; and 118 mg of calcium.

Turkey and Rice Salad

½ cup Vegetable French Dressing (page 344)
3 cups chopped, cooked turkey
2 cups cooked brown rice
2 cups cooked peas
½ cup chopped celery
½ cup chopped tomatoes
½ tsp. salt-free herb seasoning

Prepare Vegetable French Dressing according to recipe instructions. Combine remaining ingredients. Pour dressing over salad and toss. Cover and chill 1 to 2 hours. Serves 4.

(Serving = 1 lean protein; 1 starchy carbohydrate; ¼ lean, fibrous vegetable)
NUTRIENTS: 309 calories; 35.0 grams of protein; 11.7 grams of fat; 27.5 grams of carbohydrates; 539 mg of sodium; 608 mg of potassium; and 40 mg of calcium.

Summer Chicken Salad

2 cups chopped, cooked chicken

3 hard-boiled egg whites, chopped

2 cups cooked green beans

½ cup thinly sliced water chestnuts

2 tbsp. chopped pimientos

½ cup chopped celery

½ cup chopped green onion

½ cup chopped cucumber

¼ cup nonfat yogurt

2 tbsp. rice wine vinegar

1 tsp. dried marjoram

1 tsp. dried vegetable flakes

½ tsp. salt-free herb seasoning

⅛ tsp. black pepper

In a salad bowl, combine chicken, egg whites, green beans, water chestnuts, pimientos, celery, green onion, and cucumber. In a small bowl, combine remaining ingredients. Pour over salad. Toss. Chill several hours before serving. Serves 4.

(Serving = 1 lean protein; 1 lean, fibrous vegetable)
NUTRIENTS: 150 calories; 19.7 grams of protein; 2.5 grams of fat; 14.0 grams of carbohydrates; 222 mg of sodium; 327 mg of potassium; and 88 mg of calcium.

Citrus Turkey Salad

½ cup Lime Ginger Dressing (page 342)

4 cups shredded Boston lettuce

2 cups chopped, cooked turkey

3 hard-boiled egg whites, sliced
1½ cups cooked kidney beans
1 cup chopped tomatoes
½ cup chopped celery
¼ cup chopped onion
¼ tsp. garlic powder

Prepare Lime Ginger Dressing according to recipe instructions. Chill thoroughly. In a large salad bowl, combine lettuce and remaining ingredients. Pour chilled dressing over salad and toss. Serves 4.

(Serving = 1 lean protein; ½ starchy carbohydrate; 1 lean, fibrous vegetable)
NUTRIENTS: 253 calories; 34.3 grams of protein; 1.9 grams of fat; 21.9 grams of carbohydrates; 123 mg of sodium; 903 mg of potassium; and 65 mg of calcium.

Southern Pea Salad

3 cups cooked black-eyed peas
1 cup chopped tomatoes
⅓ cup chopped green onion
2 tbsp. chopped green chilies
1 tsp. chopped canned jalapenos
¼ cup nonfat yogurt
½ tsp. dried marjoram
1 tsp. dried celery flakes
2 tbsp. rice wine vinegar
¼ tsp. garlic powder
⅛ tsp. black pepper

In a salad bowl, combine black-eyed peas, tomatoes, green onion, green chilies, and jalapenos. In a small bowl, combine remaining ingredients. Pour over vegetables. Toss. Chill several hours before serving. Serves 4.

(Serving = 1 starchy carbohydrate; ½ lean, fibrous vegetable)
NUTRIENTS: 95 calories; 6.3 grams of protein; 0.8 grams of fat;
16.5 grams of carbohydrates; 11 mg of sodium; 411 mg of potassium;
and 41 mg of calcium.

English Pea and Rice Salad

2 cups cooked brown rice
1 cup cooked peas
½ cup chopped celery
2 tbsp. chopped pimientos
¼ cup nonfat yogurt
¼ cup chicken broth, defatted
1 tbsp. chopped fresh parsley
1 tsp. dried summer savory
⅛ tsp. black pepper

In a salad bowl, combine brown rice, peas, celery, and pimientos. In a small bowl, combine remaining ingredients. Pour over vegetables. Toss. Chill several hours before serving. Serves 4.

(Serving = 1 starchy carbohydrate)
NUTRIENTS: 154 calories; 5.3 grams of protein; 5.8 grams of fat;
27.6 grams of carbohydrates; 480 mg of sodium; 161 mg of potassium;
and 46 mg of calcium.

Fiesta Bean Salad

⅓ cup Yogurt Thousand Island Dressing (page 347)
3 cups cooked kidney beans
1 cup julienned zucchini
½ cup sliced celery
½ cup sliced red onion, separated into rings
3 hard-boiled egg whites, sliced

Prepare Yogurt Thousand Island Dressing according to recipe instructions. In a salad bowl, combine remaining ingredients. Pour dressing over salad. Toss. Chill several hours before serving. Serves 4.

(Serving = ¼ lean protein; 1 starchy carbohydrate; ½ lean, fibrous vegetable)
NUTRIENTS: 197 calories; 14.3 grams of protein; 0.7 grams of fat; 36.3 grams of carbohydrates; 199 mg of sodium; 675 mg of potassium; and 72 mg of calcium.

Triple Bean Salad

¼ cup Spicy Vinaigrette (page 343)
1½ cups cooked lima beans
1½ cups cooked garbanzo beans
1½ cups cooked French-style green beans
2 tbsp. chopped pimientos
2 tbsp. chopped fresh parsley

Prepare Spicy Vinaigrette according to recipe instructions. In a salad bowl, combine remaining ingredients. Pour dressing over salad. Toss to coat. Chill several hours before serving. Serves 4.

(Serving = 1 starchy carbohydrate; ½ lean, fibrous vegetable)
NUTRIENTS: 383 calories; 22.1 grams of protein; 4.2 grams of fat;
67.3 grams of carbohydrates; 23 mg of sodium; 1105 mg of potassium;
and 157 mg of calcium.

Red Potato and Pea Salad

2 lbs. new potatoes

2 cups frozen peas

1 tbsp. cornstarch

⅔ cup chicken broth, defatted

1 tsp. dried dill weed

1 tbsp. lemon juice

½ tsp. dried parsley flakes

⅛ tsp. garlic powder

¼ tsp. hickory liquid smoke

Wash new potatoes. Cut in half. Cook in boiling water until just
tender. Cool. Cut into chunks. Cook peas until just tender. In a
small saucepan, combine cornstarch and broth. Cook over
medium heat until thickened. Stir constantly. Remove from
heat. Add remaining ingredients. In a salad bowl, combine
potatoes, peas, and thickened sauce. Toss. Refrigerate several
hours or overnight before serving. Serves 4.

(Serving = 2 starchy carbohydrates)
NUTRIENTS: 209 calories; 8.1 grams of protein; 0.8 grams of fat;
44.8 grams of carbohydrates; 326 mg of sodium; 864 mg of potassium;
and 82 mg of calcium.

Pea and Cauliflower Salad

3 cups cooked peas

1 cup chopped cauliflower

1 cup shredded carrots

¼ cup nonfat yogurt

1 tbsp. lime juice

1 tsp. dried mint flakes

½ tsp. dried celery flakes

1 dash white pepper

In a salad bowl, combine peas, cauliflower, and carrots. In a small bowl, combine remaining ingredients. Pour over vegetables. Toss. Chill several hours before serving. Serves 4.

(Serving = 1 starchy carbohydrate; ½ lean, fibrous vegetable)
NUTRIENTS: 111 calories; 7.9 grams of protein; 0.8 grams of fat;
19.2 grams of carbohydrates; 324 mg of sodium; 299 mg of potassium;
and 69 mg of calcium.

Potato and Green Bean Salad

3 cups cubed, cooked potatoes

3 cups cooked green beans

¼ cup nonfat yogurt

1 tbsp. dried celery flakes

1 tbsp. white wine vinegar

¼ tsp. garlic powder

1 tsp. instant minced onion flakes

⅛ tsp. black pepper

In a salad bowl, combine potatoes and green beans. In a small bowl, combine remaining ingredients. Pour over vegetables. Toss. Chill several hours before serving. Serves 4.

(Serving = 1 starchy carbohydrate; 1 lean, fibrous vegetable)
NUTRIENTS: 106 calories; 4.2 grams of protein; 0.5 grams of fat; 22.8 grams of carbohydrates; 13 mg of sodium; 493 mg of potassium; and 70 mg of calcium.

Southwestern Potato Salad

2 cups cubed, cooked potatoes
1 cup cooked kidney beans
⅓ cup chopped celery
⅓ cup chopped green onion
⅔ cup chopped tomatoes
2 tbsp. red wine vinegar
2 tbsp. chicken broth, defatted
½ tsp. garlic powder
1 tsp. chili powder

In a salad bowl, combine potatoes, kidney beans, celery, and green onion. In a small bowl, combine remaining ingredients. Pour over vegetables. Toss. Chill several hours before serving. Serves 4.

(Serving = 1 starchy carbohydrate; ¼ lean, fibrous vegetable)
NUTRIENTS: 117 calories; 5.6 grams of protein; 0.4 grams of fat; 25.3 grams of carbohydrates; 20 mg of sodium; 493 mg of potassium; and 32 mg of calcium.

Spicy Potato Salad

⅓ cup Spicy Vinaigrette (page 343)

3 cups cubed potatoes

½ cup sliced red onion, separated into rings

1 cup sliced celery

½ cup sliced radishes

1 tsp. dried vegetable flakes

½ tsp. Italian herb seasoning

Prepare Spicy Vinaigrette according to recipe instructions.
Cook potatoes in boiling water until near tender. Drain and
cool. In a salad bowl, combine potatoes, onion, celery, radishes,
and seasonings. Pour dressing over salad. Toss gently. Chill
several hours before serving. Serves 4.

(Serving = 1 starchy carbohydrate; ½ lean, fibrous vegetable)
NUTRIENTS: 88 calories; 2.7 grams of protein; 0.2 grams of fat;
19.9 grams of carbohydrates; 36 mg of sodium; 450 mg of potassium;
and 22 mg of calcium.

Asparagus Salad Vinaigrette

⅓ cup Tarragon Vinaigrette (page 343)

4 cups asparagus spears

¼ cup water

2 tbsp. chopped pimientos

Boston lettuce leaves

Prepare Tarragon Vinaigrette according to recipe instructions.
In a medium-sized, microwaveable dish, combine asparagus
and water. Cover. Microwave on high 5 to 6 minutes until

asparagus is just tender. Drain. Pour dressing over asparagus. Top with pimientos. Cover and chill several hours. Serve on lettuce leaves. Serves 4.

(Serving = 1 lean, fibrous vegetable)
NUTRIENTS: 38 calories; 3.5 grams of protein; 0.4 grams of fat;
7.5 grams of carbohydrates; 37 mg of sodium; 5 mg of potassium; and
31 mg of calcium.

Broccoli Confetti Salad

3 cups broccoli florets
⅓ cup water
3 tbsp. chicken broth, defatted
3 tbsp. lemon juice
2 tbsp. minced green onion
¼ tsp. garlic powder
¼ tsp. dry mustard
⅛ tsp. black pepper
1 cup alfalfa sprouts
2 hard-boiled egg whites, chopped
¼ cup sliced radishes

In a microwaveable dish, combine broccoli and water. Cover and microwave 6 minutes. Drain. In a small covered jar, combine broth, lemon juice, green onion, garlic powder, dry mustard, and pepper. Shake well. Pour over broccoli. Cover and chill several hours. To serve, combine broccoli and alfalfa sprouts. Top with egg whites and radishes. Serves 4.

(Serving = 1 lean, fibrous vegetable)
NUTRIENTS: 51 calories; 6.4 grams of protein; 0.4 grams of fat;
5.4 grams of carbohydrates; 56 mg of sodium; 371 mg of potassium;
and 57 mg of calcium.

_____

Chilled Broccoli Salad

⅓ cup Yogurt Marjoram Dressing (page 345)
2 cups chopped broccoli florets
1 cup thinly sliced carrots
1 cup julienned jicama

Prepare Yogurt Marjoram Dressing according to recipe instructions. Place vegetables in a bowl. Pour dressing over vegetables. Toss. Chill 2 to 4 hours before serving. Serves 4.

(Serving = 1 lean, fibrous vegetable)
NUTRIENTS: 32 calories; 2.5 grams of protein; 0.2 grams of fat;
6.3 grams of carbohydrates; 28 mg of sodium; 260 mg of potassium; and
40 mg of calcium.

_____

Gala Coleslaw

4 cups shredded cabbage
2 cups shredded carrots
¼ cup thinly sliced celery
¼ cup thinly sliced green onion
¼ cup nonfat yogurt
⅛ tsp. dry mustard
1 tsp. dried dill weed
1 tsp. dried vegetable flakes

⅛ tsp. onion powder

⅛ tsp. white pepper

½ tsp. caraway seeds

In a salad bowl, combine cabbage, carrots, celery, and green onion. In a small bowl, combine remaining ingredients. Pour over vegetables. Toss. Cover and chill several hours. Serves 4.

(Serving = 1 lean, fibrous vegetable)
NUTRIENTS: 59 calories; 2.7 grams of protein; 0.6 grams of fat; 13.3 grams of carbohydrates; 61 mg of sodium; 452 mg of potassium; and 96 mg of calcium.

Summer Cauliflower Salad

½ cup Spicy Vinaigrette (page 343)

2 cups cauliflower florets

¼ cup water

1½ cups sliced zucchini

½ cup julienned green pepper

¼ cup chopped pimientos

Prepare Spicy Vinaigrette according to recipe instructions. In a medium-sized, microwaveable dish, combine cauliflower and water. Cover. Microwave 4 minutes. Drain. Add zucchini, green pepper, and pimientos. Pour dressing over vegetables. Cover and chill several hours or overnight. Stir twice. Drain to serve. Serves 4.

(Serving = 1 lean, fibrous vegetable)
NUTRIENTS: 38 calories; 2.3 grams of protein; 0.3 grams of fat;

8.4 grams of carbohydrates; 218 mg of sodium; 323 mg of potassium; and 25 mg of calcium.

_____

Marinated Cucumbers

4 cups sliced cucumbers
1 onion, sliced and separated into rings
1 tomato, wedge cut
1½ cups cider vinegar
½ cup water
½ tsp. dried marjoram
1½ tsp. salt-free herb seasoning
⅜ tsp. black pepper

In a 2-quart bowl, layer cucumbers and onion. Place tomatoes on top. Combine remaining ingredients. Pour over vegetables. Refrigerate several hours or overnight. Stir occasionally. Serves 6.

(Serving = 1 lean, fibrous vegetable)
NUTRIENTS: 38 calories; 1.2 grams of protein; 0.2 grams of fat; 10.9 grams of carbohydrates; 7 mg of sodium; 305 mg of potassium; and 31 mg of calcium.

_____

Dilled Cucumbers and Radishes

¼ cup Yogurt Dill Dressing (page 345)
3 cups sliced cucumbers
1 cup sliced radishes
½ cup sliced green onion

Prepare Yogurt Dill Dressing according to recipe instructions. Place vegetables in a bowl. Pour dressing over vegetables. Toss. Chill 2 to 4 hours before serving. Serves 4.

(Serving = 1 lean, fibrous vegetable)
NUTRIENTS: 20 calories; 1.0 grams of protein; 0.1 grams of fat; 4.5 grams of carbohydrates; 7 mg of sodium; 159 mg of potassium; and 25 mg of calcium.

Beans and Cauliflower Dijonnaise

⅓ cup Mustard Dill Vinaigrette (page 342)
2 cups frozen green beans
½ cup water
2 cups cauliflower florets

Prepare Mustard Dill Vinaigrette according to recipe instructions. In a medium-sized, microwaveable dish, combine green beans and water. Cover. Microwave on high 6 minutes. Add cauliflower. Microwave 3 minutes. Drain. Pour dressing over vegetables. Toss. Cover and chill several hours or overnight. Stir twice. Drain to serve. Serves 4.

(Serving = 1 lean, fibrous vegetable)
NUTRIENTS: 35 calories; 2.6 grams of protein; 0.3 grams of fat; 7.7 grams of carbohydrates; 10 mg of sodium; 269 mg of potassium; and 45 mg of calcium.

Marinated Green Bean Medley

½ cup Italian Vinaigrette (page 339)
1½ cups frozen green beans
¼ cup water
1½ cups sliced zucchini
1 tomato, wedge cut
1 small onion, sliced and separated into rings
2 tbsp. chopped fresh parsley

Prepare Italian Vinaigrette according to recipe instructions. In a medium-sized, microwaveable dish, combine green beans and water. Cover. Microwave on high 6 to 8 minutes until near tender. Drain. Add zucchini, tomatoes, onion, and parsley. Pour vinaigrette over salad. Toss. Cover. Chill several hours or overnight. Stir twice. Drain to serve. Serves 4.

(Serving = 1 lean, fibrous vegetable)
NUTRIENTS: 48 calories; 2.2 grams of protein; 0.3 grams of fat; 11.7 grams of carbohydrates; 216 mg of sodium; 370 mg of potassium; and 44 mg of calcium.

Savory Red and Green Salad

⅓ cup Basil Vinaigrette (page 338)
1 cup chopped tomatoes
½ cup chopped fresh parsley
½ cup chopped green onion
6 cups torn Boston lettuce
2 tbsp. Toasted Oats (page 379)

Prepare Basil Vinaigrette according to recipe instructions.

In a salad bowl, combine tomatoes, parsley, green onions, and vinaigrette. Toss. Chill several hours. Add lettuce and toss. Sprinkle with Toasted Oats and serve. Serves 4.

(Serving = 1 lean, fibrous vegetable)
NUTRIENTS: 61 calories; 3.5 grams of protein; 0.8 grams of fat; 11.6 grams of carbohydrates; 14 mg of sodium; 462 mg of potassium; and 53 mg of calcium.

Classic Caesar Salad

1 clove garlic, pressed
1 tbsp. safflower oil
1 head romaine lettuce
1 egg (yolk to be discarded)
1 small lemon
1 tsp. paprika
½ tsp. salt-free herb seasoning
⅛ tsp. black pepper
¼ tsp. red wine vinegar
¼ tsp. dry mustard

Crush garlic and soak in oil. Set aside while preparing salad. Wash romaine. Drain thoroughly. Dry with paper towels. Tear romaine into bite-size pieces. Place romaine in a chilled bowl. Coddle egg in boiling water for 1 minute. Break egg and discard yolk. Add egg white to romaine and toss. Cut lemon in half. Thoroughly squeeze juice over romaine. Toss. Add paprika, herb seasoning, pepper, red wine vinegar, and dry mustard. Toss thoroughly. Remove garlic from oil. Discard garlic. Pour oil over romaine and toss. Serve immediately. Serves 4.

(Serving = 1 lean, fibrous vegetable)
NUTRIENTS: 39 calories; 1.2 grams of protein; 3.5 grams of fat;
0.9 grams of carbohydrates; 14 mg of sodium; 78 mg of potassium; and
18 mg of calcium.

Summer Spinach Salad

⅓ cup Lemon Soy Dressing (page 341)
6 cups spinach, washed and torn
2 cups fresh sprouts (mung, bean, or alfalfa)
½ cup thinly sliced cucumber

Prepare Lemon Soy Dressing according to recipe instructions.
Shake well and chill. In a salad bowl, combine spinach, sprouts,
and cucumber. Toss. Just before serving, pour dressing over
salad and toss. Serves 4.

(Serving = 1 lean, fibrous vegetable)
NUTRIENTS: 44 calories; 5.4 grams of protein; 0.6 grams of fat;
4.1 grams of carbohydrates; 74 mg of sodium; 560 mg of potassium; and
105 mg of calcium.

Salad a L'Orange

⅓ cup Lemon Mustard Vinaigrette (page 340)
½ tsp. dried orange peel
4 cups torn Boston lettuce
4 cups torn fresh spinach
1 cup sliced mushrooms
¼ cup chopped pimientos
1 small red onion, sliced and separated into rings

Prepare Lemon Mustard Vinaigrette according to recipe instructions. Add orange peel to vinaigrette. Chill several hours. In a large salad bowl, combine lettuce, spinach, mushrooms, pimientos, and red onion. Shake salad dressing and pour over salad. Toss and serve immediately. Serves 4.

(Serving = 1 lean, fibrous vegetable)
NUTRIENTS: 35 calories; 2.6 grams of protein; 0.4 grams of fat; 6.7 grams of carbohydrates; 27 mg of sodium; 308 mg of potassium; and 62 mg of calcium.

Dilled Tomatoes

½ cup Lemon Dill Vinaigrette (page 340)
4 cups wedge-cut tomatoes
2 tbsp. chopped fresh parsley
2 tbsp. finely chopped green onion

Prepare Lemon Dill Vinaigrette according to recipe instructions. Place tomato wedges in a medium bowl. Combine vinaigrette, parsley, and green onion. Mix well and pour over tomatoes. Cover and chill several hours. Drain to serve. Serves 4.

(Serving = 1 lean, fibrous vegetable)
NUTRIENTS: 55 calories; 2.6 grams of protein; 0.5 grams of fat; 11.2 grams of carbohydrates; 5 mg of sodium; 559 mg of potassium; and 23 mg of calcium.

Gazpacho Salad

2 cups chopped tomatoes

1 cup chopped cucumber

¼ cup chopped green onion

¾ cup chopped green pepper

½ cup vegetable juice

2 tbsp. lemon juice

1 tsp. salt-free herb seasoning

½ tsp. garlic powder

1 tsp. dried cilantro

1 tsp. dried parsley flakes

In a salad bowl, combine all ingredients. Chill 2 to 4 hours before serving. Serves 4.

(Serving = 1 lean, fibrous vegetable)
NUTRIENTS: 43 calories; 1.9 grams of protein; 0.3 grams of fat;
9.1 grams of carbohydrates; 95 mg of sodium; 418 mg of potassium;
and 22 mg of calcium. _____

Basil Vinaigrette

⅓ cup red wine vinegar

⅓ cup chicken broth, defatted

2 tbsp. dried basil

½ tsp. garlic powder

¼ tsp. black pepper

1 tsp. dried thyme

In a small covered jar, shake all ingredients. Refrigerate and use as needed. Makes ⅔ cup.

NUTRIENTS: 18 calories; 0.4 grams of protein; 0.4 grams of fat; 4.7 grams of carbohydrates; 495 mg of sodium; 88 mg of potassium; and 10 mg of calcium.

Italian Vinaigrette

⅔ cup cider vinegar

¼ cup dry white wine

2 tbsp. safflower oil

1 tsp. salt-free herb seasoning

1 tsp. garlic powder

½ tsp. paprika

1 tsp. Italian herb seasoning

In a small covered jar, shake all ingredients. Refrigerate and use as needed. Makes 1 cup.

NUTRIENTS: 312 calories; 0.1 grams of protein; 27.2 grams of fat; 10.9 grams of carbohydrates; 3 mg of sodium; 215 mg of potassium; and 16 mg of calcium.

Lemon Chive Dressing

¼ cup white wine vinegar

2 tbsp. lemon juice

⅓ cup chicken broth, defatted

1 tsp. paprika

1 tsp. dry mustard

1 tsp. chopped fresh chives

½ tsp. dried oregano

¼ tsp. onion powder

In a small covered jar, shake all ingredients. Refrigerate and use as needed. Makes ⅔ cup.

NUTRIENTS: 15 calories; 0.4 grams of protein; 0.4 grams of fat; 3.7 grams of carbohydrates; 495 mg of sodium; 68 mg of potassium; and 9 mg of calcium. _____

Lemon Dill Vinaigrette

½ cup white wine vinegar
½ cup chicken broth, defatted
¼ cup lemon juice
2 tsp. dried dill weed
2 tsp. dried basil
½ tsp. dried oregano
1 tsp. garlic powder
¼ tsp. black pepper

In a small covered jar, shake all ingredients. Refrigerate and use as needed. Makes 1½ cups.

NUTRIENTS: 26 calories; 0.7 grams of protein; 0.6 grams of fat; 7.1 grams of carbohydrates; 742 mg of sodium; 133 mg of potassium; and 16 mg of calcium. _____

Lemon Mustard Vinaigrette

½ cup red wine vinegar
¼ cup lemon juice

¼ cup chicken broth, defatted

½ tsp. garlic powder

2 tsp. dried parsley flakes

1 tsp. dry mustard

½ tsp. paprika

In a small covered jar, shake all ingredients. Refrigerate and use as needed. Makes 1 cup.

NUTRIENTS: 21 calories; 0.4 grams of protein; 0.3 grams of fat; 6.7 grams of carbohydrates; 371 mg of sodium; 127 mg of potassium; and 12 mg of calcium.

Lemon Soy Dressing

⅓ cup lemon juice

⅓ cup chicken broth, defatted

2 tbsp. low-salt soy sauce

2 tbsp. minced green onion

2 tsp. dried parsley flakes

¼ tsp. garlic powder

In a small covered jar, shake all ingredients. Refrigerate and use as needed. Makes ¾ cup.

NUTRIENTS: 39 calories; 2.7 grams of protein; 3.8 grams of fat; 2.7 grams of carbohydrates; 1697 mg of sodium; 173 mg of potassium; and 40 mg of calcium.

Lime Ginger Dressing

¼ cup chicken broth, defatted

2 tbsp. rice wine vinegar

2 tbsp. lime juice

1 tsp. dried vegetable flakes

1 tsp. dried cilantro

1 tsp. grated, fresh, ginger root

⅛ tsp. white pepper

In a small covered jar, shake all ingredients. Refrigerate and use
as needed. Makes ½ cup.

*NUTRIENTS: 11 calories; 0.4 grams of protein; 0.3 grams of fat;
2.8 grams of carbohydrates; 371 mg of sodium; 52 mg of potassium;
and 7 mg of calcium.*

Mustard Dill Vinaigrette

⅔ cup cider vinegar

¼ cup chicken broth, defatted

2 tsp. Dijon mustard

2 tsp. dried celery flakes

1 tsp. onion powder

2 tsp. dried parsley flakes

1 tsp. dried dill weed

In a small covered jar, shake all ingredients. Refrigerate and use
as needed. Makes 1 cup.

*NUTRIENTS: 26 calories; 0.4 grams of protein; 0.3 grams of fat;
8.9 grams of carbohydrates; 371 mg of sodium; 166 mg of potassium;
and 15 mg of calcium.*

Spicy Vinaigrette

⅔ cup cider vinegar

⅓ cup chicken broth, defatted

1½ tsp. dry mustard

1 tsp. dried basil

1 tsp. dried oregano

1 tsp. paprika

¼ tsp. garlic powder

¼ tsp. cayenne pepper

In a small covered jar, shake all ingredients. Refrigerate and use as needed. Makes 1 cup.

NUTRIENTS: 74 calories; 9.7 grams of protein; 1.3 grams of fat; 8.5 grams of carbohydrates; 22 mg of sodium; 220 mg of potassium; and 15 mg of calcium.

Tarragon Vinaigrette

½ cup tarragon vinegar

¼ cup chicken broth, defatted

2 tbsp. chopped pimiento

2 tbsp. chopped dill pickle

½ tsp. onion powder

2 tsp. dried parsley flakes

¼ tsp. black pepper

¼ tsp. dried lemon peel

In a small covered jar, shake all ingredients. Refrigerate and use as needed. Makes 1 cup.

NUTRIENTS: 35 calories; 0.8 grams of protein; 0.6 grams of fat; 9.6 grams of carbohydrates; 371 mg of sodium; 127 mg of potassium; and 16 mg of calcium. _____

Vegetable French Dressing

½ cup cider vinegar
½ cup vegetable juice
2 tbsp. lemon juice
¼ cup chopped onion
¼ cup chopped cucumber
2 tsp. dried vegetable flakes
½ tsp. dried celery flakes
½ tsp. garlic powder
⅛ tsp. black pepper

In a blender, combine all ingredients. Blend until well mixed. Chill several hours before serving. Makes 1½ cups.

NUTRIENTS: 62 calories; 1.5 grams of protein; 0.1 grams of fat; 16.3 grams of carbohydrates; 363 mg of sodium; 491 mg of potassium; and 43 mg of calcium. _____

Yogurt Cucumber and Radish Dressing

½ cup nonfat yogurt
½ cup chopped cucumber
¼ cup sliced radishes
¼ cup chopped green onion
1 tsp. dried celery flakes

⅛ tsp. garlic powder

In a small bowl, combine all ingredients. Chill several hours before serving. Makes 1½ cups.

NUTRIENTS: 80 calories; 4.9 grams of protein; 2.0 grams of fat; 11.3 grams of carbohydrates; 64 mg of sodium; 311 mg of potassium; and 159 mg of calcium.

Yogurt Dill Dressing

½ cup nonfat yogurt
2 tbsp. tarragon vinegar
1½ tsp. dried dill weed
1 tsp. salt-free herb seasoning

In a small bowl, combine all ingredients. Chill several hours before serving. Makes ⅔ cup.

NUTRIENTS: 62 calories; 3.8 grams of protein; 1.9 grams of fat; 8.3 grams of carbohydrates; 57 mg of sodium; 206 mg of potassium; and 138 mg of calcium.

Yogurt Marjoram Dressing

½ cup nonfat yogurt
2 tbsp. white wine vinegar
2 tsp. dried marjoram
1 tsp. dried vegetable flakes

In a small bowl, combine all ingredients. Chill several hours before serving. Makes ⅔ cup.

NUTRIENTS: 62 calories; 3.8 grams of protein; 1.9 grams of fat; 8.3 grams of carbohydrates; 57 mg of sodium; 206 mg of potassium; and 138 mg of calcium. _____

Yogurt Mint Dressing

½ cup nonfat yogurt
2 tbsp. lime juice
2 tsp. dried mint flakes
1 tsp. dried celery flakes
⅛ tsp. white pepper

In a small bowl, combine all ingredients. Chill several hours before serving. Makes ⅔ cup.

NUTRIENTS: 56 calories; 3.8 grams of protein; 1.9 grams of fat; 5.9 grams of carbohydrates; 57 mg of sodium; 161 mg of potassium; and 135 mg of calcium. _____

Yogurt Thousand Island Dressing

½ cup nonfat yogurt
1 tbsp. tomato paste
1 tbsp. dried vegetable flakes
½ tsp. instant minced onion flakes
¼ tsp. garlic powder
⅛ tsp. black pepper

In a small bowl, combine all ingredients. Chill several hours before serving. Makes ½ cup.

NUTRIENTS: 69 calories; 4.4 grams of protein; 2.0 grams of fat; 8.9 grams of carbohydrates; 64 mg of sodium; 301 mg of potassium; and 146 mg of calcium.

12

❦ *Hints for Desserts*

Helpful Hints

Store strawberries (and other berries) unwashed in a clean and airtight container. Berries keep their flavor for several days if properly refrigerated.

Make whipped toppings from nonfat milk products. Skim milk, nonfat dry milk, and evaporated skimmed milk will eventually whip if cold enough. Sweeten with vanilla and sugar substitute.

Sugar is sugar no matter what the source. Avoid sugar, whether it's from sugar cane, beets, molasses, brown sugar, honey, corn syrup, or fructose.

NutraSweet should not be used in cooked desserts because prolonged exposure to heat causes sweetness loss. Add immediately after cooking.

Vanilla adds sweetness to recipes. Increase vanilla amount to give an apparent sweetness boost.

Use nonstick cooking sprays instead of greasing pans and sheets.

Substitute dry-curd cottage cheese or Mock Cream Cheese (page 370) for cream cheese.

Substitute nonfat yogurt or Mock Sour Cream (page 369) for sour cream.

Substitute evaporated skimmed milk for creams in recipes.

Use skim milk in place of whole milk.

Avoid toppings which contain coconut oils.

Sweet Potato Chiffon Pie

1 tbsp. unflavored gelatin

¼ cup water

1 cup evaporated skimmed milk

2 cups mashed, cooked sweet potatoes

1 tsp. cinnamon

¼ tsp. ground ginger

¼ tsp. nutmeg

12 packets sugar substitute

1 tsp. vanilla extract

1 tsp. maple flavoring

3 egg whites

One 9-inch baked and cooled Basic Pie Crust (page 353)

Soften gelatin in water for 2 minutes. In a small saucepan, combine evaporated milk and softened gelatin. Heat until gelatin dissolves. Remove from heat. In a mixing bowl, combine sweet potatoes, cinnamon, ginger, nutmeg, sugar substitute, vanilla, and maple flavoring. Beat until smooth. Add gelatin mixture. Beat until blended. Chill 20 minutes, until slightly thickened. Beat egg whites until stiff. Fold into sweet potato mixture. Pour into pie shell. Chill several hours until firm. Serves 8.

NUTRIENTS: 201 calories; 8.4 grams of protein; 6.3 grams of fat; 28.8

grams of carbohydrates; 98 mg of sodium; 358 mg of potassium; and 159 mg of calcium.

Strawberry Chiffon Pie

One 3-oz. pkg. sugar-free strawberry gelatin
¾ cup boiling water
1 pint fresh strawberries
1 tbsp. lemon juice
4 packets sugar substitute
1 tsp. strawberry extract
2 egg whites
1 recipe Whipped Dessert Topping (page 355)
One 9-inch baked and cooled Lemon Pie Crust (page 354)

In a mixing bowl, dissolve gelatin in boiling water. Set aside.
Wash and hull strawberries. In a blender, combine strawberries, lemon juice, sugar substitute, and strawberry extract.
Blend until berries are crushed. Combine berries with gelatin.
Chill 20 to 30 minutes until partially set. Stir occasionally. Beat
egg whites until stiff peaks form. Fold into strawberry mixture.
Fold in Whipped Dessert Topping. Pour into pie shell. Chill
several hours until firm. Serves 8.

NUTRIENTS: 154 calories; 6.1 grams of protein; 6.6 grams of fat; 18.6 grams of carbohydrates; 34 mg of sodium; 244 mg of potassium; and 70 mg of calcium.

Pink Lemonade Pie

1 cup evaporated skimmed milk

1 envelope unflavored gelatin

½ cup water

1 packet sugar-free pink lemonade drink mix

1 tsp. lemon extract

½ tsp. dried lemon peel

1 tsp. vanilla extract

1 cup Mock Cream Cheese (page 370)

6 packets sugar substitute

One 9-inch baked and cooled Lemon Pie Crust (page 354)

In a mixing bowl, chill evaporated milk in the freezer until ice crystals form around edges. In a small saucepan, soften gelatin in water for 2 minutes. Heat until gelatin is dissolved. Remove from heat. Stir in drink mix, lemon extract, lemon peel, vanilla, Mock Cream Cheese, and sugar substitute. Chill until mixture begins to thicken. Remove bowl from freezer. Place in a large bowl of ice cubes. Whip chilled milk 8 to 10 minutes until stiff peaks form. Immediately fold into thickened gelatin mixture. Pour into pie shell. Chill several hours until firm. Serves 8.

NUTRIENTS: 168 calories; 7.2 grams of protein; 8.2 grams of fat; 17.3 grams of carbohydrates; 46 mg of sodium; 225 mg of potassium; and 117 mg of calcium.

Basic Pie Crust

¾ cup oat flour

¼ cup rye flour

¼ cup oat bran

3 tbsp. safflower oil

3 tbsp. ice water

2 tbsp. nonfat buttermilk

Preheat oven to 375 degrees. In a mixing bowl, combine flours
and oat bran. Stir in oil, ice water, and buttermilk. Knead 3 or
4 times. Form into a ball. Cover. Chill 15 minutes. Place
between 2 sheets of wax paper. Roll into 12-inch circle. Place
in 9-inch pie pan. Trim and finish edges. Prick holes in bottom
and sides of crust. Bake 12 to 15 minutes until lightly browned.
Cool. Makes 1 pie crust. Serves 8.

*NUTRIENTS: 103 calories; 2.5 grams of protein; 6.1 grams of fat; 10.8
grams of carbohydrates; 1 mg of sodium; 82 mg of potassium; and 7 mg of
calcium.*

Lemon Pie Crust

1¼ cups oat flour

¼ cup rye flour

½ tsp. dried lemon peel

3 tbsp. safflower oil

3 tbsp. skim milk

Preheat oven to 375 degrees. In a mixing bowl, combine flours
and lemon peel. Stir in oil and milk. Press mixture on bottom
and sides of 9-inch pie pan. Bake 12 to 15 minutes until lightly
browned. Cool. Makes 1 pie crust. Serves 8.

*NUTRIENTS: 120 calories; 3.0 grams of protein; 6.4 grams of fat; 13.6
grams of carbohydrates; 2 mg of sodium; 96 mg of potassium; and 15
mg of calcium.*

Whipped Topping

½ tsp. unflavored gelatin

2 tbsp. water

½ cup nonfat dry milk

2 packets sugar substitute

1 tsp. lemon juice

½ tsp. vanilla extract

¼ cup ice water

Chill mixing bowl and beaters in the freezer. In a small microwaveable bowl, soften gelatin in 2 tablespoons water for 2 minutes. Microwave 20 to 30 seconds until gelatin is dissolved. Cool to lukewarm. Remove bowl from freezer. Combine nonfat dry milk, sugar substitute, lemon juice, vanilla, and ice water. Place in a large bowl of ice cubes. Whip 6 to 10 minutes, gradually adding gelatin mixture, until stiff peaks form. Makes 2 cups.

NUTRIENTS: 287 calories; 28.6 grams of protein; 0.6 grams of fat; 41.2 grams of carbohydrates; 424 mg of sodium; 1421 mg of potassium; and 995 mg of calcium.

Whipped Dessert Topping

¾ tsp. unflavored gelatin

½ cup evaporated skimmed milk, divided use

2 packets sugar substitute

1 tsp. lemon juice

½ tsp. vanilla extract

In a microwaveable bowl, soften gelatin in 2 tablespoons

evaporated milk for 2 minutes. Microwave 20 to 30 seconds until gelatin is dissolved. In a mixing bowl, combine dissolved gelatin with remaining evaporated milk. Chill in freezer until ice crystals form around edges. Whip until soft peaks form. Add sugar substitute, vanilla, and lemon juice. Whip until stiff. Cover. Refrigerate. Use as whipped cream. Keeps several days. Makes 2 cups.

NUTRIENTS: 99 calories; 9.7 grams of protein; 0.3 grams of fat; 14.5 grams of carbohydrates; 147 mg of sodium; 423 mg of potassium; and 369 mg of calcium.

Carrot Oatmeal Cookies

1½ cups oat flour
½ cup rye flour
1 cup old-fashioned oatmeal
1 tsp. baking powder
½ tsp. baking soda
¼ tsp. ground ginger
3 egg whites
¼ cup safflower oil
⅓ cup nonfat yogurt
2 tsp. pineapple extract
½ tsp. coconut extract
1 tsp. vanilla extract
1 cup cooked carrots
8 packets sugar substitute
2 tsp. water

Preheat oven to 375 degrees. In a mixing bowl, combine oat flour, rye flour, oatmeal, baking powder, baking soda, and ginger. Add egg whites, oil, yogurt, and extracts. Mix until blended. Stir in carrots. Drop by rounded teaspoonfuls onto baking sheets. Bake 10 to 12 minutes. Remove from oven. Combine sugar substitute and water. Brush over cookies. Cool. Makes 48 cookies. Serves 12.

NUTRIENTS: 150 calories; 5.1 grams of protein; 6.3 grams of fat; 19.2 grams of carbohydrates; 20 mg of sodium; 168 mg of potassium; and 26 mg of calcium.

Oatmeal Bars

1 cup oat flour
1 cup old-fashioned oatmeal
½ cup rye flour
½ cup nonfat dry milk
1 tsp. cinnamon
¼ cup safflower oil
¼ cup water
1 tsp. butter flavoring
1 tbsp. cornstarch
¼ cup water
1 cup grated Granny Smith apple
½ cup mashed, cooked sweet potatoes
1 tsp. maple flavoring
8 packets sugar substitute
1 tbsp. water

Preheat oven to 375 degrees. In a mixing bowl, combine oat flour, oatmeal, rye flour, dry milk, and cinnamon. Add oil, ¼ cup water, and butter flavoring. Stir until dough holds together. Set aside. In a small saucepan, combine cornstarch, ¼ cup water, and grated apple. Heat and stir until thickened. Stir in sweet potatoes. Press half of the cookie dough into an 8" x 8" x 2" pan. Spread on sweet potato mixture. Crumble remaining dough over filling. Press down. Bake 30 to 35 minutes until golden brown. Remove from oven. Combine sugar substitute and 1 tablespoon water. Brush over top. Cool. Cut into bars. Makes 16 bars. Serves 8.

NUTRIENTS: 236 calories; 7.8 grams of protein; 9.0 grams of fat; 33.3 grams of carbohydrates; 46 mg of sodium; 335 mg of potassium; and 115 mg of calcium.

Maplelike Oat Crinkles

1½ cups oat flour
½ cup rye flour
½ cup old-fashioned oatmeal
1 tsp. baking powder
¼ tsp. baking soda
⅓ cup nonfat yogurt
¼ cup safflower oil
1 tsp. butter flavoring
1 tsp. vanilla extract
1 tsp. maple flavoring
2 egg whites
8 packets sugar substitute
2 tsp. water

Preheat oven to 375 degrees. In a large bowl, combine oat flour, rye flour, oatmeal, baking powder, and baking soda. Add yogurt, oil, butter flavoring, vanilla, maple flavoring, and egg whites. Stir until blended. Drop by rounded teaspoonfuls onto baking sheet. Bake 10 to 12 minutes until golden. Makes 36. Serves 9.

NUTRIENTS: 171 calories; 5.4 grams of protein; 8.0 grams of fat; 20.5 grams of carbohydrates; 15 mg of sodium; 161 mg of potassium; and 26 mg of calcium.

Apple-Cranberry Crisp

2 cups cranberries
4 Granny Smith apples, thinly sliced
1 tsp. cinnamon
½ tsp. nutmeg
¼ cup water
12 packets sugar substitute
2 tbsp. oat flour
¾ cup old-fashioned oatmeal
⅓ cup oat bran
3 tbsp. rye flour
4 packets sugar substitute
2 tbsp. safflower oil

In a mixing bowl, combine cranberries, apples, cinnamon, nutmeg, ¼ cup water, 12 packets sugar substitute, and 2 tablespoons oat flour. Pour into 10-inch microwaveable dish. Cover with waxed paper. Microwave on high for 5 minutes. Combine oatmeal, oat bran, rye flour, 4 packets sugar substitute, and oil. Sprinkle over apple mixture. Microwave 8 to 10 minutes until tender and bubbly. Serves 8.

NUTRIENTS: 147 calories; 3.3 grams of protein; 5.0 grams of fat; 25 grams of carbohydrates; 1 mg of sodium; 184 mg of potassium; and 14 mg of calcium.

13

Snacks, Dips, and Mini-Meals

Helpful Hints

Low-fat cottage cheese (1% fat) may be substituted for dry-curd cottage cheese. Rinse low-fat cottage cheese before using. Drain thoroughly, squeezing out any excess moisture.

Hollow out a purple cabbage to use as an attractive serving bowl for dips. Serve with a variety of fresh vegetables.

Spray air-popped popcorn with nonstick cooking spray. Shake on garlic powder, butter sprinkles, salt-free herb seasoning, or other seasonings.

A bowl of bean soup, heated in the microwave, makes a great mini-meal.

Store vegetables for a snack. To store vegetables, moisten a white paper towel. Wrap cut vegetables in it. Place in a plastic bag or airtight container. Store in refrigerator for several days.

Make dips from nonfat yogurt or Mock Sour Cream (page 369).

Don't keep high-salt, -fat, or -sugar snack foods in the house.

Make fruit slushes by using sugar-free drink mixes, fresh fruit, and ice mixed in a blender.

Black Bean Dip

2 cups cooked Cuban Black Beans (page 185)
1 tbsp. lime juice
1 tbsp. minced fresh cilantro
½ cup chunky picante sauce
¼ cup Mock Sour Cream (page 369)
Spicy Corn Chips (page 374)

In a small saucepan, combine Cuban Black Beans, lime juice, and cilantro. Heat until bubbly. Mound beans on a serving plate. Top with picante sauce and Mock Sour Cream. Serve with chips. Makes 2 cups. Serves 8.

NUTRIENTS: 34 calories; 1.9 grams of protein; 0.3 grams of fat; 6.1 grams of carbohydrates; 222 mg of sodium; 110 mg of potassium; and 15 mg of calcium. (Does not include Spicy Corn Chips.)

Dilled Shrimp Dip

⅔ cup dry-curd cottage cheese
⅓ cup nonfat yogurt
2 tsp. lemon juice
1 tsp. horseradish
½ tsp. dried dill weed
1 cup shredded cucumber, drained
½ cup chopped, cooked shrimp
2 tbsp. chopped green onion

In a blender, combine cottage cheese, yogurt, lemon juice, horseradish, and dill weed. Blend until smooth. Squeeze all liquid from shredded cucumber. Add and blend until mixed.

Stir in shrimp and green onion. Chill. Makes 2½ cups.
Serves 8.

*NUTRIENTS: 44 calories; 7.7 grams of protein; 0.5 grams of fat;
1.8 grams of carbohydrates; 58 mg of sodium; 102 mg of potassium;
and 53 mg of calcium.*

Onion Dip

1 cup dry-curd cottage cheese
½ cup nonfat yogurt
1 tbsp. lemon juice
1 tbsp. dry white wine
2 tbsp. instant minced onion flakes
1 tsp. onion powder
½ tsp. garlic powder
2 tsp. no-salt-added, beef-flavored instant bouillon

In a small bowl, combine all ingredients. Cover and chill several
hours. Makes 1½ cups. Serves 6.

*NUTRIENTS: 18 calories; 2.0 grams of protein; 0.4 grams of fat;
1.2 grams of carbohydrates; 18 mg of sodium; 30 mg of potassium;
and 36 mg of calcium.*

Mock Gaucamole

1 cup chopped, cooked asparagus
2 tbsp. chopped onion
1 clove garlic, pressed
2 tbsp. canned chopped green chilies

½ cup dry-curd cottage cheese

2 tbsp. skim milk

1 tbsp. lemon juice

½ tsp. salt-free herb seasoning

⅛ tsp. black pepper

In a blender, combine all ingredients. Blend until smooth. Cover and chill. Makes 1½ cups. Serves 6.

NUTRIENTS: 13 calories; 1.5 grams of protein; 0.1 grams of fat; 1.8 grams of carbohydrates; 7 mg of sodium; 60 mg of potassium; and 20 mg of calcium.

Refried Bean Dip

2 cups Refried Frijoles (page 190)

¾ cup picante sauce

⅓ cup dry-curd cottage cheese

¼ cup sliced green onion

1 tbsp. minced fresh cilantro

¼ tsp. garlic powder

½ tsp. salt-free herb seasoning

Tortilla Chips (page 373)

In a large saucepan, combine all ingredients except chips. Cook over low heat until bubbly. Serve with chips. Makes 3 cups. Serves 12.

NUTRIENTS: 46 calories; 3.1 grams of protein; 0.2 grams of fat; 8.2 grams of carbohydrates; 86 mg of sodium; 138 mg of potassium; and 25 mg of calcium. Does not include tortilla chips.

Herbed Cucumber Dip

1 cup nonfat yogurt
¼ cup chopped cucumber
2 tbsp. chopped green onion
1 tbsp. chopped pimiento
1 tbsp. chopped fresh parsley
1 tbsp. picante sauce
¼ tsp. salt-free herb seasoning
⅛ tsp. garlic powder

In a small bowl, combine all ingredients. Cover. Chill. Makes
1½ cups. Serves 6.

Note: This dish is an excellent sauce for chilled salmon that has
been grilled or broiled. Serve with potato salad for a mini-meal.

NUTRIENTS: 23 calories; 1.4 grams of protein; 0.7 grams of fat;
2.9 grams of carbohydrates; 33 mg of sodium; 71 mg of potassium;
and 48 mg of calcium.

Spinach Dip

1 cup dry-curd cottage cheese
½ cup nonfat yogurt
2 tbsp. lemon juice
½ cup chopped onion
2 tbsp. vegetable flakes
1 tsp. salt-free herb seasoning
¼ tsp. black pepper
⅛ tsp. Tabasco sauce
One 10-oz. pkg. frozen chopped spinach, thawed
¼ cup finely chopped fresh parsley

In a blender, combine cottage cheese, yogurt, lemon juice, onion, vegetable flakes, herb seasoning, pepper, and Tabasco sauce. Blend until smooth. Squeeze all water from spinach. Add spinach and parsley to blended mixture. Cover and chill several hours. Makes 2 cups. Serves 8.

NUTRIENTS: 22 calories; 2.4 grams of protein; 0.4 grams of fat; 2.7 grams of carbohydrates; 34 mg of sodium; 120 mg of potassium; and 56 mg of calcium.

Chili Bean Dip

2 cups cooked kidney beans
⅓ cup chopped tomatoes
¼ cup chopped onion
1 tbsp. red wine vinegar
1 tsp. chili powder
¼ tsp. ground cumin
1 tsp. dried parsley

In a blender, combine all ingredients. Blend until smooth. Cover. Chill. Makes 2 cups. Serves 8.

NUTRIENTS: 60 calories; 3.8 grams of protein; 0.3 grams of fat; 11.0 grams of carbohydrates; 2 mg of sodium; 198 mg of potassium; and 20 mg of calcium.

Green Pea Dip

2 cups cooked peas
¼ cup chopped onion

2 cloves garlic, pressed
⅓ cup Mock Mayo (page 369)
1 tbsp. lemon juice
½ tsp. chili powder
½ tsp. salt-free herb seasoning
⅛ tsp. black pepper

In a blender, combine all ingredients. Blend until smooth.
Cover. Chill. Makes 2 cups. Serves 8.

NUTRIENTS: 36 calories; 3.3 grams of protein; 0.2 grams of fat;
5.4 grams of carbohydrates; 107 mg of sodium; 50 mg of potassium;
and 22 mg of calcium.

Garbanzo Bean Spread

½ cup chopped onion
1 clove garlic, pressed
¼ cup water
3 cups cooked garbanzo beans
½ cup Mock Mayo (page 369)
2 tbsp. lemon juice
1 tsp. dried basil
½ tsp. dried oregano
1 tbsp. minced fresh parsley

In a small skillet, cook onion and garlic in water until tender. In
a blender, combine garbanzo beans, Mock Mayo, lemon juice,
basil, and oregano. Add onion mixture. Blend until smooth. Stir
in parsley. Cover and chill. Makes 3 cups. Serves 12.

Note: Spread on sliced turkey to make a mini-meal.

NUTRIENTS: 184 calories; 10.7 grams of protein; 2.4 grams of fat; 31.2 grams of carbohydrates; 16 mg of sodium; 410 mg of potassium; and 80 mg of calcium.

Mock Sour Cream

1 cup dry-curd cottage cheese
½ cup nonfat yogurt
2 tbsp. skim milk
¼ tsp. salt-free herb seasoning

In a blender, combine all ingredients. Blend until smooth. Makes 1½ cups. Serves 12.

Note: Mock Sour Cream will keep in the refrigerator for several days. Add chives and serve over baked potatoes.

NUTRIENTS: 9 calories; 1.1 grams of protein; 0.2 grams of fat; 0.7 grams of carbohydrates; 10 mg of sodium; 18 mg of potassium; and 21 mg of calcium.

Mock Mayo

1 cup dry-curd cottage cheese
2 tbsp. safflower oil
1 tbsp. cider vinegar
½ tsp. salt-free herb seasoning

In a blender, combine all ingredients. Blend until smooth. Cover. Chill. Makes 1 cup. Serves 16.

*NUTRIENTS: 18 calories; 0.5 grams of protein; 1.7 grams of fat;
0.1 grams of carbohydrates; 3 mg of sodium; 0 mg of potassium; and
5 mg of calcium.*

Mock Cream Cheese

1 cup dry-curd cottage cheese
1 tbsp. safflower oil
1 tbsp. nonfat dry milk
2 tsp. skim milk

In a blender, combine all ingredients. Blend until smooth.
Makes 1 cup. Serves 16.

*NUTRIENTS: 12 calories; 0.7 grams of protein; 0.9 grams of fat;
0.4 grams of carbohydrates; 7 mg of sodium; 12 mg of potassium; and
13 mg of calcium.*

Yogurt Cheese

One 16-oz. container nonfat yogurt

Place a double-thick layer of cheesecloth or paper coffee filters
inside a colander or strainer. Place colander in a deep bowl.
Colander must not touch bottom of bowl. Spoon yogurt into
colander. Cover. Chill overnight. Discard drained liquid. Chill
Yogurt Cheese. Makes 1 cup. Serves 16.

*NUTRIENTS: 14 calories; 1.0 grams of protein; 0.5 grams of fat;
1.5 grams of carbohydrates; 14 mg of sodium; 40 mg of potassium; and
34 mg of calcium.*

Garbanzo Nuts

1 cup dry garbanzo beans, soaked overnight and drained
2 tsp. low-salt soy sauce plus 2 teaspoons water
seasonings to taste
    (onion powder, garlic powder, or paprika)

In a large stock pot, cover beans with water 3 inches higher than beans. Bring to a boil. Cook 10 minutes. Reduce heat. Cover. Simmer 1 to 1½ hours until tender. Drain well. Preheat oven to 350 degrees. Spread beans in a single layer on a nonstick baking pan. Sprinkle with diluted soy sauce and seasonings to taste. Bake 55 to 70 minutes until dry, browned, and toasted. Stir occasionally. Cool. Store in airtight container. Makes 3 cups. Serves 12.

NUTRIENTS: 61 calories; 3.5 grams of protein; 0.9 grams of fat; 10.2 grams of carbohydrates; 54 mg of sodium; 138 mg of potassium; and 26 mg of calcium.

Mock Peanut Butter

1 cup dry garbanzo beans, soaked overnight and drained
2 cups reserved cooking liquid from beans
2 tbsp. cornstarch
1 tbsp. vanilla extract
½ tsp. almond extract
2 tsp. cinnamon
6 packets sugar substitute

In a large stock pot, cover beans with water 3 inches higher than beans. Bring to a boil. Cook 10 minutes. Reduce heat. Cover.

Simmer 1 to 1½ hours until almost tender. Reserve 2 cups cooking liquid. Set aside. Drain beans well. Preheat oven to 350 degrees. Spread beans on a nonstick baking pan. Bake for 55 to 70 minutes until dry, browned, and toasted. Stir occasionally. Grind toasted beans in a food processor or blender. In a medium saucepan, combine cornstarch, vanilla, almond extract, and cinnamon. Mix in reserved cooking liquid. Heat and stir until thickened. Add ground beans and sugar substitute. Store in airtight container. Keep refrigerated. Makes 3 cups. Serves 24. Note: Use as stuffing for celery sticks. Spread on rice cakes or crackers.

NUTRIENTS: 32 calories; 1.7 grams of protein; 0.4 grams of fat; 5.9 grams of carbohydrates; 1 mg of sodium; 117 mg of potassium; and 3 mg of calcium.

Shrimp Cocktail

½ cup picante sauce
¼ cup ketchup
½ tsp. horseradish
1 tsp. lemon juice
½ lb. cooked shrimp, peeled and deveined

In a small bowl, combine all ingredients except shrimp. Chill 1 to 2 hours. Serve with chilled shrimp. Serves 4.

NUTRIENTS: 81 calories; 10.9 grams of protein; 8.7 grams of fat; 3 grams of carbohydrates; 395 mg of sodium; 236 mg of potassium; and 45 mg of calcium.

Irish Nachos

½ recipe Herbed Potato Skins (page 211)
2 cups Bean Dip (page 365)
1 cup picante sauce
1 cup chopped tomatoes
¼ cup chopped green onion
¼ cup Mock Sour Cream (page 369)
¼ cup Mock Guacamole (page 364)

On a large serving plate, arrange Herbed Potato Skins. Top
with Bean Dip. Pour picante sauce over beans and potatoes.
Sprinkle with tomatoes and green onion. Top with Mock Sour
Cream and Mock Guacamole. Serves 4.

*NUTRIENTS: 143 calories; 8.5 grams of protein; 1.1 grams of fat;
25.9 grams of carbohydrates; 501 mg of sodium; 560 mg of potassium;
and 83 mg of calcium.*

Tortilla Chips

12 corn tortillas
seasonings to taste
      (onion powder, garlic powder, ground cumin,
      chili powder, or salt-free herb seasoning)

Preheat oven to 400 degrees. Lightly spray tortillas with
nonstick cooking spray. Cut each tortilla into 6 pie-shaped
wedges. Arrange wedges in a single layer on a nonstick baking
sheet. Sprinkle with seasonings to taste. Bake 6 to 7 minutes
until crisp. Cool. Store in airtight container. Serves 4.

NUTRIENTS: 189 calories; 4.5 grams of protein; 1.8 grams of fat; 40.5 grams of carbohydrates; 0 mg of sodium; 9 mg of potassium; and 180 mg of calcium.

Potato Chips

2 baking potatoes
seasonings to taste
 (onion powder, garlic powder, salt-free herb
 seasoning, chili powder, cheese sprinkles, or dill weed)

Preheat oven to 350 degrees. Using a food processor, slicer, or vegetable peeler, slice potatoes into thin, uniform slices. Spray 2 shallow baking sheets with nonstick cooking spray. Arrange potatoes in a single layer on sheets. Spray potatoes lightly with nonstick cooking spray. Sprinkle with seasonings to taste. Bake 12 to 15 minutes until lightly browned. Serves 2.

NUTRIENTS: 100 calories; 2.6 grams of protein; 0.1 grams of fat; 21.1 grams of carbohydrates; 4 mg of sodium; 503 mg of potassium; and 9 mg of calcium.

Spicy Corn Chips

¾ cup water
2 tbsp. safflower oil
1 tsp. chili powder
½ tsp. garlic powder
¼ tsp. ground cumin
1 cup yellow cornmeal

Preheat oven to 375 degrees. In a small saucepan, combine water, oil, chili powder, garlic powder, and cumin. Bring to a boil. Remove from heat. Stir in cornmeal. Mix well. Cool slightly. Lightly spray 2 baking sheets with nonstick cooking spray. Using 1 level teaspoon of dough, shape into balls. Place balls on baking sheets 3 inches apart. Cover with wax paper. Flatten each ball with 3-inch diameter, flat-bottomed glass until very thin. Remove wax paper. Bake 10 to 12 minutes until lightly browned. Cool on racks. Store in airtight container. Makes 54. Serves 6.

NUTRIENTS: 108 calories; 1.7 grams of protein; 5.2 grams of fat; 14.1 grams of carbohydrates; 271 mg of sodium; 46 mg of potassium; and 59 mg of calcium.

Chicken and Rice Pitas

1 cup chopped, cooked chicken
½ cup cooked brown rice
¼ cup Mock Mayo (page 369)
1 green onion, chopped
1 tsp. dried parsley flakes
1 tsp. dried vegetable flakes
¼ tsp. garlic powder
Whole wheat pita bread

In a small bowl, combine all ingredients, except pita bread. Spoon chicken mixture into shells. Serves 2.

NUTRIENTS: 278 calories; 25.0 grams of protein; 7.6 grams of fat; 28.8 grams of carbohydrates; 326 mg of sodium; 446 mg of potassium; and 89 mg of calcium.

Chicken Tostados

1 cup Refried Bean Dip (page 365)
4 corn tortillas
1 cup diced cooked chicken
¼ cup Mock Guacamole (page 364)

Spread Refried Bean Dip on tortillas. Sprinkle chicken over beans. Warm in microwave. Top with Mock Guacamole. Serves 2.

NUTRIENTS: 305 calories; 24.5 grams of protein; 3.7 grams of fat; 44.3 grams of carbohydrates; 208 mg of sodium; 395 mg of potassium; and 186 mg of calcium.

Garbanzo Rollups

1 cup Garbanzo Bean Spread (page 368)
1 cup chopped, cooked turkey
6 large Boston lettuce leaves

In a small bowl, combine Garbanzo Bean Spread and turkey. Spoon mixture in center of lettuce leaf. Roll up. Serves 2.

NUTRIENTS: 500 calories; 46.0 grams of protein; 7.8 grams of fat; 62.3 grams of carbohydrates; 93 mg of sodium; 1127 mg of potassium; and 166 mg of calcium.

Oven-Dried Jerky

2 lbs. turkey breast, partially frozen
¼ cup low-salt soy sauce
1 tbsp. Worcestershire sauce
1 tsp. hickory liquid smoke
1 tsp. onion powder
½ tsp. garlic powder
¼ tsp. black pepper

Remove skin and fat from turkey. Cut into ⅛-inch thick slices, about 1½ inches wide. In a bowl, combine remaining ingredients. Arrange turkey strips in a shallow dish. Pour soy mixture over turkey. Cover. Refrigerate overnight. Shake off excess liguid. Arrange turkey in a single layer on cake racks. Place racks on shallow pan. Set oven temperature at lowest setting (150 to 200 degrees). Bake 4½ to 5½ hours until turkey has turned brown and is dry to the touch. Pat off any beads of oil with paper towels. Turn off oven. Cool to room temperature. Remove from oven. Store in airtight containers in refrigerator. Serves 8.

NUTRIENTS: 137 calories; 28.2 grams of protein; 2.2 grams of fat; 0.1 grams of carbohydrates; 357 mg of sodium; 393 mg of potassium; and 8 mg of calcium. _____

Crispy Cornmeal Crackers

1 cup plus 3 tablespoons yellow cornmeal
½ cup oat flour
½ tsp. baking soda

½ tsp. salt-free herb seasoning
½ cup nonfat buttermilk
3 tbsp. safflower oil
¼ tsp. Worcestershire sauce
prepared butter-flavored mix
seasonings to taste
    (caraway seed, garlic powder, onion powder,
    dill weed, or chili powder)

Preheat oven to 350 degrees. In a mixing bowl, combine cornmeal, flour, baking soda, and herb seasoning. Add buttermilk, oil, and Worcestershire sauce. Mix until dough forms a ball. Knead on oat-floured surface for 8 minutes. Spray 2 baking sheets with nonstick cooking spray. Using level teaspoons of dough, shape into balls. Place balls on baking sheets 3 inches apart. Cover with wax paper. Flatten each ball with 3-inch diameter, flat-bottomed glass until ⅛ inch thick. Bake 6 to 8 minutes until golden brown. Remove to a rack. Brush lightly with prepared butter mix. Sprinkle with desired seasonings. Makes 4 dozen. Serves 8.

NUTRIENTS: 139 calories; 3.0 grams of protein; 6.2 grams of fat; 18.2 grams of carbohydrates; 263 mg of sodium; 91 mg of potassium; and 78 mg of calcium. _____

Delicious Caraway Crackers

2 cups oat bran
½ cup buckwheat flour
½ cup oat flour
2 tbsp. caraway seed

½ tsp. onion powder

⅓ cup safflower oil

½ cup water

Preheat oven to 300 degrees. Spray 2 baking sheets with nonstick cooking spray. In a large bowl, combine bran, flours, caraway, and onion powder. Add oil. Slowly add water. Stir until dough holds together as a ball. Place half of dough on each baking sheet. Cover with wax paper. Roll as thin as possible. Repeat for other half. Cut into 2-inch squares. Bake 30 minutes until lightly browned. Separate crackers on sheet. Cool on wire racks. Makes 5 dozen. Serves 10.

NUTRIENTS: 150 calories; 4.3 grams of protein; 8.5 grams of fat; 17.8 grams of carbohydrate; 3 mg of sodium; 140 mg of potassium; and 4 mg of calcium.

_____

Toasted Oats

1 cup old-fashioned oatmeal

Preheat oven to 325 degrees. Spread oatmeal in a thin layer on a shallow baking sheet. Bake 20 to 30 minutes until toasted. Stir occasionally. Cool. Store in airtight container. Makes 1 cup.

Note: Combine rye flakes with oatmeal to make homemade dry cereal. Sprinkle with cinnamon or allspice when toasting. Eat dry or serve with milk.

NUTRIENTS: 390 calories; 14.2 grams of protein; 7.4 grams of fat; 68.2 grams of carbohydrates; 2 mg of sodium; 352 mg of potassium; and 53 mg of calcium.

14

Sauces and Seasonings

Helpful Hints

Refer to the chart Using Herbs and Spices (page 12) to try new combinations of spices.

Replace oil or fat in marinades, sauces, and salad dressings with defatted chicken broth, vegetable broth, lemon juice, lime juice, vinegar, tomato juice, vegetable juices, low-salt soy sauce, or wine vinegars.

To thicken sauces, reduce liquid by rapid boiling.

Thicken gravies and sauces with oat bran, oat flour, cornstarch, or nonfat dry milk instead of flour and butter.

Use evaporated skimmed milk or nonfat dry milk to make cream sauces.

Tangy Barbecue Marinade

¼ cup red wine vinegar
¼ cup low-salt soy sauce
½ cup chicken broth, defatted
¼ tsp. black pepper
¼ tsp. cayenne pepper
1 tsp. dried parsley flakes
1 tsp. onion powder

¼ tsp. garlic powder

¼ tsp. ground cloves

In a small bowl, combine all ingredients. Makes 1 cup.

NUTRIENTS: 90 calories; 4.7 grams of protein; 7.4 grams of fat; 14.3 grams of carbohydrates; 3142 mg of sodium; 516 mg of potassium; and 83 mg of calcium.

Soy Sauce Marinade

¼ cup low-salt soy sauce

1 tbsp. hickory liquid smoke

2 tbsp. cider vinegar

In a small bowl, combine all ingredients. Makes ½ cup.

NUTRIENTS: 54 calories; 4.0 grams of protein; 6.8 grams of fat; 3.2 grams of carbohydrates; 2400 mg of sodium; 309 mg of potassium; and 63 mg of calcium.

Spicy Enchilada Sauce

1 large onion, quartered

One 28-oz. can tomatoes

1 clove garlic

1 tsp. ground cumin

2 tsp. salt-free herb seasoning

1 tsp. dried oregano

One 6-oz. can tomato paste

One 7-oz. can chopped green chilies

1 cup water

In a blender, combine onion, tomatoes, and seasonings. Blend until smooth. Pour into a large skillet. Add tomato paste, green chilies, and water. Bring mixture to a near boil. Reduce heat. Cover. Simmer 30 minutes. Makes 5 cups.

NUTRIENTS: 371 calories; 16.0 grams of protein; 2.5 grams of fat; 81.5 grams of carbohydrates; 1157 mg of sodium; 3106 mg of potassium; and 191 mg of calcium.

Basic Gravy for Mashed Potatoes

2 tbsp. cornstarch
¾ cup potato broth
1 cup chicken broth, defatted
¼ tsp. ground oregano
¼ tsp. dry mustard
⅛ tsp. black pepper

Dissolve cornstarch in potato broth. In a medium saucepan, combine all ingredients. Cook over medium heat and stir until thickened. Makes 2 cups.

NUTRIENTS: 57 calories; 1.3 grams of protein; 1.1 grams of fat; 20.6 grams of carbohydrates; 1484 mg of sodium; 25 mg of potassium; and 15 mg of calcium.

Gravy with Mushrooms

1 cup sliced mushrooms
1 cup chicken broth, defatted
¼ tsp. garlic powder

½ tsp. onion powder

1 tsp. dried vegetable flakes

⅛ tsp. black pepper

2 tbsp. cornstarch

¾ cup potato broth

In a medium saucepan, combine mushrooms, chicken broth, garlic powder, onion powder, vegetable flakes, and pepper. Simmer 5 to 7 minutes until mushrooms are tender. Dissolve cornstarch in potato broth. Add to mushroom mixture. Cook over medium heat and stir until thickened. Makes 2 cups.

NUTRIENTS: 77 calories; 3.1 grams of protein; 1.3 grams of fat; 23.8 grams of carbohydrates; 1484 mg of sodium; 25 mg of potassium; and 57 mg of calcium.

Gravy With Onions

1 large onion, thinly sliced

2 cups chicken broth, defatted

⅛ tsp. ground sage

¼ tsp. dried chervil

¼ tsp. dried celery flakes

½ tsp. Kitchen Bouquet

⅛ tsp. black pepper

2 tbsp. cornstarch

¼ cup water

Spray a large skillet with nonstick spray. Add onion and cook over high heat until onion is browned. Stir frequently. As onion gets dry and begins to stick, add water. Stir and continue cooking until onion is translucent and lightly browned. Add broth, sage, chervil, celery flakes, Kitchen Bouquet, and pepper. Dissolve cornstarch in water. Add to onion mixture. Cook over medium heat and stir until thickened. Makes 2 cups.

NUTRIENTS: 116 calories; 4.1 grams of protein; 2.3 grams of fat; 30.7 grams of carbohydrates; 2978 mg of sodium; 207 mg of potassium; and 57 mg of calcium.

Hot Sauce

2 tomatoes, quartered
1 large onion, quartered
2 cloves garlic
2 jalapeno peppers
¼ cup chopped green pepper
One 7-oz. can chopped green chilies
One 15-oz. can tomato sauce
¼ cup red wine vinegar
1 tsp. salt-free herb seasoning
1 tsp. ground oregano
1 tsp. chili powder
½ tsp. ground cumin

In a blender, combine all ingredients. Process until mixed. Makes 4 cups.

NUTRIENTS: 326 calories; 13.3 grams of protein; 2.5 grams of fat; 80.1 grams of carbohydrates; 2680 mg of sodium; 2937 mg of potassium; and 268 mg of calcium.

Lemon Dill Sauce

2 tbsp. cornstarch

¼ cup water

1 cup chicken broth, defatted

2 tsp. dried dill weed

2 tbsp. lemon juice

1 tsp. dried parsley flakes

¼ tsp. garlic powder

½ tsp. hickory liquid smoke

Dissolve cornstarch in water. Cook broth and dissolved cornstarch until thickened. Stir in remaining ingredients. Makes 1⅓ cups.

NUTRIENTS: 41 calories; 0.4 grams of protein; 0.3 grams of fat; 19.6 grams of carbohydrates; 371 mg of sodium; 7 mg of potassium; and 4 mg of calcium.

Mushroom Sauce

1 tbsp. cornstarch

2 tbsp. water

1 cup sliced mushrooms

2 tbsp. chopped green onion

1 tbsp. low-salt soy sauce

1 cup chicken broth, defatted

1 tsp. dried parsley flakes

¼ tsp. dried rosemary, crumbled

¼ tsp. garlic powder

½ tsp. bacon-flavored sprinkles

Dissolve cornstarch in water. In a medium skillet, cook mushrooms and green onions in soy sauce until tender. Stir frequently. Add broth, parsley flakes, rosemary, and garlic powder. Heat 2 to 3 minutes. Add dissolved cornstarch. Heat and stir until sauce is thickened. Stir in bacon sprinkles. Makes 1½ cups.

NUTRIENTS: 79 calories; 4.4 grams of protein; 3.0 grams of fat; 16.2 grams of carbohydrates; 2086 mg of sodium; 124 mg of potassium; and 77 mg of calcium.

Spaghetti Sauce

1 cup chopped onion
1 clove garlic, pressed
½ cup water
One 28-oz. can tomatoes
One 16-oz. can tomato sauce
¼ tsp. black pepper
2 tsp. dried oregano
1 tsp. salt-free herb seasoning
1 tsp. dried basil
1 tsp. dried celery flakes

In a large saucepan, cook onion and garlic in water until tender. Add remaining ingredients. Simmer, uncovered, 30 to 50 minutes until thickened. Makes 4 cups.

NUTRIENTS: 397 calories; 17.3 grams of protein; 3.1 grams of fat; 87.7 grams of carbohydrates; 3767 mg of sodium; 4039 mg of potassium; and 264 mg of calcium.

White Sauce

2 tbsp. cornstarch
¼ cup water
1 cup chicken broth, defatted
¼ tsp. garlic powder
1 tsp. grated fresh ginger root
½ tsp. salt-free herb seasoning
2 tbsp. rice wine vinegar

Dissolve cornstarch in ¼ cup water. In a medium saucepan, combine broth, garlic powder, ginger root, herb seasoning, and rice wine vinegar. Bring to a boil. Reduce heat. Stir in dissolved cornstarch. Heat and stir until sauce is thickened. Makes 1 cup.

NUTRIENTS: 63 calories; 1.3 grams of protein; 1.1 grams of fat; 23.0 grams of carbohydrates; 1484 mg of sodium; 70 mg of potassium; and 18 mg of calcium.

Spicy Salsa

1 cup finely chopped tomatoes
½ cup finely chopped onion
1 tbsp. finely chopped green chilies
1 finely chopped jalapeno pepper
3 tbsp. vegetable juice
1 tbsp. lemon juice
¾ tsp. salt-free herb seasoning

In a small bowl, combine all ingredients. Chill for 1 hour before serving. Makes 1¼ cups.

NUTRIENTS: 99 calories; 4.0 grams of protein; 0.6 grams of fat; 21.3 grams of carbohydrates; 190 mg of sodium; 787 mg of potassium; and 46 mg of calcium.

Jalapeno Tomato Salsa

1 cup chopped tomatoes

⅓ cup chopped onion

2 cloves garlic, pressed

1 finely chopped jalapeno pepper

¼ tsp. salt-free herb seasoning

½ tsp. dried oregano

1 tsp. dried parsley flakes

1 tbsp. lime juice

In a small bowl, combine all ingredients. Chill for 1 hour before serving. Makes 1 ¼ cups.

NUTRIENTS: 78 calories; 3.4 grams of protein; 0.5 grams of fat; 16.9 grams of carbohydrates; 14 mg of sodium; 611 mg of potassium; and 31 mg of calcium.

Herb Seasoning Mix

1 tbsp. black pepper

1 tbsp. onion powder

1 tbsp. celery seeds

2 tsp. cream of tartar

1½ tsp. dried orange peel

1½ tsp. garlic powder

1½ tsp. arrowroot

1 tsp. dried marjoram

½ tsp. white pepper

½ tsp. dried thyme

½ tsp. dill weed

¼ tsp. dry mustard

¼ tsp. cayenne pepper

¼ tsp. dried lemon peel

1 packet sugar substitute

In a blender, combine all ingredients. Grind until well mixed and very fine. Using a funnel, pour into a shaker. Cover. Use as a salt substitute. Makes ½ cup.

Table of Equivalent Amounts

Table of Equivalent Amounts

Item	PURCHASED QUANTITY/WEIGHT	PREPARED YIELD
Asparagus	1 lb. fresh 1 lb. frozen	2 cups 3 cups
Beans, dry	1 lb. raw (2 cups)	6 cups cooked
Beets	1 lb. (4 medium)	2 cups
Black-eyed peas	1 lb. frozen	3 cups
Broccoli	1 lb. fresh 1 lb. frozen	4 cups 4 cups
Brown rice	1 lb. raw (2 cups)	6 cups cooked
Cabbage	1 lb.	4 cups shredded, raw; 2 cups shredded, cooked
Carrots	1 lb. (6 - 7) 1 lb. frozen	3 cups sliced or shredded 3 cups
Cauliflower	½ medium head 1 lb. frozen	3 cups raw; 2 cups cooked 3 cups cooked
Celery	2 large stalks	1 cup sliced

Item	PURCHASED QUANTITY/WEIGHT	PREPARED YIELD
Chicken	1 whole chicken	8 oz. cooked
Breast, split, chopped, skinned, and boned		1½ cups
Corn	1 lb. frozen (3 cups)	2 cups cooked
Corn, ears	12 medium	2½ cups cooked
Cucumber	1 lb. (2 medium)	4 cups sliced
Eggplant	1½ lbs.	3 cups diced raw; 2½ cups diced, cooked
Green beans	1 lb. fresh 1 lb. frozen	3 cups 4 cups
Green peppers	1 medium	1 cup chopped
Green onions	4 onions	¼ cup chopped
Greens for salad	2 cups loosely packed 4 cups loosely packed	1 serving raw 1 serving cooked (1 cup)
Herbs	1 tbsp. fresh ½ ounce fresh	1 tsp. dried ¼ cup packed or 2 tbsp. chopped

Item	PURCHASED QUANTITY/WEIGHT	PREPARED YIELD
Leeks	3	1 cup chopped
Lemon	1 medium	2 - 3 tbsp. juice; 1 tbsp. grated peel
Lima beans	10 oz. frozen	2 cups
Lime	1 medium	1½ tbsp. juice
Mushrooms	8 oz. fresh 1 cup freeze dried One 4 oz. can	2 cups sliced raw; ½ cup cooked ¼ cup reconstituted 2 tbsp. drained
New potatoes	1 lb. fresh (5 small)	1½ cups peeled/diced
Onion	1 medium	1 cup chopped or sliced
Peas	1 lb. fresh 1 lb. frozen	1 cup shelled 3 cups
Potatoes	1 lb. (2 medium)	1½ cups peeled/diced
Radishes	7 - 8	¼ cup sliced
Shrimp	1 lb.	15 - 18 jumbo 26 - 30 medium 60 - 65 tiny

Item	PURCHASED QUANTITY/WEIGHT	PREPARED YIELD
Shrimp, cont.	12 oz. raw shrimp in shell 4½ - 5-oz. can	8 oz. shelled shrimp (1 cup) 1 cup
Split pea, dry	1 lb. raw (2 cups)	4½ cups cooked
Spinach	10 oz. pkg fresh or 1 bundle 1 lb. frozen (3 cups)	6 cups raw (packed), or 2 cups cooked 2 cups cooked
Sweet potatoes	1 lb. (2 medium)	1½ cups peeled/diced
Tomatoes	1 lb. (3 medium)	1½ cups chopped
Zucchini	1 lb.	3½ cups sliced

Appendix B

Table of Substitutions

| *Table of Substitutions*

Item	AMOUNT	SUBSTITUTIONS
cornstarch	1 tbsp.	2 tsp. arrowroot
garlic, fresh	1 clove	⅛ tsp. garlic powder or ⅛ tsp. instant minced garlic
ginger, fresh	1 tsp.	¼ tsp. ground ginger
herbs, fresh	1 tbsp.	1 tsp. dried herb
lemon peel, spice	1 tsp.	1 tsp. fresh lemon peel, grated
lemon juice, fresh	2 tbsp.	2 tbsp. concentrate
lime juice, fresh	2 tbsp.	2 tbsp. concentrate
mushrooms, fresh	8 oz.	1½ cups freeze dried
onions	1 medium, chopped	1 tbsp. onion powder or 2 tbsp. instant minced onions
orange peel, spice	1 tsp.	1 tsp. fresh orange peel, grated
salt, table	½ tsp.	1 tsp. salt-free herb seasoning

Appendix C

Index

Index

CLIFF SHEATS